How to Win the Premier League

IAN GRAHAM

T0333172

CENTURY

II

Century
20 Vauxhall Bridge Road
London SW1V 2SA

Century is part of the Penguin Random House group of companies
whose addresses can be found at global.penguinrandomhouse.com.

First published by Century in 2024

www.penguin.co.uk

A CIP catalogue record for this book is available from the British Library.

ISBN 9781529934632

Typeset in 12/14.75pt Dante MT Std by Jouve (UK), Milton Keynes
Printed and bound in Great Britain by Clays Ltd, Elcograf S.p.A.

The authorised representative in the EEA is Penguin Random House Ireland,
Morrison Chambers, 32 Nassau Street, Dublin D02 YH68

www.greenpenguin.co.uk

Penguin Random House is committed to a
sustainable future for our business, our readers
and our planet. This book is made from Forest
Stewardship Council® certified paper.

How to Win the Premier League

In memory of Philip Stanley Graham

Contents

PART ONE — THE ROAD TO ANFIELD

1. The Best Team in the Land   3
2. Tottenham Hotspur   19
3. False Red Dawn   39
4. Heavy Metal Football   55
5. Winning the Lot   75

PART TWO — HOW FOOTBALL WORKS

6. Gambling on Data   101
7. What to Expect if You're Expecting Goals   121
8. The Value of Possession   141
9. Track Your Man   157
10. Paying for Performance   175

PART THREE — MORE THAN A GAME

11. Schrödinger's Manager   189
12. Goat War   205
13. Zebra Farmers: Why Transfers Fail   219
14. Home Is Where 30% More Goals Are   235
15. Stats and Snake Oil   251
16. Stats and Crude Oil: The Future of Football   267

Conclusion: How Not to Win the Premier League   279
Acknowledgements   283
Notes   285
Index   297

PART ONE

The Road to Anfield

The Best Team in the Land

*Statistical thinking will one day be as necessary
for efficient citizenship as the ability to read and write*

Samuel S. Wilks paraphrasing H. G. Wells, 1951

*'Cause he's fitba' crazy, He's fitba' mad.
The fitba it has ta'en away the wee bit sense he had*

James Curran, 1885

Never Give Up

Liverpool Football Club were about to play FC Barcelona in a competitive game for only the 10th time in their history.[1] I worked for Liverpool and had the privilege of being allocated two tickets for the game. But I'd decided not to go. It was May 2019 and we'd reached the semi-finals of the Champions League – football's most prestigious club competition.

Frankly, I'd had enough. Since I joined Liverpool in 2012, we'd come agonisingly close to winning the Premier League in 2014. We'd lost the Europa League final in 2016, having led at half-time. We'd lost the Champions League final against Real Madrid in 2018. Now, in 2019, we had just lost the semi-final first leg in Barcelona 3–0. Coming back from that deficit was very unlikely. I felt jaded and couldn't face another glorious failure. Then my friend Jin got in touch. He realised it was a long shot but said he would regret it if he didn't ask: did I have a spare ticket for the game? I told him that I did and that I would not be going.

He asked me, quite rightly, if I was out of my mind. It was the Champions League semi-final! It was Barcelona! It was Lionel Messi! I realised he was right – I'd never seen Messi play live before. It was worth going to the game if only to watch the world's greatest player.

My job was the reason I didn't want to be there. As director of research at Liverpool it was my responsibility to source, analyse and interpret data about football matches. One of the applications of data analysis in football is predicting outcomes. At Liverpool, my colleagues and I had developed a set of statistical models that took raw performance data – information about shots, saves and goals – and turned it into estimates of team strength. Each team's attacking and defensive capabilities – their ability to score goals and stop goals being conceded – were then used to produce forecasts of games and competitions.

Given the 3–0 loss in the first leg, our algorithms estimated our chance of progressing to the final was 3.5%. Our statistical model of team strength rated Barcelona's team a whopping 20% stronger than Liverpool's. Liverpool's home advantage in the second leg would make it an evenly matched game but we had to win by at least four goals, or take the tie into extra-time by winning exactly 3–0. My approach to football is the exact opposite of the romantic way in which fans view the game: I see everything through the lens of probability, which is estimated using objective evidence. And for this game, the evidence suggested our probability of success was extremely low.

It was well known at the training ground that my department produced these forecasts. When the canteen staff asked what our chances were and I told them the bad news, their reaction was: 'That's a higher chance than I thought!' My pessimism was somehow a cause for optimism among my colleagues.

Even by Anfield's standards, the atmosphere that night was electric. Luis Suárez – Liverpool's best player from 2011 to 2014, but now playing for Barcelona – had scored in the first leg and celebrated wholeheartedly. This had angered the Liverpool fans and now, as he was about to take the kick-off, 50,000 people were screaming 'Fuck off Suárez! Fuck off Suárez!' In my job I was paid to take a sober, dispassionate view of football, but I was at Anfield as a fan and I happily joined in the chant.

The game was very open, and very entertaining. Strangely, our low chance of success allowed me to take a lot more pleasure in the match than I usually did. Since we were going to lose anyway I could just enjoy the spectacle without worrying about the result. But after six minutes, Barcelona's Jordi Alba made a poor clearance, heading it straight to Sadio Mané. Sadio played in Jordan Henderson, whose shot was only parried by the goalkeeper and Divock Origi could not miss. We were 1–0 up.

Barcelona created several dangerous chances but the first half finished with Liverpool still 1–0 ahead. After 53 minutes, Trent Alexander-Arnold created a good chance for Gini Wijnaldum, who scuffed a terrible shot that somehow squeezed past the goalkeeper: 2–0. Barcelona kicked off but immediately lost the ball and within 30 seconds Gini had scored again with a brilliant header to make it 3–0. The atmosphere at Anfield went from electric to nuclear. Every touch of the ball by Suárez was met with venom and derision from our fans. By the time the third goal went in I'd shouted so much that I'd lost my voice. I had to ask Jin to shout at Suárez on my behalf. I spent the second half jabbing him in the ribs as the signal to hurl some abuse.

My nerves had increased in direct proportion to our chances of victory. But after 78 minutes, Trent took a lightning-quick corner, having noticed the Barcelona defence was asleep, and Divock hit an unstoppable shot for a 4–0 lead. Barcelona's habit of losing concentration and complaining to match officials when defending corners had been highlighted by my colleagues in the Video Analysis department. As a result, our players and ball-boys had been primed to restart the game quickly from corners. The video analysts deserved tremendous credit for their insights.

We had reached the Champions League final in the most dramatic and unlikely of circumstances. Maybe, after seven years of working for Liverpool, we would finally win a trophy. Like every other Liverpool fan, I was buzzing when I left Anfield that night. But the data analyst in me was eager to evaluate the game.

The Outside View

That night, as I drove home, data was being pushed to our computer servers in the cloud. Video analysts working in our suppliers' collection centres had transcribed the details of every on-ball action – passes, shots, tackles, fouls – and uploaded them. At the same time, cameras at Anfield had recorded the movements of all the players and the ball. This video was then converted using computer vision algorithms into a trace of each player's location. These player positions – recorded 25 times per second – were also now available to be analysed.

When the data arrived at around 5am the next morning, several automatic processes were triggered. First, validation: an algorithm checked that the data was of high enough quality for our models to produce sensible results. Next, composition: the on-ball events were synchronised with the player positions to give a unified history of the game. Finally, analysis: the synchronised data was pushed through our statistical models. These models produced a statistical interpretation of the game, judging the contribution of each player to the result. Based on the performances of each player, further algorithms updated our ratings of team strengths and player abilities.

In the stands I watched the game as a fan, exhilarated and elated. The next morning, with the data processed and the results of our algorithms displayed before me, I analysed the game rationally. The game I remembered from the night before was not quite the same as the game I reviewed the next day.

We had won 4–0, but the result could so easily have been different. In hindsight, it seemed almost inevitable that we would achieve the result we needed. Mohamed Salah, injured for the game, had watched from the stands wearing a T-shirt that said 'Never give up'. But every game is subject to the arbitrary power of chance. We can all remember games where the outcome might have been different but for a mishit cross or a lucky deflection. Given the goal-scoring chances that occurred in the game, our 4–0 victory was far from guaranteed. Using data to analyse what *might* have happened leads to a less certain, more probabilistic view. Its value lies in separating performance, or signal, from luck, or noise. It allows us to better understand the strengths and weaknesses of our team by discounting a lucky win or appreciating a good performance that nevertheless ended with an unlucky loss.

The shots that occurred in the game meant that we estimated the 'fair score' to be 2.0 goals to Liverpool and 0.9 goals to Barcelona. This 'fair' goal difference of +1.1 predicted by our model was not enough to win the tie. The fair score had been calculated using a method that has become known as 'Expected Goals'.

Expected Goals

Goals are rare in football – there are only 2.7 per Premier League game. A goal usually (but not always) follows a shot and there are 10 times as many shots as there are goals so it makes sense to analyse them. The shots may tell us something about the performance of the teams that the goals do not.

Different shots have different chances of being converted into goals. Every football fan knows that a penalty has a better chance of becoming a goal than most shots that occur in open play. And most fans intuitively understand that a shot taken from inside the opposition's 18-yard box has a higher chance of hitting the back of the net than a shot from outside the box. 'Expected Goals', introduced in 1997 by Richard Pollard and Charles Reep,[2] simply quantifies the conversion chance of each shot.

The statistical model they built revealed that a shot from 30 yards had only a 1% chance of being converted into a goal. Just inside the box that increased to 10%, then the chances rapidly improved: 20% from the penalty spot, and 50% inside the six-yard box. They showed that defensive pressure led to a lower conversion chance, and that shots from set-piece situations had a lower conversion chance than similar shots in open play.

Why 'Expected' Goals?

Pollard and Reep used the term 'Weighted Shots', which was a good name. Each shot is weighted by its chance of converting into a goal, so 'Weighted Shots' makes perfect sense. 'Expected Goals' is a terrible name. 'Expected' refers to the number of goals we'd see, on average, given the conversion chance assigned to the shot. For example, penalties are converted into goals about 75% of the time. After 100 penalties we'd expect 75 goals – or expect 0.75 goals per penalty.

The semi-final with Barcelona had been closer than I remembered. Divock's first goal had an excellent conversion chance of 40%. But it had been followed by two Barcelona chances: a 12% shot from Messi and an 18% shot from Coutinho. On the stroke of half-time, Barcelona's Jordi Alba had a 33% shot superbly saved by our goalkeeper, Alisson Becker. In the second half, Virgil van Dijk – Liverpool's best defender – saw his header saved from a corner: a 36% chance. Conversely, based on the probability of success, our three goals in the second half added up to only 0.41 Expected Goals.

I replayed the game in a computer simulation with goals being scored according to each shot's individual conversion chance. The simulation resulted in a 4–0 or better result for Liverpool only 5% of the time, plus a 4% chance of taking the tie into extra-time.

Next I looked at how much the shooters had capitalised on their Expected Goals. Taking a shot from a given location in a given situation is one thing; taking it well is another. When accounting for the trajectory of each shot and the position of the goalkeeper – 'Post-Strike Expected Goals' – the calculation changed: a 2.0–0.9 win became a 3.4–1.7 win. Both teams' shot-takers had taken shots of above-average quality.

Divock's two goals were particularly well taken. He shot accurately and he shot where the goalkeeper wasn't. But Barcelona's players had also shot accurately: their 0.9 Expected Goals had increased to 1.7 thanks to accurate shooting – no surprise, with Messi and Suárez in their team. Barcelona's 1.7 Post-Strike Expected Goals had resulted in zero actual goals: our goalkeeper Alisson had a strong claim to have been named man of the match.

Success

In the final we played Tottenham Hotspur, the team I had consulted for between 2007 and 2012. Our model predicted a 60% chance of victory. It was a terrible game. Liverpool's centre-forward, Roberto Firmino, was not fully fit, and neither was Tottenham's Harry Kane. Sadio Mané won a penalty in the second minute, which was converted by Salah. Liverpool mostly defended for the next 90 minutes. We survived a late onslaught from Spurs but Divock Origi scored with only a few minutes remaining to effectively end the game and secure his legacy as a Liverpool legend. We'd finally won a trophy.

I'd watched the game in the stands with my colleagues from the Scouting department. The initial euphoria at the final whistle had died down and we were watching the players celebrate and get ready for the presentation of the trophy. There was a tap on my shoulder: it was Steven Gerrard, the former Liverpool captain and one of the club's greatest ever players. He'd watched from the row behind ours. He told us he'd never been so nervous at a game – as a player, manager or spectator. I agreed, saying it had been unbearable to watch. He hadn't been worried about the game, he explained, but watching our extreme anxiety for 90 minutes – biting our nails and putting our heads in our hands at every Spurs chance – had rubbed off on him. 'I wouldn't have been nervous at all if I wasn't sat behind you idiots, watching you kick every ball.'

Several days of celebration passed before I looked at the analysis of the final. In the last 20 minutes of the game, Spurs had created 0.82 Expected Goals compared to our paltry 0.16. I was right to have been nervous.

The next season, 2019/20, we won the Uefa Super Cup and the Fifa Club World Cup, while making the best start in Premier League history. In March we found ourselves 25 points clear at the top of the table, having won 27 of our first 29 games. We were going to be champions. It was so overwhelmingly likely to happen that I'd been asked by the head of our Ticketing department to forecast which game would be the most likely to see us crowned champions. Then Covid-19 struck. It looked as though a certain first league title in 30 years, and a first Premier League title, would be denied us by the pandemic. But football returned, behind closed doors, in June 2020. We finally won the Premier League title. Liverpool winning the league title should have been an occasion for joy, but it wasn't. It felt very strange to me: the world was still in the grip of the pandemic, and football was simply not important.

We continued to vie with Manchester City – the most dominant team the Premier League has ever seen – for the league title, coming second in 2021/22 and finishing runners-up in the Champions League again. We also won the FA Cup and the League Cup. I was gratified to have played a part in returning Liverpool to their historic position as one of the best clubs in Europe.

My story about helping return Liverpool to success focuses on data analysis: this was my role and it gave us an edge over our rivals, especially in the transfer market. But I must stress that building a successful football club is a team effort: without the foresight and long-term thinking of John W. Henry, Tom Werner, Mike Gordon and the rest of Fenway Sports Group, my work would have had little impact. Without the arrival of Jürgen Klopp and the decision-making ability of Michael Edwards as sporting director, my contribution would also have failed to make a difference, to say nothing of the hard work of my colleagues in the Academy, Video Analysis, Sports Science, Scouting and Medical departments. My data analysis team increased our chances of success and identified future stars for Liverpool but the theoretical edge it gave only became a reality thanks to the hard work and talent of our owners and my colleagues.

Of course, the ultimate success of a team depends on its players. The players who started the Champions League final were nearly all signed with the help of data analysis. Liverpool's most expensive incoming transfer in history at that point was Virgil van Dijk – a brilliant centre-back who, incredibly, was not already playing for a big Champions League club. When we signed Virgil in January 2018, he became the most expensive centre-back ever (he has since been surpassed by Matthijs de Ligt, Harry Maguire and Joško Gvardiol). Goalkeeper Alisson Becker became the most expensive goalkeeper ever when he signed in the summer of 2018, until Chelsea signed Kepa Arrizabalaga three weeks later. The transfer fees we paid for Van Dijk and Alisson were much higher than Liverpool had usually paid. Their price was high because they were both clearly brilliant players. They shone brightly in our data analysis, but their talent shone brightly to scouts, coaches, the media, and anyone with even a passing interest in football.

Our owners, Fenway Sports Group, had always been very willing to invest Liverpool's revenues into the playing squad, but we had to live within our means. On this occasion, however, we were able to pay high fees for obvious superstars thanks to a previous success story. Philippe Coutinho signed for Liverpool in January 2013 from Internazionale and had become the star player of our team. In January 2018 Barcelona, desperate to make prestigious signings after Neymar's buyout clause was met by Paris Saint-Germain, had paid us a barely believable £142 million to sign Coutinho.

If Alisson and Van Dijk were obvious stars, two other members of our defence were not. Joël Matip was one of our first signings under Jürgen Klopp, and had arrived in summer 2016 on a free transfer from the German team Schalke 04. A gangly and rather awkward looking player, he had amassed an impressive amount of experience – 175 Bundesliga starts by the age of 24. His apparent awkwardness was a turn-off for some of our scouts, who had doubts about his pace and his ability in the air. The most worrying thing was that he seemed to be making the same mistakes week after week. Our scouts were not alone in their opinion. We faced very little competition for his services – in January 2016, Newcastle United were the only other English team interested in signing him, but they were relegated at the end of the season. Despite his lack of popularity among scouts at nearly every club, our data analysis concluded that his performances for Schalke were easily above the Premier League centre-back average. At such a young age and a free transfer, he was an obvious signing to us if no one else.

Andy Robertson at left-back was another undervalued player. Liverpool signed him in 2017 from Hull City, who had been relegated from the Premier League with the worst defensive record of any club, conceding 80 goals. He was one of the best attacking full-backs in the league – his passing and dribbling looked very impressive in our data analysis. His defending was a cause for concern, but my worries were eased by Jürgen, who prioritised a full-back's attacking abilities over his defensive ones. It's fair to say that Robertson's defending for Liverpool has exceeded my expectations. Midfielder Gini Wijnaldum had also joined from a relegated club, Newcastle, and was similarly undervalued.

Our defensive midfielder, Fabinho, had joined in summer 2018 for a relatively large fee. A member of Monaco's title-winning 2016/17 team, he remained at the club until 2018, while his team-mates Tié-moué Bakayoko, Bernardo Silva and Benjamin Mendy signed for Chelsea and Manchester City. Still only 24, we considered him one of the best young defensive midfielders not already playing for a big Champions League rival, and the Scouting department agreed. He could also play as a right-back, potentially giving us more bang for our buck.

Our forward line of Mo Salah, Roberto Firmino and Sadio Mané all carried some baggage when they signed for Liverpool. Salah had 'failed' at Chelsea – he had not really failed but his playing time had been extremely limited. Because of this, he was considered a Premier League failure. We consequently faced little competition for his signature from our Premier League rivals despite his success playing for Fiorentina and Roma in Italy. Firmino had scored only 38 goals in 140 Bundesliga appearances for mid-table Hoffenheim, and Mané 21 in 67 for similarly mid-table Southampton.

Our data-based opinion of all these players was much, much more positive than the opinion of the rest of the footballing world. For various reasons, they had been overlooked and undervalued by other clubs. At Liverpool we had, through luck and judgement, hit upon an effective method for identifying talent and signing players.

Liverpool's ex-sporting director Michael Edwards has often said that if data, scouts and manager all agree on a player, that player rarely fails. Michael is a critical and argumentative man, as am I. I once recorded a fourth percentile score on a psychological test for agreeableness among a sample of science postgraduates, a group not generally known for their agreeableness. Me and Michael argued and argued about blind spots in data analysis and video analysis of players. I also had endless debates about the relative merits of players with Dave Fallows and Barry Hunter, the leaders of our Scouting department. 'Argumentative' is an adjective that can also easily be applied to Jürgen Klopp. But we used our tendency towards argument and criticism as a positive force. Michael's criticism of my data analysis motivated me to improve it. My criticism of scouting motivated the scouts to consider the merits of less aesthetically pleasing players. Michael's animated discussions with Jürgen persuaded him to sign players that were maybe not his first choice. Every player we ever considered underwent an exhaustive qualitative, quantitative and financial examination.

Luck also played a part. No one – certainly not me – expected Andy Robertson to become a world-class defender. We were confident that Firmino and Mané would be excellent players for

Liverpool but they exceeded my expectations. If Salah had not 'failed' at Chelsea, we would certainly have faced stiff competition to sign him in 2017. If Paris Saint-Germain had not signed Neymar for such a huge fee, Barcelona would not have been so desperate to sign Coutinho, and we would not have had the funds to sign Alisson and Van Dijk. We were lucky that Jürgen was not in work when Liverpool were looking for a new manager – our previous attempt to sign players combining data, scouting and manager opinion had previously failed badly when Brendan Rodgers was manager.

How We Changed Football

In this book I want to do three things. First I want to tell the story of data analysis in football, using my own experiences to guide the way – from obscurity and moderate success at Tottenham, through a disastrous start at Liverpool with Brendan Rodgers, to historic successes with Jürgen Klopp. I will explain the cultural differences that had to be overcome and the cognitive biases I encountered and had to work around in order for data analysis to have a chance of making a difference. I will also tell the story of the other early adopters of data analysis in football, Brentford and Brighton & Hove Albion.

Second, I want to challenge the way that you view the game. I will do this by explaining the most important concepts of data analysis and showing how they have impacted the Premier League using first-hand examples from Liverpool as well as case studies from other teams. Football is a very low-scoring game: it is diffi-cult to draw conclusions from any particular result. But there are statistical tools that can help us untangle skill from luck, or signal from noise. Expected Goals is a good example. Measuring the quality of each shot by its chance of conversion shows that not all chances are created equally. Most players never even take a shot in a game (even Mo Salah takes fewer than four per game on average), so we have to analyse the impact of actions other than shots. 'Possession Value' analyses every chain of possession in order to estimate the value of a pass that may not directly lead to a shot. Expected Possession Value revealed just how much players like Andy Robertson and Trent Alexander-Arnold add to a team through the quality of their passing and dribbling. These tools were the cornerstones of our work at Liverpool and dictated our transfer policy: if a player did not rate highly in our models, he was not signed.

Finally, we'll apply some statistical thinking to diverse questions about the game. We'll explore why hiring the right manager is so difficult, and reveal the work we did to demonstrate that Jürgen Klopp was a brilliant fit for Liverpool. We'll discover whether Lionel Messi was a better player than Cristiano Ronaldo, and why nearly half of all transfers fail. We will demonstrate the importance of home advantage, and analyse how it decreased when games were played in empty stadiums after Covid – thereby providing hard evidence that fans make a difference. We'll explain the importance of set-pieces in goal-scoring (and conceding). And, looking ahead, we'll also explore how the limitless spending power of state-owned clubs has distorted football's landscape.

When I began working at Liverpool, in 2012, detailed data on top-flight men's football was difficult and expensive to source. Data was impossible to source for the women's game. Things have changed and, as with other aspects of the sport, women's football data is rapidly improving. The ground is fertile for a data-driven approach to be applied to the women's game, with some enlightened data suppliers making full seasons of Women's Super League (WSL) data freely available. But my work at Liverpool was almost exclusively for the men's team.

The data-driven view of football has been caricatured as clinical and accused of taking the passion out of the game. Nothing could be further from the truth, as you would know if you had the misfortune of sitting next to me at a game. At Anfield I occasionally sat next to Caroline, one of the training ground's canteen staff, who would quite rightly complain about both the frequency and intensity of my shouting, swearing and 'jumping about like a bloody lunatic' over the course of the match. Football is a game of passion, and as the Scottish philosopher David Hume said: 'Reason is, and ought only to be, the slave of the passions, and can never pretend to any other office than to serve and obey them.' At Liverpool we strove to understand the game analytically in order to increase our chances of success, because we were passionate about winning. Data analysis is also accused of taking the beauty and magic away from football. Again, I believe the opposite is true. A better understanding of the game leads to a much richer appreciation of its beauty. Florence Nightingale's phrase 'To understand God's thoughts we must study statistics, for these are the measure of His purpose' sums up my opinion on the use of data in sport.

Some sports have changed immeasurably since embracing data analysis. Formula One, once the preserve of risk-seeking mavericks, has become a sport where careful engineering, logistics and resource management are prized over exciting overtaking manoeuvres. Michael Lewis captured baseball's data revolution in his book, *Moneyball*. But one of the outcomes of the revolution was slower games and fewer hits. The baseball executive Theo Epstein admitted that analytics had 'unwittingly had a negative impact on the aesthetic value of the game'.[3] These sports have arguably become less fun since the geeks assumed control.

Other sports have fared differently. The distribution of basketball shots is unrecognisable from a decade ago, with large numbers coming from the three-point line. Limited-overs cricket has become a more exciting spectacle since data analysis showed that high-risk, high-reward attempts to hit a four or a six led to a better chance of winning than more cautious batting. I would argue football has also become more exciting, with a faster tempo, higher-quality attempts on goal, and tactics like gegenpressing. Gegenpressing tacitly accepts the risk of a higher chance of conceding a goal in return for the reward of a higher chance of scoring one. I have a pet theory: the quality of a sport can be gauged by whether data analysis makes it more entertaining or less entertaining. Football is, of course, the best sport, and data analysis has improved it so far. Let's find out how.

2.

Tottenham Hotspur

It is a capital mistake to theorize before one has data.
Insensibly one begins to twist facts to suit theories,
instead of theories to suit facts

Sherlock Holmes (Arthur Conan Doyle)

Sensible Soccer, Science and Statistics

Growing up in rural South Wales I had little connection to any club. My closest team – Swansea City – were in the Third Division when I became interested in football, but even they were an hour's drive away, and nobody in my family cared about football. Most of my classmates supported Liverpool – they were the most successful team in the 1980s, and children always love to follow a successful team. By coincidence I shared a name with one of their greatest strikers – Ian Rush – who was also Welsh. I couldn't not become a Liverpool fan.

I was always a very geeky fan. There wasn't much football on TV in the 1980s, so instead I read about it – a series of children's books on the histories of Liverpool, Manchester United, Celtic, Rangers, Everton and Arsenal. The Ladybird book *World Cup 86* made an enormous impression on me. I spent hours poring over an old book of football statistics that included every league table in history – I couldn't believe how many times in the 1960s Bradford (Park Avenue) AFC had finished bottom of Third Division North and had successfully 'applied for re-election' (relegation from the Third Division being impossible back then) given how bad they were.

I was also obsessed with Subbuteo, the game where you could 'flick to kick' miniature players around a miniature pitch. My dad had stapled the fabric pitch to a wooden board to make for a better playing surface. I occasionally convinced my brother and a couple of friends in the village to play a tournament but most of the time I had to play games against myself. Every summer there was a full league and cup calendar, with Liverpool, Celtic, Brazil, Watford, West Germany and Italy competing in the first division, and Liverpool (away kit), Holland, Coventry City and Scotland competing in the second division. After each round of fixtures I would update the results and league tables using the Amstrad computer that my mother had borrowed from the local college, where she taught word processing. By some fluke, Liverpool won the double and Liverpool (away kit) were promoted to the first division, replacing relegated West Germany.

Come the 1990s, I became addicted to Sensible World of Soccer, a computer game where you controlled the action on the pitch, but could also sign and sell players. I would scour the globe for bargains, foreshadowing my future career. I would always sign Dynamo Brest's speedy wingers – they helped many of my teams to Champions League glory.

The other sport that I loved in the 1980s was American football. NFL highlights were shown every Sunday evening in the UK and its exotic glamour made it very popular. I loved the glut of statistics – passing yardage for quarterbacks, sacks for defenders – and I loved the way that they *meant* something. Passing for 300 yards in a game usually indicated a very good performance. Football, as far as I was aware, had nothing similar.

Football was always just a hobby for me – I always assumed I'd have a career in science or engineering. I studied physics at university, and by 2005 I had done a Ph.D. in biological physics, using ideas from statistical physics to try to understand the chemical-sensing network of *E. coli* bacteria. Despite barely passing my Ph.D., I applied to be a postdoctoral researcher working on the challenging topic of polymer[1] physics. I enjoyed the work, but it was tough going. People much cleverer than me had advanced the theory of polymer physics, and the pieces that remained unexplained were by definition very difficult to explain. After nine months' work I was nowhere near publishing a paper, which is lethal to a young scientist's future employment prospects.

Even though I liked the work, the money was bad (£14,000 per year) and so was the security (a two-year fixed-term contract). I could sense the end of my scientific career was nigh, given my failure to produce any new research. At the time, my partner worked at the University of Cambridge Local Examinations Syndicate. The head statistician there had seen an advert on an academic job listings website that asked: 'Would you like to analyse football statistics for a living?' I leapt at the opportunity. I had always loved football but had no idea that it was possible to have a career analysing the information it produced.

The company I worked for, Decision Technology, is a management consultancy specialising in behavioural economics. Its main business is doing experiments and analysis to help supermarkets decide which special offers to run, or banks to optimise the interest rates on credit cards. Its co-founder, Henry Stott, used football as an advertising tool. His idea was that football was a captivating example of how data analysis adds insight. Prospective clients were sent Premier League and World Cup forecasts. This would pique their interest in Decision Technology, while the forecasts also showcased the company's analytical skills.

In the early days, our main football client was Danny Finkelstein at *The Times*. Every week we would analyse a football topic – red cards, home advantage, substitutions – and send a report to Danny. He would write up the analysis for his 'Fink Tank' column, which appeared in the paper every Saturday.

Searching for Signal

Football teams seemed like obvious clients for our services, but no one was interested. Part of the problem was that detailed player data didn't exist. But the main issue was that no one employed by a football club knew about or cared about data analysis. That would soon change. Damien Comolli, who had been a scout at Arsenal under Arsène Wenger and sporting director at Saint-Etienne, was headhunted in 2005 for the role of director of football at Tottenham Hotspur. Spurs were unusual – very few teams in England had a director of football at the time.

Damien had been given a mission at Spurs: a top-four finish, which Spurs had not yet achieved in the Premier League era and which would bring Champions League football and much larger revenue. The problem was that Spurs wanted to achieve this using a lot less money than the 'big four' teams who usually topped the table – Manchester United, Arsenal, Chelsea and Liverpool. Damien had read *Moneyball* and felt that data analysis could be applied to football. He had employed a French company called Amisco to provide Spurs with technical reports, but they were not predictive. 'They were telling me what the weather was like yesterday, but I was trying to understand what the weather will be next week,' he told me.

Damien began a mission to understand sports data. He visited baseball's Oakland A's and met their general manager, Billy Beane, who showed him what could be done with baseball statistics. Player performances could be measured, but also projected, and an estimate of a player's impact on a team's number of wins could be made. Damien told Beane that he wanted something similar for football but didn't really know where to start. Beane told him: 'You should speak to Finkelstein' – he had been reading our column in *The Times*. Billy Beane's matchmaking gave us our first opportunity to work with a club.

The data problem was also solved. A media company, Opta, had started to produce detailed 'Event Data'. For every on-ball 'event', like a pass, tackle or dribble, Opta would record the player's identity, some context for the event (was it a header, a chipped pass or a pass along the ground?), and where on the pitch the event happened.

The data was finally granular enough that I could develop a Possession Value model.

> ## 'Possession Value' Models
>
> The system that we used to analyse players for Spurs was an early example of a 'Possession Value' model, originally introduced by Pollard and Reep in 1997 and recently popularised by Arsenal data scientist Karun Singh as 'Expected Threat'. We've seen how Expected Goals takes one step back from goals to analyse the quality of the shots that may lead to goals. Taking another step back we can analyse the passes that lead to shots. And moving one step back again we can think about the passes that lead to passes that lead to shots. And we can keep stepping back in order to consider the impact of any action on the pitch in terms of how it might increase our team's chance of scoring. This allows us to say something about the contribution of midfielders and defenders.
>
> The name I coined for this sort of model was 'Goal Probability Added'. It is not a catchy name, but it is descriptive. The idea is to estimate the probability of scoring a goal from a given game situation. One way of doing this is by looking at possessions. Imagine a player has possession in midfield, in open play, just inside his own half. What is the chance that his team scores a goal before losing possession? The easiest way to estimate this is to count all of the occasions where a team had possession in a similar situation and count the number of those occasions where a goal was scored before possession was lost. A rough estimate might be that for every 1,000 occasions a team has possession just inside their own half, four goals are scored – a goal probability of 0.4%. We can ask the same question for any game situation. For example, a possession on the

edge of the opposition box might lead to 17 goals for every 1,000 possessions – a goal probability of 1.7%.

We looked at a range of different game situations – open play, set-pieces, defensive possession and controlled possession – and assigned a goal probability to each area of the pitch for each situation. The results are intuitive – obvious even – to any fan: possession is on average more valuable the closer you are to the opposition goal. Controlled possession is more valuable than defensive possession. Set-piece possession is more valuable than open-play possession far away from the box, because you can retain possession with a short free-kick or put the ball in the box from a corner or wide free-kick. But close to and inside the opposition box, open-play possession is more valuable than set-piece possession, because the opposition typically packs the box to defend set-pieces.

With all these situations labelled, and a goal probability attached to each, we can start to analyse player impact. In our example, if the player in possession just inside their own half (0.4% chance of a goal on this possession) makes a successful pass to the edge of the box (1.7% chance of a goal), he has helped to increase his team's chance of a goal by 1.3%. If he loses the ball he has decreased his team's chance of a goal by 0.4%. These changes in goal probability are the foundations upon which player ratings are built.

By 2007, Opta had collected event data for the big five European leagues – the English Premier League, French Ligue 1, German Bundesliga, Italian Serie A and Spanish La Liga. They'd also collected the two European competitions – the Uefa Champions League and the Uefa Cup. I spent the summer developing my Possession Value model, and by autumn 2007 it was ready to show to Spurs.

Their old training ground, Spurs Lodge, was in the leafy suburb of Chigwell, right on the north-east edge of Greater London, just inside the M25. After a typically fraught commute along London's North Circular Road I was nervously sitting in Damien's office, explaining to him how the model I'd created worked. Then came the critical moment – revealing which players were the most highly rated in the model. Years later I asked Damien what had convinced him of the value of our approach. His answer was simple: 'All the best players in the world were at the top of your model's ratings.' Damien's job was to identify talent and if the model had identified the same set of players as elite, then it must be doing something right.

I was thrilled to be working for a big Premier League club. Spurs had been in the doldrums for a few years, nearly always finishing mid-table in the Premier League. They finished fifth in 2005/06 (remember 'Lasagne-gate'?)[2] and 2006/07 but by 2007/08 were back to their habitual mid-table position. Spurs are a big club, one of only seven ever-presents in the Premier League at the time. It was exciting to be able to see the players at Spurs Lodge. I remember an exceptionally polite Luka Modrić shaking my hand and wishing me a very good morning, and saying hello to Gareth Bale who, being injured, was sat on his own in the canteen stoically eating a breakfast of beans on toast.

Disaster Strikes

Our first transfer window working for Spurs was the summer of 2008. Spurs had won the League Cup that spring, and the future looked reasonably bright, but the transfer window would bring massive upheaval.

One of Damien's successful signings, the charismatic Bulgarian forward Dimitar Berbatov, had had a magnificent season. Manchester United were desperate to sign him. Spurs played a game of brinkmanship, extracting the maximum amount of money from United by waiting until very late in the window before agreeing to the transfer. The upside was that more money was indeed extracted – the transfer fee of £30.75 million was the second highest ever between Premier League clubs at the time.[3] The downside, however, was that there was little time to replace him, and many of the available players we'd identified had already been transferred. Spurs ended up signing Roman Pavlyuchenko from Spartak Moscow. Pavlyuchenko had played well in Euro 2008, but we had no data on the Russian league so could not really offer an opinion on his value to Spurs.

To compound Spurs' problems in attack, Liverpool unexpectedly bid for their other striker, Robbie Keane. Damien, knowing Berbatov would be leaving, demanded a high fee of £19 million and was surprised when Liverpool agreed to pay it. Spurs had made a lot of money, but would go into the season having replaced Berbatov and Keane with Pavlyuchenko and Fraizer Campbell, a young loan signing from Manchester United.

Goalkeeper was another position where we provided advice. Our goalkeeper ratings, based on Post-Strike Expected Goals (see box), indicated that Paul Robinson had been among the worst performers in the Premier League for shot-stopping since 2006/07. The outstanding candidate to replace him was Hugo Lloris. Lloris, then a 20-year-old playing at Nice in France, had had one of the best goalkeeping seasons in Europe according to our model. Damien had told me that Lloris wanted to come to Spurs and I was very excited about the first signing that would be made with the help of data. But my dreams were soon shattered: Lloris received some bizarre advice that if he signed for Spurs he would not be considered for the French national team. He signed for Lyon instead. Lloris continued to live up to the incredibly high expectations set by his first season, and eventually arrived at Spurs in 2012.

Post-Strike Expected Goals

Expected Goals (see box in Chapter 1) assigns a conversion chance to a shot given its distance to goal, angle, phase of play and so on. But when it comes to assessing goalkeepers, Expected Goals is not the right tool to use.

At first glance, saving goals seems like the mirror-image of converting goals, and all Expected Goals does is to measure conversion chance. A keeper who saves shots with a high conversion chance is probably performing well. However, there is a problem. Every single shot has a positive conversion chance according to Expected Goals. But goalkeepers do not have to save off-target shots. And it is difficult to save shots smashed into the top corner, and easy to save shots scuffed straight at the goalkeeper.

Post-Strike Expected Goals adds information about the trajectory of the shot in order to create a revised conversion chance. An Expected Goals conversion chance of 30% becomes 0% if the shot is off-target, maybe 10% if the shot is hit close to the goalkeeper, and maybe 90% if the shot is hit into the top corner.

Expected Goals asks 'What is the chance of a goal given a shot?' Post-Strike Expected Goals changes the question to 'What is the chance of a goal given a shot whose trajectory we know?' It allows us to calculate a difficulty-adjusted save percentage for goalkeepers. For example, a goalkeeper who faces only penalties is not expected to have a high save percentage, whereas a goalkeeper who only faces shots aimed at him is expected to have a very high save percentage.

The back-up choice for goalkeeper was Heurelho Gomes. Spurs had been beaten in the Uefa Cup by PSV Eindhoven that season, and Gomes was the star of the penalty shoot-out. We didn't have data for the Dutch league, but we did have data on Gomes's games in the Champions League and Uefa Cup. His shot-stopping had looked fine in those games, but it was only 20 games over two seasons. We were not very certain about his qualities. But Spurs' scouting was also very positive on Gomes, so Damien felt comfortable signing him. The signing was certainly helped by Gomes saving a penalty kick in the shoot-out against Spurs, and playing very well over the two legs, conceding only one goal when two goals might have been expected.

Gomes turned out to be an excellent shot-stopper for Spurs – among the best in the league in his first two seasons. But he was liable to the occasional spectacular mistake. We were often asked by Spurs whether our analysis of Gomes was correct. It was a case of what psychologist Daniel Kahneman calls 'availability bias'.[4] Dramatic events, personal experiences and vivid examples lead to biases in evaluating performance. Some of Gomes's mistakes had cost Spurs points, and so he sometimes looked really bad on *Match of the Day*. Our work suggested Spurs should accept his occasional howlers because he was extremely good at shot-stopping. A save is usually not as emotional or as vivid an event as a goal. And if a goalkeeper has skills such as quick reactions or pre-emptive positioning, then saves that might look spectacular from a lesser player can look routine from a better one. Ironically, Gomes's excellence made him look a less impressive player than he really was.

Another player I was excited about was Giovani dos Santos, signed from Barcelona. He also rated extremely highly in our model, but over only 1,400 minutes, the equivalent of only about 15 full games. When discussing Dos Santos with Damien, I did not put enough emphasis on his low number of minutes: it is easier to look excellent in a run of 15 games than it is to look excellent in a run of 30 games. The fact that Spurs' manager Juande Ramos really liked the player helped. The scouting reports were also positive, so Damien felt it made sense to sign him. But Dos Santos did not prosper at Spurs – and his chances were not helped by Ramos getting sacked eight games into the season. Spurs had started the campaign very badly, drawing two and losing six of their first eight games of the 2008/09 season. Damien left Spurs along with Ramos, and I was worried that Decision Technology's contract would be cancelled. These worries were not eased when Harry Redknapp was appointed manager and Damien's role of director of football was made redundant.

Harry's Game

Damien had signed Gareth Bale from Southampton in 2007 as a precocious 17-year-old. But he had made a bad start at Spurs. He was injured for a large portion of his first season, and now in 2008/09 he was not a regular starter under new manager Harry Redknapp.

The club were considering using Bale as a makeweight in a deal with Middlesbrough to sign Stewart Downing. To my great surprise, data was being used in the press to support the idea that Bale was not a good player. Bale's problem was that Spurs had not won any of the first 22 Premier League games that he had started. This fact led to the incorrect conclusion that he must be a bad player. My analysis of Bale showed something very different. In the 22 games Bale started, he had been impressive despite the team's repeated failure to win. Often playing at left-back, he was doing as much attacking as a typical winger. Spurs' defence suffered because of it, but Bale's personal contribution was fine – still only a teenager, he rated as an average Premier League full-back, albeit one with an extremely lopsided profile of good attacking and poor defending.

There was some scepticism about our analysis so I looked at the rest of the squad in terms of the points the team won when they started compared to when they did not start. This type of analysis, known as 'plus-minus', was popular and somewhat useful in basketball but I did not believe it was a valid approach in football. Bale was clearly the worst performer in terms of points won when starting, but two of the other worst performers by this metric were Jonathan Woodgate and Ledley King, both of whom had played for England. Woodgate and King had injury problems and their game-time was managed. They tended to play against tougher opposition so had an excuse for a lower number of points won when playing. But the conclusion that they were among Spurs' worst players was ridiculous enough to convince Spurs that they shouldn't pay too much attention to their failure to win when Bale started. Bale soon moved up a line, playing on the left wing, and immediately prospered. In 2013 Real Madrid paid £85.3 million to secure his services.

After Damien left Spurs, my meetings were with head of video analysis Ryan Groom. Ryan was a thoughtful advocate of data analysis but had many calls on his time. Redknapp's assistant coach, Joe Jordan, had an insatiable appetite for video analysis and most of our meetings were interrupted by Joe asking Ryan when the next cut of video would be ready. We finally stopped meeting at Spurs Lodge and relocated to a local pub to avoid the constant interruption. In those pub meetings we discussed some Brazilian players. Leandro Damião had played for Brazil and scored at a very high rate, but on further inspection many of his goals had been scored in the state championships against small clubs. The state championships were the equivalent of Arsenal, Spurs and Chelsea playing in a league against Barnet, Leyton Orient and Dagenham & Redbridge. His goal-scoring exploits at that level needed to be taken with a very large pinch of salt.

Spurs slowly began to make progress. In January 2009, the hole left by Berbatov and Robbie Keane was filled by Jermain Defoe, an ex-Spurs player who had played for Redknapp at Portsmouth, and, er, Robbie Keane, who had barely played at Liverpool. In a perfect illustration of the insanity of the transfer market, he was re-signed by Spurs for £12 million, £7 million less than Liverpool had paid for him six months previously.

Spurs ended 2008/09 in eighth place and began the summer 2009 transfer window with a plan to sell striker Darren Bent. Spurs had signed Bent from Charlton for a club-record £16.5 million in 2007, but Harry Redknapp was not a fan. After Bent failed to finish a seemingly easy chance, he famously said his wife 'Sandra could have scored that'.[5] Our opinion of Bent was high and our advice was not to sell, but he was transferred to Sunderland for £10 million, potentially rising to £16.5 million based on performances.

Bent's replacement at Spurs was Peter Crouch, who, like Defoe, had played for Redknapp at Portsmouth. Crouch was joined by Niko Kranjčar, who had also played for Redknapp at Portsmouth. It was an early lesson for me that would reappear throughout my career: managers tend to like players who have played for them before. It makes a lot of sense – the manager knows the character of the player and his strengths and weaknesses: a lot of risk is removed from the transfer. Crouch played for two seasons at Spurs and played well. He only scored 12 goals in two seasons but created many chances and goals for his team-mates. He was transferred to Stoke City in summer 2011 for a small profit – no mean feat for a player the wrong side of 30. Crouch's transfer was a success, but even so Spurs had lost out by selling Bent. In his 18-month spell at Sunderland he scored 24 goals and his value skyrocketed. In January 2011 Bent signed for Aston Villa for £18 million, potentially rising to £24 million. His first 18 months at Villa were successful, scoring 16 goals excluding penalties.

It's All Bullshit, Isn't It?

Harry Redknapp was keen to bring his old Portsmouth video analyst to Spurs. Michael Edwards had worked for Portsmouth since 2003 and became Spurs' head of video analysis in November 2009. He would also become responsible for the club's relationship with Decision Technology. I was not thrilled at this prospect. Bizarrely, Spurs' board had decided that Harry did not need to know about data analysis and Decision Technology, and I assumed that Michael was a Redknapp loyalist. Our first meeting confirmed my worst fears.

Space was at a premium at Spurs Lodge. My first meeting with Michael, on a cold, grey November day, was in the draughty education room used by the Academy. 'Pleased to meet you, Michael,' I said. He replied: 'My friends call me Eddy.' The default formula for a training ground nickname is first syllable of surname plus the letter 'Y'. Eddy was wearing the usual video analyst's uniform of

Spurs training kit. He was quite short and skinny, and wearing a pair of glasses even thicker than mine. The strange look was topped off with a spiky haircut. Eddy would later tell me that when Sunderland's manager Mick McCarthy spotted him at Fratton Park, he exclaimed: 'Fuck me, it's Jedward.'

We waited for some Academy players to file out before sitting down to talk. As I was opening my laptop, Eddy made his opening move: 'All this data analysis in football is bullshit, isn't it?' I soon found out that this behaviour is quite typical. Eddy is aggressive and combative and takes a special delight in confronting and calling out nonsense wherever he sees it. He had been a youth footballer in Peterborough's Academy but was released, having been deemed too small to succeed in the professional game. After gaining a degree in informatics and trying out teaching IT (a role to which he was definitely not suited) he had been offered a job by a friend who was working for Prozone, football's first real data company.

Prozone had installed video cameras in football stadiums, and recorded each game on VHS. After every game, the tapes were driven to the company's Leeds office, where they were painstakingly transcribed into the first version of 'Tracking Data', where all of the players' positions on the pitch are captured. At Portsmouth, Eddy's job was to present a statistical report for each game to the coaching team. The problem was that he thought the statistics were garbage. And at the time he was right. First, the coaches didn't care about statistics, and second, the statistics didn't represent what he believed to be important about the game. I had come to the same conclusion while developing my Possession Value model. Pass completion percentages were meaningless – it is easy to complete 100% of passes if they are all back towards the goalkeeper. The passes that make a difference by breaking the defensive line are risky by definition and players making those passes have much lower completion rates.

The main use of Prozone was physical data – how much distance the player had covered, how many sprints he had made and so on. This had some use for planning training sessions, but the physical data did not have much correlation with team success. Instead, it was used as a motivational tool – a way for the manager to criticise players for being lazy if their total distance was low. Players immediately began to game the system. When the ball was out of play, one Portsmouth player started sprinting to the touchline to take a throw-in.

Given his experiences with data, it was no wonder Eddy was sceptical. I began to explain the Possession Value model to him. Move from defensive to controlled possession, get a reward. Move the ball up the pitch, get a reward. The rewards get higher the closer to the opposition goal you go. Lose possession, receive a penalty. I thought I was getting somewhere, but 'it's bollocks though, isn't it? You can't tell how much pressure a player's under. The backwards pass might be his best option.' The only way to get someone to trust a mathematical model is to explain it honestly, including its shortcomings as well as its strengths, so I admitted that we could not directly see in the data how much pressure a player was under. The data was certainly an incomplete view of the game and it did not capture some of the things that Eddy knew were important. But it did consistently, if imperfectly, record every action of every player in every game.

Dean Oliver, author of *Basketball on Paper* and one of my sports data heroes, has spoken eloquently on this topic. 'A good scout, a good analyst, they go and they watch the game,' he said. 'Your eyes see the game much better than the numbers. But the numbers see all the games. And that's a big deal! They see all the detail and they really get you a lot of the story. Watching on video and going to games, those add different components to what the numbers can give you.' This is the point of view that Eddy slowly came round to, though I didn't realise it during that first meeting. The meeting was a brutal three hours of being loudly told in colourful language the manifold shortcomings of my work. Afterwards, somewhat rattled, I sat in the Spurs Lodge car park trying to collect my thoughts. I remember calling my boss Henry and saying: 'I don't think we'll be working with Spurs for much longer. Their new video analyst doesn't believe in data.' Thankfully, I was wrong.

Spurs continued to improve on the pitch and, motivated by Eddy's endless nitpicking, I had refined our Possession Value. My colleague Mark Latham developed a model to understand a player's positional role in a team, so we also had a way of identifying players playing in a style that Spurs were interested in, as well as providing a judgement on what impact they'd have on results.

In Eddy, we had an advocate who believed in and understood our models, and also understood their strengths and weaknesses. His youth football career gave him strong opinions on what was captured well by our analysis and what wasn't. One player who caused a difference of opinion was Luka Modrić. According to our system he was a perfectly good young attacking midfielder, which was out of step with Eddy's opinion that he was by far the best player in the squad. When ever-greater offers for Modrić's services came in from Europe, our opinion was Spurs should certainly consider selling if there was a reasonable replacement available. Eddy did not agree with that advice. Looking back, and knowing now what was missing from those early models, Eddy was right and we were wrong. Modrić's dribbling and passing looked good, but not world-class. Eddy could see, watching every game in detail on video, that Modrić passed, received and dribbled in very tight spaces, and often relieved pressure for his team. These were aspects that were difficult to glean from the data: at that time they were not directly collected. This experience with Modrić became our template for understanding players. Data analysis defined the starting point for our evaluation of a player, and Eddy's judgement would refine that starting point. For the most part, there was good agreement between the model and Eddy's view but in special cases, like Modrić, Eddy would consider a player to be better or worse than the model suggested.

The summer 2010 transfer window was the test of our improved method of work. Harry Redknapp's exciting style of play required attackers, and there was a shortlist of four. Liverpool's Ryan Babel, Wigan's Charles N'Zogbia, Everton's Steven Pienaar and a Dutchman playing for Real Madrid. Rafael van der Vaart was an outstanding attacking midfielder who had been Hamburg's star player before moving to Spain in 2008. At Madrid, he was a bit-part player, start-ing only 31 league games in two seasons, and usually being subbed off in the games he did start. The other players on the shortlist had lots of Premier League experience, something that Premier League managers love and something that is priced accordingly by the market, attracting a big mark-up on transfer fees.

Van der Vaart had been brilliant in Spain, even though he was not a regular starter. He'd also been excellent in the Bundesliga. The other options were all good Premier League players, but Van der Vaart was clearly the best choice according to our model, and Eddy agreed. He was signed on deadline day. I was ecstatic. He started brilliantly for Spurs – over two seasons at White Hart Lane he exceeded my expectations and played better even than he had at Madrid. But Harry was not a fan. Van der Vaart was not his choice, and this seemed to outweigh the evidence in front of his eyes. If Van der Vaart had not been such a talented player, I think Harry would have dropped him. Despite his being a very early example of data helping to sign a player, Van der Vaart is not a fan of statistics. He recently said: 'The "data people" need to get out of the football world as soon as possible. Otherwise I will quit watching football in three years' time. I am being serious.'[6]

There were other highlights, such as recommending signing Emmanuel Adebayor and keeping Kyle Walker. There were also dis-appointments such as missing out on Mesut Ozil, then playing for Werder Bremen. It is strange to think that data was not readily avail-able for players 15 years ago, and Premier League clubs' knowledge of foreign markets was much more patchy than it is today. A rough guide to the better players, which is exactly what our model pro-vided, gave Spurs a head start in identifying potential transfers. Despite this, lots of Spurs' foreign signings at the time – Modrić, Pavlyuchenko, Gomes, Sandro – were signed from leagues where detailed data did not yet exist. In fact, Van der Vaart was the only data-driven signing from a non-UK club.

Looking back at my experiences with Spurs, we made a differ-ence. Decision Technology's advice played an important part in helping Spurs turn the 'big four' into the 'big six', along with Manchester City. In 2009/10 and 2011/12 the club finished fourth, achieving their highest ever positions and points totals in the Premier League at the time. They qualified for the Champions League for the first time.

From 1992 to 2008, Spurs were a mid-table Premier League team averaging 51 points per season. Over the course of their relationship with Decision Technology they improved to a Champions League level team, winning on average 69 points per season between 2008 and 2019. My own period working with Spurs, until 2012, was not quite statistically significant – they won 63 points per season between 2008 and 2012. But this improvement was achieved with a low net transfer spend. Over those seasons Spurs bought low and sold high, and their five-season spend was only the seventh highest in the league, lower than Stoke City's and Aston Villa's, and only just higher than Sunderland's. Spurs' wage bill also remained much lower than their Champions League rivals.

Many factors were important in Spurs' success: Harry Redknapp's leadership of the squad, Daniel Levy's financial acumen and running of the club, and Eddy's expert video analysis and translation of our advice. Our work at Decision Technology also played its part. We helped move the odds in Spurs' favour by recommending good signings, suggesting the club keep its best players, and steering the club away from questionable signings. The work at Spurs was rewarding but as a third party I was often far removed from the real decision-making at the club. Spurs were, I think, happy with the work we did. But I felt very frustrated. As exciting as it was to be advising a big Premier League team, I had little insight into how or why decisions were made. Sometimes our recommendations were followed and sometimes they were not, and the reasons why were usually not shared. I believed we could add much more to the decision-making process, but Spurs kept Decision Technology at arm's length. Soon enough another ingredient was added to my frustration: Eddy left.

Eddy had worked closely with Harry and his coaches for years at

Portsmouth, but their relationship soured a little after the Van der Vaart signing. In 2010 Harry had confronted Eddy on the subject: 'Van der Vaart. Van der fucking Vaart. He's your signing, Eddy, not mine.' Harry's coaches chipped in: 'This data analysis is all bullshit. You know it's bullshit, why are you using it to sign players?' The coaches' complaints were unfair. Eddy had been asked by the board to translate our data analysis and aid their decision-making. He recommended Van der Vaart but didn't sign him. Eddy soon left Spurs and most of the fun of working for Spurs left with him. Maybe it was time for me to think about a change too.

3

False Red Dawn

To find out what happens to a system when you interfere with it,
you have to interfere with it (and not just passively observe it)

George Box

The American Invasion

Decision Technology's deal with Spurs was exclusive: we were not allowed to work with any other Premier League team. But we were allowed to work for teams in other leagues, so the company sent me on an evangelising mission to spread the good word about data analysis. The mission failed – I'm not a great salesman – but I did believe in the message. Effective data analysis would give teams an edge by improving their decision-making process, particularly in the transfer market.

By early 2012 I'd expended a lot of time and effort trying to sell Decision Technology's services. I'd spoken to clubs in Germany, France and the United States. Some were very interested in our work, but somehow they were never quite ready to sign a contract. Spurs had started to enjoy some success but apparently the story was not compelling enough to make other teams queue up for our services.

Moneyball told the story of how Billy Beane and the Oakland A's baseball team massively overperformed their small budget by using statistical analysis to identify undervalued players. Yet even the film adaptation of the same name, starring Brad Pitt and released in

2011, wasn't sufficient to convince clubs of the value of data. This was despite Beane, the film's main protagonist, saying of football: 'There is so much emotion going into football, there must be a lot of inefficiency. And that means that there is a lot of opportunity.'[1] If Brad Pitt couldn't convince them, what chance would I have? Meanwhile, Fenway Sports Group (FSG), then known as New England Sports Ventures and led by John W. Henry, had purchased Liverpool in October 2010. John is an American billionaire who earned his fortune using statistical methods in the stock market, having started out trading soya bean futures. Back in 2002, FSG bought the Boston Red Sox, a major league baseball team. John was convinced that the statistical approach pioneered by Beane and the Oakland A's could be applied successfully to a big budget team. The 'cursed' Red Sox had not won a World Series since 1918, but their new data-driven approach proved very successful. In 2004, the Red Sox won their first World Series in 86 years. They won it again in 2007 and 2013. John believed the same methods would be successful in football.

When FSG bought Liverpool, my heart sank. Finally, here was a club owner who would be willing to listen to our arguments about data analysis, and likely to buy into them on a much grander scale than Spurs. And here I was working at Decision Technology, which was locked into a long-term exclusive contract with Tottenham bloody Hotspur.

There was soon a reason for hope, however. It came from Damien Comolli. In late 2010 he was hired by Liverpool as director of football strategy. Maybe he would try to secure our services.

Meeting Fenway

In April 2012, I was on my way back from the office – sitting on the train, staring out the window, feeling mildly despondent – when my phone rang. It was a familiar voice: 'Would you like to meet John Henry? He's coming to Liverpool on Thursday, and he wants to meet you.'

In November 2011, Eddy had been headhunted by Damien Comolli to join Liverpool as their head of performance and analysis, and we'd been discussing if there might be a way for Decision Technology to break free from the Spurs contract and work for Liverpool instead. Now he was calling to ask if I wanted to meet John Henry. We both knew his question was rhetorical. We both knew I wouldn't be able to resist.

The meeting was arranged one morning a few days later, but I was running very late as my train had hit a sofa left on the line just outside Crewe. As I watched the debris being removed from the railway tracks, feeling agitated about being late for such an important appointment, Eddy called again:

'Just so you know, Damien's gone.'

'What do you mean, he's "gone"?'

'He's left the club. He's not working for Liverpool any more.'

'Oh. Do you still want me to come to the meeting? Is it still on?'

'Yes, they still want to meet you.'

A couple of hours later, I was waiting in Damien's former office at Melwood. The window looked out over the training pitches, though training had finished for the day by the time I arrived. No trace of Damien's presence remained.

Eddy, John Henry and Tom Werner – Liverpool's chairman – walked in.

Tom, an American TV producer, exuded showbiz warmth. 'How *are* you? It's *so* great to meet you. We're *really* excited to hear about your work.' John, in contrast, said nothing. Tom and Eddy sat down. I sat down. John continued standing and not speaking. The contrast between him and Tom was disconcerting. If there was a World Cup of Silence, John would have made it to at least the semi-finals.

Eventually, still standing, he placed both hands on the table and leaned towards me. In a quiet voice, staring directly at me, he said slowly: 'Ian, I have an advantage over you. No, wait. I have a tremendous advantage over you. A *tremendous* advantage.'

I didn't know what to do with this information. I replied: 'Er, OK.'

'I have a tremendous advantage over you because I know that

you're a Liverpool fan, and I know that you're going to come and work for us.'

The recent history of Liverpool had not been happy. American businessmen Tom Hicks and George Gillett had bought the club in 2007. Results on the pitch had sharply declined, exacerbated by the defensive approach of new manager Roy Hodgson. Off the pitch, the club's debts – created by Hicks and Gillett's leveraged buyout – caused their creditors to force a sale. In October 2010, John W. Henry and FSG bought the club for £300 million.

Now, in April 2012, John Henry had offered me my dream job. I didn't actually agree there and then to come and work for the club, but John was correct in knowing that I would. Eddy's blunt but elegant solution to the problem of that exclusive Spurs contract was to have Liverpool hire me instead.

The meeting ended abruptly – there was more hiring and firing to be done. John and Tom filed out of the office. Eddy had to chaperone them for the next couple of hours but would be back for lunch. I was left alone in Damien's old office. I opened up my laptop and tried to do some work but I couldn't concentrate. The BBC Sport website's top story was about the upheaval at Liverpool – some other senior training ground staff had already been given the boot. I was in the eye of the storm. Eddy finally turned up at 5pm, the hiring and firing complete; his day had been much busier than mine.

Liverpool were in disarray. They'd finished the previous season with 58 points, their fourth worst Premier League season ever in terms of points per game. By the end of the season in May 2012 they had recorded their worst ever Premier League season points tally of 52. I would start in June 2012. There was a lot to be done. Since summer 2009, Liverpool had sold some of their world-class players – Xabi Alonso, Javier Mascherano and Fernando Torres. And the players who had arrived had mostly failed to make an impact. The money spent on players such as Alberto Aquilani, Andy Carroll, Christian Poulsen, Paul Konchesky and Charlie Adam had been wasted. To make things worse, Liverpool would soon be desperately short of forwards. Craig Bellamy and Maxi Rodríguez were out of contract and Dirk Kuyt had a bizarre clause in his contract, allowing him to join a Dutch team for a bargain price. The squad was expensively assembled but had performed poorly, and Liverpool's chances of success seemed slimmer than ever given the strength of Manchester United, Arsenal and Chelsea, and the fact that Manchester City and Tottenham Hotspur had turned the 'big four' into the 'big six'.

In between being offered the job and accepting it, I had to recuse myself from Spurs work. Spurs had sacked Harry Redknapp at the end of 2011/12. Liverpool and their manager (and club legend) Sir Kenny Dalglish had also decided to part company. Both clubs had a very short shortlist of managers: Roberto Martínez or Brendan Rodgers. The conflict of interest meant I couldn't continue advising Spurs.

I was ignorant of it at the time, but FSG's headhunting process had started a couple of months earlier. I was in Boston representing Decision Technology at the MIT Sloan Sports Analytics Conference – America's annual meet-up for sports stats geeks. The conference was dedicated to American sports, but 'soccer' had a growing presence there. I'd spoken at its first dedicated soccer event the previous year. Eddy, by then working for Liverpool, was also in attendance. On the final day of the conference, he asked me: 'Would you like to meet Bill James tomorrow?' This is the geek's equivalent of asking a Liverpool fan if they'd like to meet Kenny Dalglish. Bill James was the *real* star of *Moneyball*, the little-known statistician slowly inventing a body of work that would redefine how performance was measured in baseball, and eventually lead to its statistical revolution. James had been hired by John Henry in 2003 to work for the Boston Red Sox and now I had the chance to meet him.

It was a freezing cold blustery Sunday, so we decided to take a cab from downtown Boston to Fenway Park, home of the Red Sox. On the way I asked Eddy how he'd managed to arrange the meeting with Bill James: 'John Henry suggested it. Bill can tell us how data is used in baseball and give us some good advice on how to really make a difference to a team.'

The stadium was deserted – the season would not start for

another month and it took a little time to convince the security guard that we really did have a meeting scheduled at the stadium. We were led up a few flights of stairs to the offices, where Bill and his colleague Tom Tippett were waiting. Bill greeted us warmly and offered us a coffee. Then we sat down to talk. Bill started off by asking about football: 'I don't know a lot about soccer. You've got all those different leagues over there in Europe. How can you tell if a player from one league would be any good in another?' I was impressed by his politeness – how thoughtful that the king of baseball stats was showing an interest in our sport. I answered his question: promotion, relegation, cup games and European games mean we can create a kind of exchange rate of goals across leagues. It's harder to score in the Premier League, so we use the exchange rate to downgrade goals scored in other leagues.

Tom Tippett did know about football. He was another John Henry hire, joining the Red Sox after developing a baseball computer simulation engine. He wanted to know how the exchange rate worked for different teams. It's easier to score against Bochum than Bayern Munich, right? I answered: yes, the exchange rate was team-specific. What about the transfer market? How did that work? And how do you adjust performances based on the player's role in the team? What could data say about defending? How do player skills change with age? I was happy to try to answer the questions – back in 2012 it was a novelty to meet anyone the slightest bit interested in football data analysis. A conversation with two baseball executives who appeared to be fascinated by the subject was wonderful. But after about 90 minutes I started to wonder when we'd get to ask them about the secrets of the Red Sox.

Before we had a chance to ask our questions, the meeting was over. Bill was kind enough to give us a tour of Fenway Park but he'd stopped talking shop. Walking around the baseball diamond, Bill pointed out the distance between the plates and observed that baseball players were very underrated as athletes. It was freezing outside but the atmosphere got a little frostier when I gave my opinion that footballers are by far the better all-round athletes. I also remember

Bill expounding his theory of 'conservation of fan joy'. The idea is that when a big team wins, its many fans are a little bit happy – they were expected to win after all. But when a small team wins its fans are ecstatic, with the result that the total amount of joy, regardless of the result, remains constant.

Heading back to downtown Boston, I said to Eddy: 'That was weird. We didn't get to ask them about baseball at all.' Eddy agreed. I never actually asked anyone at FSG, but in retrospect I think Bill and Tom had been asked to give an opinion on my suitability as a future employee and Eddy's as a more senior employee. They did a thorough job.

Bill was kind enough to get back in touch a week later with his thoughts regarding a data-based strategy for football. He deduced, correctly, that the challenges in football are much bigger than in baseball. In his sport, there was a huge record and tradition of statistics, and many 'fanalysts' who analysed them. Football had no such thing. The injection of money into baseball had also led to owners insisting on professionalism and accountability from a team's decision-makers, a process that was only just starting in football. Some of his advice – such as fostering a community of analytically minded fans – we didn't follow, but should have. The advice that we did follow, and the most important piece of advice he gave, was: do not waste your time talking to people who are not receptive to what you do. Luckily, in John Henry, Mike Gordon and the rest of FSG, we had owners who were receptive, and demanded a data-driven and accountable approach to running a club.

A Camel is a Horse Designed by a Committee

In the weeks leading up to my first day at Liverpool, I could barely sleep. It was the club I'd supported since I was a child. The new owners had proven in baseball that they'd adopt a data-driven approach. I would be working with Eddy again. The combination of his expert opinion on players, honed during his years as a video analyst, and my data analysis would make us unstoppable in the transfer market. Eddy had also recruited Barry Hunter and Dave Fallows, who would soon arrive from Manchester City. They would overhaul Liverpool's Scouting department and give us an edge when it came to finding young players.

But everything immediately went wrong. Before I, and the other new hires, started, Liverpool had to replace their manager. Kenny Dalglish had been appointed after Roy Hodgson's disastrous tenure, and had won the League Cup in February 2012, but Premier League results in 2011/12 had been disappointing so FSG and Kenny decided to part ways. The choice of replacement was between two: Brendan Rodgers, who'd overachieved at Swansea City, winning promotion and then guiding his team to a mid-table finish in their first Premier League season; or Roberto Martínez, who had managed underdogs Wigan Athletic successfully in the Premier League for three years. Brendan was the stronger candidate and was chosen for the job. FSG, with the help of Eddy and the club's managing director Ian Ayre, were concurrently searching for a director of football to replace Damien. The search was unexpectedly cut short. Brendan used a media interview on his first day in the job to say: 'I am better when I have control . . . I wouldn't directly work with a director of football . . . If you want to have a sporting director, get him in and then you can pick your manager from there but if you do I won't be the manager.'[2]

Brendan was right. We should have appointed a sporting director first. Now he'd made it impossible. It would have been nice to have known Brendan's feelings on the matter before he took the job. Instead a compromise was reached. A committee would be formed, consisting of Brendan, Ian Ayre, Eddy, Dave and Barry. I was an unofficial member – thankfully I didn't have to join the meetings in person. The Transfer Committee, as it came to be known, was no different to how many other clubs worked – Spurs made sporting decisions in a similar way. The difference was that at Liverpool the committee became a matter of public knowledge.

In 2012, Brendan's top transfer priority was Joe Allen, a very good

22-year-old Welsh midfielder who'd enjoyed a successful first Premier League season playing for Brendan at Swansea City. As one of my first jobs at Liverpool, I was asked by the owners for my opinion of Allen. His responsibility at Swansea was to keep possession ticking over in the middle of their midfield, an important element of Brendan's Barcelona-lite style of football. Brendan saw Allen as fundamental to his team's style of play. Statistically speaking, Allen's pass completion of 91% was excellent. Of Premier League midfielders that season to play at least 2,000 minutes, only his team-mate Leon Britton managed a higher success rate. Successful passing is *correlated* with good results, but does it *cause* good results?

Through the lens of Possession Value, I could see that many of Allen's passes were quite safe, and they did not increase Swansea's chance of scoring much more than the passes of the average Premier League midfielder. The passing of Liverpool midfielders Steven Gerrard and Lucas Leiva was much more effective in terms of increasing our chance of scoring a goal. This was despite them having much lower raw pass completion percentages than Allen.

None of this is to say that Joe Allen is a bad player. He is an excellent player. As a Welshman, I know very well that Allen was for many years Wales's third best player, behind only Gareth Bale and Aaron Ramsey. Wales usually struggled when Allen wasn't playing. However, his superficially high pass-completion success rate could not really be expected to improve Liverpool's midfield. His characterisation by Brendan as the 'Welsh Xavi' was very unfair. His skills would bring value to many Premier League teams, but his value to Liverpool was marginal. Swansea, knowing Brendan's admiration, set Allen's fee at a very high £15 million. I was uncomfortable at the prospect of spending a large fraction of our transfer budget on a midfielder when there were other positions that needed to be urgently filled.

Brendan's next priority was Gylfi Sigurdsson. Like Joe Allen, Brendan's focus on Sigurdsson was an object lesson in cognitive bias. Both had Premier League experience and both had played for Brendan before. The problem was that the strongest facet of

Sigurdsson's play was his set-piece delivery. But Steven Gerrard took the set-pieces at Liverpool: the marginal value of a second right-footed set-piece expert was small. It was very uncomfortable to start our relationship opposing every one of Brendan's suggestions but his ideas of the players needed to improve our squad were very different to Eddy's and to mine.

Meanwhile, our squad was desperately short of strikers. Dirk Kuyt, Craig Bellamy and Maxi Rodríguez had been allowed to leave, and we needed replacements. Our priority was Daniel Sturridge, who was surplus to requirements at Chelsea. However, Brendan was against the idea. His preference at centre-forward was Fabio Borini, yet another player who had played for him at Swansea. To make matters worse, Brendan told the owners he would not play Andy Carroll, the striker signed for £35 million 18 months previously as Fernando Torres' replacement. Tom Werner asked me if I would speak with Brendan about Carroll.

My first meeting with Brendan didn't start well. I explained our statistical approach. Brendan's comment, which was quite perceptive, was: 'This is just the old Graham Taylor long-ball approach, isn't it?' Charles Reep had indeed worked with Taylor at Watford and, using ideas similar to Possession Value, had advocated a long-ball approach. Reep's model was sound but his conclusion – that the long-ball game was more effective – was not. It didn't matter; I'd lost Brendan's interest. I now had to bring up the subject of Andy Carroll.

'Brendan, I know your style of play doesn't suit a player like Andy Carroll. I agree there's no place for him in your long-term plans. But the owners paid a lot of money for him. If we can increase his value this season and sell him next summer that means more money to spend next year. I'm not suggesting you start Carroll in every game, but at Anfield, against smaller teams who only care about defending their own box, why not bring him on as a substitute if we've failed to break them down after 60 minutes? Just as a Plan B? He'll score a few goals and we can sell him next summer.' Carroll's market value was at a low point – he had only scored six Premier League goals in his 18 months at Liverpool, and would not attract a high transfer fee if he was to leave, as Brendan wanted. We knew that it would be impossible to recoup all of Carroll's huge transfer fee, but if we could raise market interest in his skills through playing him we might recoup a decent fraction of it.

Brendan did not think much of my suggestion. He told me that his Plan A was so good that a Plan B was not necessary. I considered asking him to reconsider in the manner of Oliver Cromwell: 'I beseech you, in the bowels of Christ, think it possible that you may be mistaken.' But I felt my words would be wasted. It was a surprise to me, then, that Brendan brought Carroll on in his first Premier League game as Liverpool manager (we were 3–0 down to West Brom), but Carroll was quickly loaned to West Ham in the hope he would prosper by playing for another team.

This experience was a hard lesson for me. Our clever ideas about how we would modernise the running of a football club crashed and burned in the face of a manager who wanted to oversee the club in the traditional English way, by being in total control of all decision-making. 'Culture eats strategy for breakfast.'

Brendan's approach to the Liverpool job was entirely understand-able and could even be considered rational. In his shoes I may have made similar decisions. A manager's job is a precarious one: a few bad results and you are at risk of being sacked. I'm sure every man-ager has heard from new owners that they are different, they are in it for the long term, and that he will be judged on process and per-formance, not results. And many managers who have listened to this noble speech from supposedly enlightened owners have found themselves sacked a few months later. Given the pressure and instability inherent in the job, I'd want players I could trust, and you *know* you can trust players who have played for you before. In short, I'd want full control of all the decisions. Brendan has said that being a manager 'is like trying to build an aircraft while it is flying'.[3] Liver-pool had tried to put a system in place to make sure the manager could concentrate on flying the plane. But he simply did not trust the engineers responsible for building it. Brendan is not a bad manager, in the same way that Joe Allen is not a bad player. But he was the wrong manager for Liverpool's strategy. He told the world as much in that interview on day one. He wanted full control, and that power struggle would define the next three years at Liverpool.

SAS to the Rescue

We'd gone into the season with a lopsided squad and by the end of December we were ninth, having won only 28 points from the opening 20 games, Liverpool's third lowest total after 20 games in the Premier League era. Our new striker Fabio Borini had been injured in September and we were totally reliant on Luis Suárez and Steven Gerrard to score our goals. In January 2013 Brendan was finally convinced that our problems in attack must be addressed. Daniel Sturridge, thankfully, was still available from Chelsea. In order to convince Sturridge of Liverpool's enthusiasm for him, Eddy prepared a video analysing the strengths and weaknesses of his game. Brendan presented the video to Sturridge, and to his credit persuaded him that he really was wanted at Liverpool, that we had a plan for him, and that he would be a regular starter.

Brendan's other target in the January 2013 transfer window was Tom Ince, a former Liverpool youth player now playing for Blackpool in the Championship. Our analysis indicated that Ince would certainly not improve Liverpool's squad. Success owes as much to luck as to skill: Kahneman says the equation for success is 'skill plus luck', and the equation for great success is 'a little more skill and a lot more luck'. We were about to get lucky. It had been more or less agreed that we would sign Ince, but Blackpool could smell desperation, and changed the terms of the deal at the last minute. The owners pulled the plug. We all agreed another attacker was needed, and Eddy had the solution.

Philippe Coutinho is one of my favourite players. Eddy had first become aware of him back in October 2010 when Spurs played Internazionale in the Champions League. Everyone remembers the tie for Gareth Bale's hat-trick in the first game, and his evisceration of the Brazilian right-back Maicon in the second game. But Eddy had seen something special in the diminutive Coutinho, who had only just turned 18 and started the first leg for Inter. He thought Coutinho was Inter's best player, and Inter was a team packed with stars like Samuel Eto'o and Wesley Sneijder. Barry Hunter, whose speciality at Manchester City had been the Italian league, was also a big fan. Data wasn't the driving force behind Coutinho's signing, but he had looked brilliant in our model while out on loan playing for Mauricio Pochettino's Espanyol. He was only 19 years old and, according to our analysis, had performed above the level of an average Premier League attacking midfielder, a very high benchmark for a teenager. His loan in Spain only lasted six months and he had played just under 1,500 minutes. As with Dos Santos a few years previously, our model liked what it saw but it had seen a limited number of games. Crucially, Coutinho was exactly the type of player that Brendan loved – skilful and technical and Brazilian. It was agreed – we would sign Coutinho instead of Tom Ince.

Over the final 18 games of the season, we won 33 points, which was close to the pace required for a top-four finish. Sturridge and Coutinho instantly became regular starters and were immediate successes. Maybe the future was bright after all.

Close but No Cigar

Over the summer transfer window we signed more players who looked good in our data analysis – Simon Mignolet, Mamadou Sakho, Iago Aspas and Luis Alberto. The player we missed out on was Diego Costa, who had played brilliantly for Atlético Madrid. He was 24 and could play as a centre-forward or a wide forward. I was extremely excited by the prospect of signing him because he looked excellent in both of these positions, although Costa did have his downsides. I remember sitting in the scouting office watching our press officer Matt McCann turn green as he watched a 'highlights' reel. Before one game he tripped up a ball-boy while warming up and the boy burst into tears. In other games there were spitting and stamping incidents. But Costa was so good it was worth considering him despite his unpleasant behaviour. However, Aston Villa striker Christian Benteke was Brendan's number one choice for Liverpool. We eventually agreed that a bid should be made for Costa, offering to pay his release clause. Unfortunately it was too late. Costa didn't want to come to Liverpool and signed a new contract at Atlético.

Despite Luis Suárez missing the first three games of the season (serving a ban for biting an opponent), we started strongly, winning each game 1–0: three goals for Sturridge and three clean sheets for our new goalkeeper Mignolet, who even saved a penalty on his debut. A slightly unlikely title challenge had begun. Our good performances at the end of 2012/13 led us to estimate that we were the fifth best team in the league, but not very far below the level of the top four. At the start of the 2013/14 season we forecast a 45% chance of Champions League qualification and a 5% chance of the title. We were stocked with attacking talent: Sturridge scored 21 goals, Suárez 31; Coutinho and Raheem Sterling continued to improve and contributed goals and assists; Gerrard and Jordan Henderson provided creativity from midfield; centre-back Martin Skrtel even scored seven goals from corners.

We were winning plenty of games – 5–3 against Stoke, 5–1 against Norwich and Arsenal, 5–0 away against Spurs – but we were conceding plenty of goals too, playing a wild counter-attacking style that was at odds with Brendan's preferred 'controlled possession' or 'death by football' approach. I preferred wild attacking for a mathematical reason: if you are stronger than your opponent you should attack, accepting that the reward of scoring a goal is worth more than the risk of conceding one. The simple reason for this is that there are three points for a win and one point for a draw – an innovation recommended by Jimmy Hill back in 1981. A draw is a bad outcome if you are the stronger team. To gain some intuition for the value of attacking,[4] imagine Arsenal have played a game against

Leyton Orient. You are told that five goals have been scored in the game but you don't know the result. How likely do you think it is that Arsenal won? Now imagine you are told that one goal was scored in the game. How likely is it that Arsenal won? Low scoring favours underdogs, and they have every right to adopt a defensive approach to the game.

By the end of March, our main rivals for the Premier League title were Manchester City, four and a half years into their Abu Dhabi funded transformation into the juggernaut of modern football. In the 34th game of the season we faced them at Anfield and won a thrilling game 3–2. With four games remaining we were seven points clear of City, having played two games more. Our destiny was in our hands and we forecast that Liverpool were title favourites with a 46% chance of winning the league (Chelsea also had a chance of winning). It was the first time we'd rated ourselves as favourites that season.

The next game, away to Norwich, was another nerve-racking encounter where we just about held on to win. I watched the game on TV. My partner walked in with 10 minutes to go, and Norwich pressing for an equaliser, to find me curled up on the floor in the foetal position unable to watch. Her advice was that I should try to disengage emotionally from the games, otherwise I'd risk having a heart attack before I was 40.

From the position of favourites, we failed to win the title, losing at home to Chelsea (a game memorable for, among other things, Mo Salah's first appearance at Anfield) and drawing 3–3 away to Crystal Palace after being 3–0 up at half-time. I was distraught – our best chance to win the title had disappeared. Despite overachieving and finishing second with 84 points, the season was a disappointment. Of the new signings, only Mignolet and Sakho had been regular starters for Liverpool, and Mignolet's good early-season form had faded badly. But our other signings, Luis Alberto and Iago Aspas, had barely featured.

Aspas had made a mistake in the crucial game against Chelsea, giving away possession from a corner kick in injury-time. Aspas had played well, though out of position, in his rare appearances for Liverpool. But the vivid and costly mistake made him an easy scapegoat and Brendan was happy to allow him to leave on loan. I was very pleased that he managed to rebuild his career, scoring 106 goals in La Liga since returning to Spain. In 2016/17 and 2017/18 he was the fourth highest scorer in Spain, behind Messi, Ronaldo and Suárez, and in 2018/19 he was third top scorer, behind Messi and Benzema.

Luis Alberto was also allowed to leave on loan. He has since built a successful career at Lazio. Eddy cites Alberto as an example of getting the qualitative, human side of signing a player wrong. Talent is not sufficient for success. The cultural misfit between Alberto and Liverpool spoiled his chances of success and is something we did not pay enough attention to in those early days.

Our star player, Luis Suárez, had agitated to leave the previous season, and Arsenal had made a bid of £40,000,001 in the belief it would trigger a release clause. John Henry tweeted: 'What do you think they're smoking over there at the Emirates?' We knew 2013/14 would be Suárez's last at Liverpool. To compound our difficulties, he had bitten the Italian player Giorgio Chiellini at the World Cup and would serve another lengthy ban. As one of the best players in the world, we expected a very high transfer fee, but his ban lasted until October and put off potential suitors – Real Madrid had intended to sign him but changed their mind because of the bite. Eventually Barcelona agreed a fee of £65 million. It was less than we hoped we'd receive at the start of the summer. The money had to be spent very wisely.

4.

Heavy Metal Football

Although we often hear that data speak for themselves,
their voices can be soft and sly

Frederick Mosteller

How Not to Spend £65 Million

Replacing the world-class Suárez was the absolute priority for Liverpool in summer 2014. Given that we had been negotiating with Barcelona over Suárez, we raised the idea that they might sell their forward Alexis Sánchez. Barcelona were open to the idea. This was great news – Sánchez was one of the few players in the world who would be a credible replacement for Suárez. Brendan was not averse to the idea but his focus was on signing Adam Lallana from Southampton. Lallana is an excellent player, but his Premier League experience, English nationality and silky skills made him a very expensive player. There was a slot for Lallana in our team, as Brendan often played with a '10' – a central attacking midfielder just behind one or two strikers – but it was Coutinho's best position, and Coutinho was a better player than Lallana. In 2013/14, Sterling and Henderson had also played in that role. Just like in summer 2012, the Transfer Committee's priorities for the squad were not the same as Brendan's. To make matters worse, we knew that Southampton had lined up Red Bull Salzburg winger Sadio Mané as Lallana's replacement, for a lower fee. I suggested we might simply cut out the middle man and sign Mané, but to no avail.

Lallana was duly signed, but by the time we switched our focus to Sánchez, Arsenal manager Arsène Wenger had stolen a march on us, having met the player during the World Cup in Brazil. I believe that Sánchez may have earned more money at Liverpool than he ended up getting at Arsenal, but his decision to go to Arsenal was already made.

We looked at many other forwards that summer, but the necessity of compromise between the different members of the Transfer Committee made it difficult to agree on any player. Brendan was still a big fan of Christian Benteke – a player he would finally sign in 2015 – but data analysis did not agree that he was suitable for Liverpool's style of play. Everyone agreed that Andy Carroll was not right for Brendan's style, and Benteke was a 'target man' in a similar mould. Eddy's idea was to sign a target man for a much smaller fee, as an experiment to see whether that type of player could succeed in Brendan's system. Rickie Lambert, then 32, had had a couple of successful seasons for Southampton and bore some resemblance in style to Benteke. For £4 million we would find out if a target man could prosper at Liverpool without risking a huge fee on Benteke.

Lambert was definitely no Suárez replacement, and time was running out to find another forward. There was a young player who looked outstanding in our Possession Value model. He had rated consistently above the Premier League average for many seasons, had lots of Premier League and European experience, was an Italy international, and was still only 24. It was incredible that he was available for only £16 million. I was very excited when Liverpool signed Mario Balotelli. Eddy agreed that he was a talented player, but controversy had followed him at every club he'd played at. Eddy's job was to weigh up different opinions about potential signings – what the data said, what the scouting and video analysis said, what the manager thought, the financial impact of signing the player, and, critically, the 'soft stuff': psychology, cultural fit and so on. Balotelli's past behaviour raised some red flags, but perhaps we could mitigate the risks. At the time Liverpool used the services of a psychologist, Steve Peters. If we could get an expert opinion on

Balotelli from a psychologist, we could be more comfortable with the signing, or decide against it. But Steve would not interrupt his holiday to talk to Balotelli. Instead, Brendan met him at Melwood and the meeting went very well. Maybe it would work out . . .

The committee reached a compromise on the signings of central defender Dejan Lovren, left-back Alberto Moreno, young midfielder Emre Can and young striker Divock Origi, who were all required to replace departing starters, or signed as prospects for the future. The other big attacking signing of the summer was Lazar Marković, a 20-year-old winger playing for Benfica. Marković looked quite good in our data analysis but, similar to Giovani dos Santos many years before, we had seen limited minutes: the Portuguese league was not fully covered by our suppliers back in 2014. In any case, Marković was not outstanding in the same way Dos Santos had been back in 2007/08, and I'd been stung by attaching too much weight to limited minutes before. Marković's fee of £20 million was very high too – that summer, Antoine Griezmann signed for Atlético Madrid for €30 million and Sadio Mané for Southampton for £11.8 million. But in every scouting department in Europe Marković was the hottest young player of the 2013/14 season and our own scouting reports were very positive. Eddy was not sure what to make of the conflicting information, so watched 20 games on video himself. He saw some very good performances but also some very bad ones. Young players can be variable in quality, so some bad games are to be expected. In retrospect, the problem was that the games where Marković was scouted happened to be his best performances of the season. This led to our scouting reports being too optimistic in their estimate of his abilities. Scouts at other clubs felt exactly the same way: upon signing Marković, many other clubs in Europe congratulated us in a way that we never again experienced for any other signing.

There is not much to say about the 2014/15 Premier League season on the pitch, other than it was not successful. Our best forward, Daniel Sturridge, suffered a series of injuries, and started only seven games. The new attackers Marković, Balotelli and Lambert started 11, 10 and seven games respectively. The goal-scoring burden was left to Raheem Sterling. Balotelli had been particularly unlucky, suffering the worst season of his career thus far in terms of finishing. We finished sixth and lost to Aston Villa in the semi-final of the FA Cup, with Benteke opening the scoring. We humiliatingly lost 6–1 to Stoke City in Steven Gerrard's final game for Liverpool. After May 2015, none of Marković, Lambert or Balotelli would play a competitive game for Liverpool again.

We'd become a laughing stock: on Bleacher Report, Duncan Castles wrote an article headlined 'Liverpool's Transfer Committee Has Been a Spectacular Failure'.[1] An anonymous Premier League manager chipped in: 'That guy [he's referring to me] was a serious nerd. And the program [the one I'd designed to analyse players] was ridiculous. The parameters were set from his own view of what a defender, midfielder or attacker should do. They were ludicrous and inaccurate.'

Target Man Acquired

I thought the 2014/15 season might have spelled the end for the Transfer Committee but I was wrong, and we were heading towards another disagreement with Brendan. Raheem Sterling, our main forward in 2014/15, had been signed by Manchester City. We could not compete with the wages that City were offering, so we accepted their £49 million bid. Once again, some forwards were needed. Despite the failed experiment with Rickie Lambert, Brendan's number one target for the summer 2015 transfer window was Christian Benteke. His obsession with Benteke made Captain Ahab's fascination with Moby Dick look like a passing fancy. Benteke had always played brilliantly against Liverpool: he'd scored five goals and assisted one in his six games against us, and looked unplayable every time he faced us. But his record against us was much better than his record against most other teams, and more importantly he did not suit Brendan's style of play. With my colleague Dafydd Steele, we had built a tool to classify players. Benteke was firmly in the 'target man' class (see box). A target man's job is to receive long balls and crosses, and use his head to score. Target men can be effective but their teams need to be set up to play to their strengths and minimise their weaknesses, and Liverpool were not.

Player Classification

When people think of a player's role, they think of the formation that his team plays and his slot in that formation. This can be useful but players interpret their roles very differently to one another, depending on the coach's instructions and their own instinctive preferences of how they like to play. The left-back in a Klopp team may rush forward to join the attack at every opportunity, but the left-back in a Tony Pulis team may stay back and defend, almost like a centre-back. The central striker could be a 'false 9' mix of striker and attacking midfielder like Firmino, a target man like Benteke, or a pure goal-scorer like Erling Haaland.

We used event data to identify these roles. We decided not to prescribe any roles up front but see which ones popped out naturally from the patterns that existed in the data. The first step was to reduce the data to its underlying components. Our data provider collected about 60 different events: 16 different flavours of pass, five flavours of shot, headers, tackles, fouls and so on. We calculated how frequently each player performed each event. We also added the location of the players' events into the mix. Do they play high up the pitch or stay back? Hug the wing, stay central or roam around? The result of assembling these statistics was a huge table containing one row per player and many columns noting event frequency and positional information.

We'd assembled about 70 different aspects of play for each player. This is too much data for anyone to digest, and in any case many of the aspects of play are correlated with one another. Players who tend to cross the ball a lot also tend to stay wide, for example. A statistical technique called Principal Component Analysis helps us to summarise these 70 aspects of play into a few underlying themes. The technique identifies which aspects vary strongly with one another and groups them together. In this way we reduced the original 70 different aspects of play down to nine distinct factors.

The factors made a lot of intuitive sense. There was 'defending', which involved clearing, blocking and preventing offsides, but also staying back on the pitch. These are aspects of play associated with central defenders. Then there was 'heading' – a job usually performed by target men and central defenders. 'Dribbling' was self-explanatory. 'Shooting' included shots, of course, but also associated behaviours like winning corners, staying high up the pitch and not recovering possession very much. Various types of passing were identified – direct long passing from midfield, short passing, crossing, creative passing and set-pieces. 'Tackling' obviously included tackling but also the rest of the dirty work that defensive midfielders must do, like fouling and picking up yellow cards.

Each player's role was described by these nine factors, and they could be used to pigeonhole players into a particular category. Centre-backs (heading and defending) and full-backs (crossing and defending) were obvious, but we found four different types of midfielder (destroyers, direct passers, all-rounders and number 10s), and three sorts of winger (defensive wingers, traditional crossers and 'wide forwards', who cut in to central positions from wide). And we found three types of forward: target men, out-and-out goal-scorers and hybrids, which were a mix of the two.

We deliberately ignored any aspect of 'quality' when we developed the tool. For example, different types of pass were included, but their impact on Possession Value was excluded. We did this to try to separate the question of *who* the player is from *how good* the player is. Classification is only about *who* the player is, which allowed us to compare apples with apples.

Target men are often misunderstood. Just because a player is tall or strong does not make him a target man. Occasionally players like Zlatan Ibrahimović or Dimitar Berbatov are described as target men, but they played in a style that had more in common with Lionel Messi than with a true target man like Andy Carroll or Christian Benteke. This may be a case of substituting a difficult question – 'What is the role of the player?' – with an easier one – 'Is he tall and does he play up front?' If you watched Ibrahimović and Berbatov for any length of time it became clear they were not target men. Other players, like Edin Džeko and Romelu Lukaku, bore more resemblance to target men, but we did not class them as such. They can do the job of a target man, partly because they are big and strong, but they shoot with their feet much more often than target men. We called players like these 'hybrid strikers' because they did some parts of the target man role and some parts of the out-and-out goal-scorer role.

In 2014, Benteke had been Brendan's preferred replacement for Suárez. And in 2015, despite the failed Rickie Lambert experiment, Benteke was yet again top of the list. By 2015, I preferred the idea of signing Lukaku from Everton. Another 'hybrid' striker, he *could* play the target man role of Benteke, but had other strengths that would fit much better with Liverpool's style of play. The plan didn't really get off the ground. Our CEO Ian Ayre was given the unenviable task of 'crossing the park' (Stanley Park) to ask Everton if they'd sell, and was told in no uncertain terms that they would never sell a player to Liverpool. In any case, it didn't matter:

Brendan's opinion was that if he was offered the choice between Lukaku and Benteke, he would choose Benteke a thousand times out of a thousand. In those early seasons, I felt that the best work of the Transfer Committee was avoiding completely unsuitable signings. Benteke is a very good footballer, but he was absolutely the wrong player for Liverpool.

The arguments about signings went on for a long time. I was thankful that I wasn't based full-time at Melwood. If I'd had to participate in the arguments every day like Eddy did, I think I'd have quit long before summer 2015. After so many years of arguing over Benteke, I was amazed that our owners might now sanction his signing. I begged them not to sign him. I did an analysis showing hardly any top teams played with a target man (the only one was Arsenal, who had Olivier Giroud). The owners floated the idea that Benteke might change his style, and not play like a target man at Liverpool. So I did another piece of work, scouring the database for any target man who had changed his style after a transfer to another club. There had been no notable or successful instances of a target man changing his spots across the many different leagues and seasons that I analysed.

Our owners and Eddy had the foresight to conduct some scenario planning, or what psychologist Gary Klein calls a 'premortem', on signing Benteke. The idea is that you imagine you've made a decision and it's turned out to be a bad decision. Then you ask yourself the reason the decision didn't work out, and what the negative outcomes are. The reason why Benteke might not work out was clear – his style did not fit Liverpool's. The negative outcome would be an unwanted player surplus to requirements. Eddy felt that Benteke's previous success in the Premier League, and the number of teams in the league who played with a target man, meant there would always be a Premier League team willing to sign him. Maybe the financial downside would not be so bad if he didn't work out at Liverpool.

I understood Brendan's feelings about Benteke. Despite his best plans, Benteke always scored against us, and really did look brilliant in those games. The emotional impact of a player scoring against your team, time and again, must be huge. All the tactics designed to stop him failed: it is very tempting to conclude that the player is brilliant, overweight the vividness of his goals, and discount the fact that a little luck may have been involved in the ball ending up in the back of your net. But the answer to the question 'Did this player play well against us?' is usually not the same answer as to the question 'Should we sign this player?'

Si, Señor

The other big signing of summer 2015 was Roberto Firmino, who, along with James Milner, would become the first unqualified success among the signings made by the Transfer Committee since Coutinho and Sturridge back in January 2013. Our data analysis was a driving force behind signing Firmino, but he did not immediately stand out as a high-value signing. We needed to dig deeper into the data in order to really understand his value, and may not have done so if Eddy had not been insistent that he was undervalued. In addition to performance analysis, we performed financial analysis for the club, and an important part of this was understanding transfer fees and salaries: what the market overpaid for and what the market underpaid for. After all, the definition of 'Moneyball' is not to improve performance but to maximise improvement in performance per pound spent. After all, nearly anyone, with notable exceptions such as the Glazer family at Manchester United, can improve performance with large enough expenditure.

Firmino was a player whose demographics led us to estimate his expected transfer fee at £19 million. He had played for four seasons at a mid-table Bundesliga club, Hoffenheim, and had only two years left on his contract. These factors indicated a modest transfer fee. The fact he played in Germany meant he was not liable to the 'Premier League experience' surcharge. The fact he was a young forward and Brazilian increased the expected fee, but the fact he had not played youth football or competitively for Brazil deflated it again. All else being equal, of course we'd prefer a player with Premier League experience and 20 caps for Brazil, but all else is not equal, and those players command a high premium.

Borussia Dortmund were also interested in signing Firmino and had already offered €25 million. We would have to pay more to secure his services. Eddy was adamant that Firmino was drastically undervalued by the market and persuaded our owners to part with £29 million to sign him. There were important points in Firmino's favour that suggested he was undervalued: he was rarely injured, and had played nearly every game for Hoffenheim over the past four years. He was excellent in the air and was excellent at creating chances for others, despite his modest goal return (he'd scored 10 or more goals in only one of his four Bundesliga seasons). He could also play in three positions.

The fact that Firmino played three positions should have been seen as a strength, but I think it was seen as a weakness – other teams didn't know what to make of him. Was he a centre-forward, an attacking midfielder or a winger? Even our own coaching staff were unsure what to do with him; the consensus was that he was a good player but they didn't quite know where to fit him in. From my point of view a multifunctional player is a huge asset: if Firmino can play in three positions, then less squad depth is needed in those positions because he can fill in there. Another unqualified success of the 2015 transfer window – free transfer James Milner – had exactly the same strength.

Even our data analysis had been tripped up by Firmino's flexibility. He'd ended up in the striker category, but didn't add enough through shooting to look very impressive as a striker. Eddy insisted that he'd played many games as a '10' so we took another look at him. My colleague Daf was given the task of analysing Firmino's role game by game. Our Player Classification tool allowed us to decide what role each player played in each game. We could use Firmino's games as a striker to compare him to other strikers, and his games as a '10' to compare him to other '10's. The result of this process was that, as a '10', he looked like one of the best young players in Europe. Most of the young players who rated better than him – Alexis Sánchez, James Rodríguez, Isco, Oscar, Pogba, Ramsey – were playing for huge Champions League teams and completely unrealistic signings for Liverpool's position in the pecking order in 2015.

Eddy credits data analysis for influencing the signing of Firmino, but we would not have spent the time we did on analysing him if Eddy had not insisted: his new process of analysing 20–30 games on video had also suggested that Firmino, while inconsistent, might just be a special talent.

A Change of Culture

Despite the signings of Firmino and Milner, Liverpool started the season disappointingly. After eight games, we'd gained 12 points. Firmino had started only three games. Benteke had started the first six, scoring two goals, but was subbed off at half-time in the sixth. The owners finally decided enough was enough, and Brendan was sacked in October 2015. There was a lot of sympathy towards him – from the outside it seemed that the Transfer Committee had made any sort of success impossible.

The press lined up to give their judgements. In the *Daily Mail*, Neil Ashton complained: 'The committee have yet to explain how they came up with the figure of £29 million to sign Brazilian forward Roberto Firmino from Hoffenheim, who finished eighth in the Bundesliga last season.' The *Independent*'s view was: 'The analytics propounded by Edwards saw some very big claims for some very average players.' Barney Ronay wrote in the *Guardian*: 'Liverpool have signed 50 players in the past five years, a team a season. The current group were signed under five different managers, to unconnected tactical plans, most recently by a mob-handed transfer committee with its own dimly conceived Moneyball-style pretensions.' (How could you, Barney?!) Jamie Carragher also weighed in, saying on Sky Sports: 'There are no wide players in the squad, there is an abundance of No 10s. I don't know how the transfer committee thought they would fit them in. There are four centre-forwards and three or four No 10s and no wide players. There are some problems with that squad in terms of the quality and the balance.'

It was true that a lot of our signings had been failures and looking in from the outside, the Transfer Committee did seem to be a complete disaster. But our owners continued to believe in the process that we'd built. Many of the players we'd signed were fifth, sixth or seventh choices because of the eternal difference of opinion between Brendan's preferences and the rest of the committee's. I'd hoped that success stories like Sturridge and Coutinho would lead to a more harmonious relationship between Brendan and the rest of the committee but it was not to be. Season after season, first-choice targets like Alexis Sánchez and Diego Costa had slipped away while we argued about their merits. Our process for identifying and filtering players was fundamentally sound, but it produced poor results. The suggested players rarely arrived, and when they did they were used grudgingly.

The test of our owners' faith in the model would be the next manager. Jürgen Klopp was the prime candidate, and there was a big cultural advantage to a German manager: they were used to working in a collaborative environment. Ideas like the Transfer Committee, which were still heretical in England in 2015, were not at all controversial in Germany. In the Bundesliga, the head coach reported to the sporting director, and had little say over player recruitment. At Liverpool, our owners could offer Jürgen a lot more power and influence than most Bundesliga managers had, and Jürgen, for his part, was used to operating in a collaborative way.

Me and Eddy had been given advance warning that Brendan would be leaving Liverpool, and were asked to analyse the careers of Jürgen and other leading candidates. There had been some doubts about Jürgen's disastrous final season with Dortmund in 2014/15 – a team that had been among the best in Europe collapsed to seventh place in Germany. We gave Jürgen a clean bill of health, and he also impressed our owners by telling them that a full squad rebuild was not necessary – an opinion at odds with the other candidates for the job. Jürgen was offered the job and we were all very happy and excited when he accepted the offer.

I'd first become aware of Jürgen in 2009 when Dortmund players started getting on to our shortlists for Spurs. I hadn't heard of most of these players, but Neven Subotić, Mats Hummels and Nuri Sahin had started to look like some of the best young players in Europe in our Possession Value model. They were soon joined by Mario Götze, Robert Lewandowski and Shinji Kagawa. When so many players from one team start to look good, you have to start watching them, and Dortmund did not disappoint. They played a very exciting, super-aggressive, gegenpressing style. John Henry had been a fan of Jürgen's style of play for a long time and so had I. The cherry on the cake was that he had won titles with players who were young and undervalued – exactly the sort of player our recruitment process was designed to find.

The Deutsche Fußball Liga

A strange coincidence meant that I'd analysed Dortmund's terrible 2014/15 season long before Jürgen arrived at Liverpool. Rewind to March 2015. I'd been invited to Frankfurt to give a presentation at the Deutsche Fußball Liga (DFL)'s annual analysts' meeting by an old acquaintance, Holger Ruhl.

Analysts representing the 18 Bundesliga teams and the 18 second division 'Zweite Bundesliga' teams were in attendance. The meeting room was one long table with row upon row of video analysts lined up to listen to what I had to say. Those at the far end of the room had to look in the opposite direction to a second screen, as the one I was standing next to was too far away for them to see. It was not the ideal set-up for giving a presentation.

I showed them some Bundesliga analysis. According to our team strength ratings and despite their terrible season Dortmund were still clearly the second-best team in Germany. At the halfway stage of the season, Dortmund had been 17th out of 18 teams in the league table, and in the relegation zone. The press smelled blood and the German tabloid *Bild* published a photo of Jürgen comforting star forward Pierre-Emerick Aubameyang, who was in tears after yet another loss. The caption was 'Echter Schrott', which roughly translates as 'Absolute Garbage'. By March, Dortmund had recovered somewhat, to 10th place. But the general opinion in Germany was that second-placed Wolfsburg or Borussia Mönchengladbach in third would be the new challengers to Bayern Munich. It was widely accepted that Dortmund were a spent force, and here was some data guy saying they were still the second-best team in the country?

I went on to say that we predicted them to finish seventh in 2014/15, generating about two points per game on average from their final eight games. This prediction was met with some disbelief. Mönchengladbach were expected to only generate 1.5 points per game. Was I saying Dortmund were a better team than Borussia Mönchengladbach? Yes I was. Dortmund had been on the receiving end of some results that were very different to their underlying performance, as measured by Expected Goals. Dortmund's Expected Goal Difference after 26 games of 'Echter Schrott' was the third best in the Bundesliga, better than both Wolfsburg's and Mönchengladbach's. They were creating and allowing a similar quantity and quality of chances as they had in previous seasons. The main difference was that their shots were not crossing the goal-line while the opposition's shots were.

You might argue that some teams have special tactics or special players that can outperform Expected Goals each season, but they are exceptions to the general rule. Over nine Bundesliga seasons, from 2007/08 to 2015/16, I collected each team's Expected Goals scored and conceded in each game. These Expected Goals can be translated into 'Expected Points': assuming each shot was converted in line with expectations[2] – a penalty 75% of the time, a 30-yard shot

1% of the time, and so on – how many points would each team have won in each game, on average?

Each season I compared the league points actually won by the teams with their Expected Points. Over nine seasons, some teams were able to outperform expectations. Bayern Munich, for example, generated 5.5 points more than expected on average. But they were able to call on the services of Germany's goalkeeper Manuel Neuer, and Robert Lewandowski, the best striker in the league. It is not a surprise that these players can score or save a little more often than expected, given that Expected Goals estimates the average shot's chance of conversion against the average goalkeeper. But even with the luxury of being able to call on these super talents, Bayern's actual points total outperformed their Expected Points by only 8% per season.

There was very little correlation between overperformance one season and overperformance the next season. Of the 69 teams who had gained more points than expected in one season, 34 of them gained fewer points than expected the next season.

This means that overachievement in one season is no guarantee of overachievement the next. And that is what Dortmund found. The narrative might be that Jürgen ruined Dortmund and his replacement, Thomas Tuchel, saved them. But the boring statistical story is that their performance returned to its expected level after a tremendously unlucky season.

Dortmund's dreadful 2014/15 resulted in 16 fewer points than expected – the third worst underperformance that I'd seen in nine Bundesliga seasons. The following season – with a new manager but more or less the same squad – they finished second, with their second highest ever points total. In that season the 78 points they won represented a moderate but unsurprising overperformance of 5.5 points.

In any case, Dortmund's 2014/15 season was nothing to be concerned about: there was no logical reason why Jürgen's bad luck should continue. We were all convinced the future would be bright.

Meeting Jürgen

In late October 2015, Eddy told me: 'You need to set up a meeting with Jürgen to explain what your department does.'

Jürgen had been announced as Liverpool manager three weeks previously. The whole of Liverpool was very excited by his arrival. He had recently brought success to Dortmund for the first time in a decade, winning the Bundesliga in 2011 and 2012, and reaching the Champions League final in 2013. He had instigated an exciting 'gegenpressing' game at Dortmund – branding it 'heavy metal football' – but had left under a cloud after that very unlucky 2014/15. John Henry had admired Jürgen's brand of football for many years and would have loved to have made him Liverpool's manager as early as 2012.

Eddy, soon to be announced as Liverpool's first sporting director, thought Jürgen needed to understand how the club was using data to help its decision-making. My experience with Brendan had been an unhappy one, and I knew that Jürgen had had little prior exposure to statistical analysis in football. It was important to me that I made a good impression.

I'd worked all week on an introductory presentation. It showed how we benchmark team strength and forecast games; how we classify players into different roles; how we model the club's income based on Liverpool's progression in different competitions; and finally how we give feedback on team performance, using Dortmund's awful 2014/15 season as an example.

The day before the meeting I asked my partner to look through the presentation. I needed a second opinion on whether it was pitched at a suitable level for someone with no background in stats. She said that it looked fine but had one suggestion: 'All that stuff where you kiss his arse, put that at the start.' It was a good suggestion – I'd begin by talking about Dortmund.

At Melwood, the offices were upstairs – as with many training grounds, downstairs is the preserve of the players and the Medical department. At the far end of reception, past 'The Champions Wall', listing the club's historic successes and a replica of the European Cup (just to remind you exactly where you are), was the staircase. Facing you at the top of the staircase was the manager's office.

If you turned right, walked past the player liaison office, the coaches' office, past the boardroom, past opposition video analysis and post-match video analysis, past the toilets, the kitchen and the print room, then at the end of the corridor you'd see an unmarked door. If you opened it, walked past the multi-faith room, an empty office and another toilet, you would have reached the scouting office. My department – Research – shared our office space with the scouts.

Jürgen had been given a tour of Melwood the day he arrived, but it was unclear if the tour had made it as far as the remote outpost of the Scouting office, and whether the Research department had even been mentioned.

Feeling more than slightly nervous, I walked from the Scouting office, back past the multi-faith room, the boardroom and all the other offices, and knocked on Jürgen's door.

'How are you? Great to meet you!' A handshake, a flash of the famous grin, and an invitation to sit down – on the sofa rather than at the desk.

'So, you are the data guy?' Yes I was, and I started the presentation.

First, a one-pager on Expected Goals for someone who hadn't seen Expected Goals before: from a given location on the pitch, kicked shots end up in the net more often than headers. Well of course, that's obvious. If you shoot from closer range, or where the goalkeeper isn't, the shot is more likely to become a goal. So far, so good.

The next question is usually 'Who cares?' Hoping to pique Jürgen's interest, the next part of the presentation was on Dortmund 2014/15 and how his success story there unravelled.

I revisited the eight worst games of the season with Jürgen. I hoped it would not be too traumatic an experience for him.

20 September 2014: Dortmund lose 2–0 away to Mainz. It was clear this game was tinged with bad luck for Dortmund without resorting to any sophisticated analysis. Dortmund's expensive new signing Ciro Immobile won a penalty when Dortmund were only one goal down, but it was saved by Loris Karius, of all people – he would join Liverpool in 2016. And the second goal was an own goal. According to Expected Goals, the 'fair score' in the game should have been 1.8–1.7 in Dortmund's favour. A Dortmund win was the likeliest result. Jürgen agreed with the analysis. 'We should have won that game! You saw it?' No, I hadn't seen it. I had just analysed the data.

25 October 2014: Dortmund lose 1-0 at home to Hanover, their fourth consecutive Bundesliga defeat. By Expected Goals, Dortmund's chances were expected to be rewarded with 1.2 goals, compared to 0.5 for Hanover. The shots that were observed in the game would lead to a Dortmund win 56% of the time and a draw 31% of the time. 'You saw that game? We fucking destroyed them! It was unbelievable we didn't score!' No, I hadn't seen the game, but I had analysed the data. Even the press sensed something odd was happening – Dortmund had won their first three Champions League games that season but couldn't buy a win in the Bundesliga. The Associated Press called it 'baffling'.

30 November 2014: Dortmund lose 2–0 away to Frankfurt and fall to last place in the league table. But they have six shots on target to Frankfurt's three, 17 total shots to Frankfurt's 10, and 35 box entries to Frankfurt's 25. Expected Goals estimated 2.2 Dortmund goals to Frankfurt's 1.1 and a 67% chance of victory given the quality and quantity of each team's chances. The game was a case study on the contribution of luck to football results. After going behind early, Dortmund created many good-quality chances, with one shot hitting the post. Frankfurt had created little since their fourth-minute goal. Then a defensive mistake after 77 minutes gave Frankfurt 0.45 Expected Goals and one actual goal, and the game was over.

17 December 2014: Dortmund draw 2–2 at home to Wolfsburg but . . . Jürgen had got the point by now. 4 February 2015: Dortmund

lose 1–0 at home to Augsburg. 14 March 2015: Dortmund draw 0–0 at home to Köln. 4 April 2015: Dortmund lose 1–0 at home to Bayern Munich. 2 May 2015: Dortmund draw 1–1 away to Hoffenheim. In each case, Dortmund deserved a better result than they got. It was the same story, time and again. Dortmund's results did not match their underlying performances, they'd just received a very large dose of bad luck. Crucially, Jürgen's intuition was in tune with what the analysis was saying.

The rest of the presentation went well. If Jürgen wasn't an overnight convert, the meeting had gone well enough that he might become the convert I was hoping for.

5

Winning the Lot

If your players are better than your opponents,
90 per cent of the time you will win

Johan Cruyff

The Rebuild: Part 1

With Jürgen installed as manager, our evidence-based strategy for running a football club finally had a chance to succeed. In Germany, the culture of elite clubs was for managers to work collaboratively with a sporting director, a culture Jürgen was happy to continue at Liverpool. Eddy was duly promoted to sporting director shortly after Jürgen's arrival.

Jürgen's brand of 'heavy metal football' and his charisma meant he was attractive to players, who were excited about the idea of playing for a Klopp team. We hoped this would give us the chance to sign our first-choice targets. The rest of the 2015/16 Premier League season was not great, but Firmino started playing regularly, and we reached the League Cup and Europa League finals.

I was very surprised and very happy that some of Jürgen's transfer priorities were also extremely highly rated in our statistical models. It was music to my ears that he highly regarded the Senegalese forward Sadio Mané. Jürgen would later describe passing up the opportunity to sign him for Dortmund as one of his biggest regrets: 'It was a wrong evaluation on my side. It is not the only wrong decision I have made, [but] this one I could correct some years later.'

I'd loved Mané for years. He had been superb playing for Red Bull Salzburg in the Europa League in 2013/14. In April 2014, me and Eddy met Red Bull's director of football, Ralf Rangnick, who was interested in our data-led approach. I showed him some results from our Possession Value model: Mané was the second-best winger in the Europa League that season. Our discussion also touched on transfer fees. Ralf believed Mané would attract a high transfer fee, but I was sceptical: no player had transferred out of Austria for more than €10 million in the past. But Austria hadn't seen a team as strong as Red Bull Salzburg in the past either, and their attacking flair attracted big-league buyers: Southampton signed Mané. The fee was reported as £11.8 million but whatever the truth Ralf was right and I was wrong. It turned out the discussion nearly led to disaster two years later.

In summer 2016 Jürgen was very keen on signing Mario Götze, who had been one of the stars of his Dortmund side in their Bundesliga title-winning seasons. Jürgen, like many managers, seemed to have an understandable penchant for players who had played for him previously. The difference in Jürgen's case was that some of the best young players in Europe had played for him previously. But Götze decided he didn't want to come. Meanwhile, Mané had continued to play very well at Southampton and scored twice against us in March 2016 after Southampton had been 2–0 down at half-time. Mané's introduction at half-time changed the game, and Southampton won 3–2. I'd been here before: Jürgen must have felt the exact same vivid emotional impact that Brendan did every time Benteke scored against us. The difference this time was that Mané was a player I thought was perfectly suited to Liverpool.

Jürgen was sold on Sadio, and the video work done by the scouts painted a consistent picture of excellence. We were unanimous: Mané was the player to sign. When Eddy met Mané's agent, he was surprised that Liverpool were interested. He asked Eddy: 'Are you the guy that stopped Sadio coming to Liverpool first time round? You and some data guy?' Our discussion with Rangnick had somehow been garbled into the completely inaccurate story that our data analysis did not rate Mané! Eddy reassured the agent that we did really like Mané, and really had done back in 2014. Our uncertainty was purely academic and only concerned the size of transfer fees of players leaving Austria.

Eddy also did some due diligence on the character of Mané. Liverpool had signed many players from Southampton so it was quite easy to get an opinion. We were dismayed to find the opinion was negative. In summary, we were advised not to sign Mané. At Southampton he was apparently unprofessional, late for training, and a 'difficult character'. Eddy's job is to weigh up these character references against the ability and fit of a player, and the finances of the transfer. He decided that the poor character reference was not important enough to stop the transfer and I'm very glad that he did. It was a lesson that canvassing opinion about a player can lead to very unreliable information. Completely contrary to the character references Eddy received, Sadio Mané was one of the most intelligent, decent, professional and hard-working players we ever signed.

There was some competition for Mané's signature. He could have chosen to sign for Manchester United instead. Playing in the Champions League is a huge draw for any player, so it was imperative that we qualified, otherwise Manchester would be the more attractive destination for Mané. We had reached the final of the Europa League in 2015/16: if we won it we would qualify for the Champions League. We lost the final to Sevilla but, surprisingly, Mané still chose Liverpool over Manchester United. Years later, Eddy asked why Mané and his agent had made this decision. The reason was that they believed in Jürgen's ability, in his enthusiasm for Mané, and they believed that something special was going to happen at Liverpool.

This was the first demonstration of Jürgen's critical importance to Liverpool. Mané had the choice of Champions League football and a higher salary at Manchester United. Or no European football at Liverpool, but the chance to play for Jürgen Klopp. And Mané chose Klopp. Two years previously we were in a similar competition with Arsenal over the signing of Alexis Sánchez, and he chose

Arsenal and Arsène Wenger. This time we had secured our first-choice target. And it was thanks to Jürgen's ability to attract players to Liverpool with the prospect of playing exciting attacking football.

I was delighted that Jürgen's opinion of Mané matched our data analysis, and my delight was about to increase further. I happened to be working from the training ground instead of from home one week when Jürgen came in and started talking to Eddy and some of the scouts: 'What about this Joël Matip? He's available on a free transfer. Maybe we should think about it.' Matip had made some very high-profile mistakes over his career and was caricatured by the phrase 'mistake every game'. And now Jürgen was suggesting we might sign him! Eddy had also disliked Matip from some video analysis that had been done years before.

Jürgen's interest gave us the impetus to look at Matip again. Objectively, he had huge experience for his age, and our Possession Value model insisted that since 2012 he'd been easily above the level of the average Premier League centre-back. Eddy ordered the video work to be done on Matip and, on reviewing it, changed his mind. At Melwood one morning, Eddy bumped into Jürgen in the corridor and said: 'Matip – I had a look, he's good!' To which Jürgen replied: 'Yes. I told you so.' Eddy's response? 'Great, let's fucking sign him then.' The second brick of the rebuild was in place. After agreeing to sign Matip, Eddy visited Germany to watch him play against Borussia Mönchengladbach. Matip slipped over on the halfway line, a mistake that led to an immediate Gladbach goal. Bayern Munich's scouts were also watching the game and their reaction left Eddy in no doubt that they'd also placed Matip in the 'mistake every game' category.

The third big signing of the summer was Georginio Wijnaldum. Jürgen and his coaches were huge fans of Wijnaldum and he had just been relegated with Newcastle United. Our data analysis indicated he was a very good player, but I was concerned about where he would fit in the team. His best position was attacking midfield, but we already had Coutinho and Lallana to play in that role.

Firmino could also play there, though Jürgen had mostly used him as a centre-forward in 2015/16.

In hindsight, it seems inevitable that Mané, Matip and Wijnaldum would become stars. But at the time, they were not stars. Each was perceived to be flawed in some way by the rest of the football world. This limited their attractiveness and meant we did not have to compete as hard as we might have to secure their services. Mané was (totally unfairly) seen as a bad character and had previously been rejected as a potential signing for Liverpool when Brendan was manager. Matip was seen by the whole scouting world as an error-ridden liability unfit for the Premier League. Wijnaldum had been tarred by the brush of relegation. Our Possession Value model suggested all three would significantly improve Liverpool's performances. But we knew from bitter experience that signing talented players was not sufficient for success. The difference in 2016 was that Jürgen thoroughly approved of all three signings and had even suggested Matip and Wijnaldum.

I had high hopes for the season and we made a great start, beating Arsenal 4–3 away in the first game. Mané, Matip and Wijnaldum all became regular starters and we qualified for the Champions League on the final day of the season. It was more nerve-racking than it should have been – 76 points is usually easily sufficient for fourth place, but five of the 'big six' had good seasons, and all 76 points were needed to keep Arsenal, with 75 points, behind us in fifth. The fact that the other big teams had good seasons meant our improvement was a little underplayed. Champions League qualification has a huge financial impact, and we now had the opportunity to invest in the squad to try to cement our place in the top four, the task we'd failed back in 2014.

The Rebuild: Part 2

By summer 2017, our recruitment process was finally working properly, to the point that I became paranoid that Eddy had stopped consulting our data analysis – I had barely spoken to him in months.

I asked him if we were now surplus to requirements but he assured me that wasn't the case. My colleague in the Research department, Mark Stevenson, had built a website to display the results of our analysis: all our player ratings were now available to browse through on demand. The reason I hadn't heard from Eddy was that he was happily using the website to sift through hundreds of players. He would log on every day to see if any interesting players had zoomed up the rankings. I improved his efficiency by telling him we only updated player ratings on Sunday nights – he only needed to check the website once a week.

Another improvement was that we were able to keep our net transfer spending low through player sales. Previously, heavy spending only followed the sale of stars like Suárez and Sterling, but now a host of promising players had begun to flow from our Academy. Eddy had totally revamped the Academy since 2012, appointing Alex Inglethorpe as its head. He started appointing coaches that senior teams would later want to hire. Many of Liverpool's youth coaches progressed to first-team roles at other clubs.[1] Eddy also set up a Loans department, managed by future sporting director Julian Ward, to improve the development of our youth players. Liverpool started to sell youth players, often after successful loans. The Academy also produced a first-team star for the first time since Steven Gerrard: right-back Trent Alexander-Arnold.

Enter Mo Salah

Back in January 2014, right in the middle of Liverpool's first title challenge in five years, we attempted to sign a little-known winger from the Swiss team Basel. Just 21 years old, he'd produced some brilliant performances in the Europa League and Champions League. Statistically he looked excellent and Eddy thought he would become a superstar. But the proposed transfer fee kept on increasing – enough to make me very nervous. It looked like we'd have to break the Swiss transfer record by 50% to secure the services of one Mohamed Salah. In the end my nervousness didn't matter. Basel stopped taking our calls. We'd been gazumped by Chelsea. The price had already increased to £12 million, way beyond the Swiss record. But Chelsea had been offered £40 million by Manchester United for Juan Mata. With money to burn, they offered Basel £20 million and Basel stopped negotiating with us. Another failure to chalk up to experience.

Mo proceeded to sit on the bench for Chelsea – then managed by José Mourinho – for a year. Next season he was loaned to Fiorentina, then to Roma, who eventually signed him. Chelsea nearly made their money back on Mo's transfer fee, but they had to pay him while he warmed the bench, and they almost certainly had to cover some of his wages in Italy. This failed transfer was an enormous waste of time for both the club and the player.

In summer 2017, Liverpool again had the opportunity to sign Mo, this time from Roma. We had little competition from within the Premier League: he'd 'failed' at Chelsea and our English rivals did not want to risk repeating Chelsea's mistake. But we knew something that other clubs seemed to be ignorant of, despite abundant evidence: lots of transfers fail, for many different reasons. If Mo's Chelsea transfer had failed because of circumstances outside his control, maybe it could be discounted.

At Chelsea, Mo competed for game-time with Eden Hazard, who was then a global superstar. The other wingers and attacking midfielders in Chelsea's squad were senior internationals for Spain, Germany and Brazil. Mo wasn't the only exceptional young talent to find minutes difficult to come by in that Chelsea team – Kevin de Bruyne played so little for Chelsea in 2013/14 that he was loaned to Wolfsburg just before Salah arrived.

When Mo did play for Chelsea – which wasn't very often – his performances were good, in line with what we'd expected from his time at Basel. Mo's 'failure' was a failure to get on to the pitch, and the competition he faced for game-time meant it really couldn't be held against him.

After leaving Chelsea for Italy, he played magnificently for two and a half seasons. His performances rated very highly in our detailed statistical models, but he shone through in the most basic data too. He scored and assisted at a rate of 0.94 goals and assists per 90 minutes in his final season for Roma – an extremely high rate for a player who did not usually play centre-forward.

We signed Mo for £37 million in 2017. To put that into context, in the same summer Arsenal signed Alexandre Lacazette for £46.5 million, Chelsea signed Alvaro Morata for £58 million and Manchester United signed Romelu Lukaku – another Chelsea 'failure' – for £75 million plus £15 million in add-ons. It was incredible to me that there was so little competition from any other big Premier League club for Mo's signature. When I asked Eddy if a Premier League rival might sign him, he told me that they were certainly interested but he was sure none would put their reputation on the line, because of that so-called failure. Subjective opinion trumped hard data for most teams, and this intrinsic bias among our competitors gave us an edge that persists to this day.

Mo was not Jürgen's first choice in 2017. He was a fan of Julian Brandt, a talented young German at Bayer Leverkusen. But among the many players we considered – Brandt included – Mo was an outlier. His ability to increase a team's chance of scoring a goal, through shooting and through creating opportunities for team-mates, was much greater than any other player on our shortlist. Jürgen was convinced to sign Salah by my colleagues. He later said: 'We were sure he [Salah] can help us. Michael Edwards, Dave Fallows and Barry [Hunter], they were really in my ear and were on it: "Come on, come on. Mo Salah, he's the solution!"'

In his first season at Liverpool, Mo scored 32 Premier League goals (an unsustainably high return according to Expected Goals, though his Expected Goals was also excellent) and became vital to Liverpool's success.

Oh, Andy, Andy

Our starting left-back since 2014 had been Alberto Moreno, signed just after he'd turned 22. We needed squad depth at left-back. James

Milner, really a midfielder, had been starting ahead of Moreno in 2016/17. Left-back always seemed to be a difficult position to recruit, but in summer 2017 we had a shortlist of five targets. Andy Robertson, the player we signed, was not top of the list. The standout left-back that summer was Benjamin Mendy. He was top of my data-driven list but he wasn't top of Eddy's: he guessed, correctly, that Manchester City would try to sign Mendy, automatically putting him outside our financial range. He also attached significant weight to the bad character references he'd received about Mendy: this was a judgement call – the previous summer he had not attached very much weight to Sadio Mané's poor references. Our second choice was Roma's Emerson Palmieri. I was a little hesitant about Emerson because we had only seen about 2,500 minutes of him since he arrived in Europe (see box). He was 23, had performed to the level of an average Premier League full-back, and was very likely to improve. I would have liked to have seen more minutes to be sure but 2,500 was just about enough to make him my second choice for our new left-back.

How Much Evidence Do You Need?

A player's performance in a game owes something to circumstance, something to opportunity, something to skill, and something to luck. When we analyse a player's performance we try to control for these factors as much as possible. The circumstances of the game can be taken into account by controlling for home advantage and the strength of the opponent. We can control for opportunity as well – if a player is played in midfield rather than up front we might expect him to contribute more through passing and less through shooting. We make these adjustments because we want to isolate the player's skill. 'Luck', 'noise' or 'unexplained stuff' is more difficult to control for. A scuffed shot combined with a goalkeeper error may lead us to overestimate a player's shooting ability. An excellent pass but an inattentive team-mate may lead to an incomplete pass and an underestimate of a player's passing ability.

After a large number of games, the skill of the player emerges from the data, but after only a few games his performance rating will contain an element of luck. One way to think about this problem is to ask: do you prefer a striker who has scored four goals in four games, or one who has scored 30 in 40? The player with four in four has the higher scoring rate, but the player with 30 in 40 has sustained his scoring over a longer period. A concept called Bayes' theorem allows us to counteract luck's influence over players who have played a small number of games. We start off with a prior assumption about a player's scoring rate – for example, we might guess that a new striker is average, and will score one goal every four games. But we know our prior assumption is just an assumption. So as the player plays more games and scores more goals Bayes' theorem tells us how to update our opinion based on the evidence we've seen. This approach predicts that the four goals in four games player will most likely perform like a four goals in 10 player over the long term, while the 30 in 40 player will perform like a six goals in 10 player in the future. We downgrade the four in four player's scoring rate much more severely, because we've seen a much smaller amount of evidence.

Here's a real Premier League example. Adam Le Fondre had one great season in the Premier League, scoring nine goals excluding penalties for Reading in 2012/13, at a rate of 0.54 goals per 90 minutes. Diego Costa had three brilliant seasons in the Premier League, scoring 52 goals for Chelsea between 2014 and 2017, at a rate of 0.53 goals per 90 minutes. Le Fondre has the higher scoring rate but Costa maintained his for longer – it's not really a fair comparison. Bayes' theorem suggests we should revise Le Fondre's rate down to 0.40 because of the low number of minutes we observed. Costa's revised rate is 0.49 – we have seen so much evidence of his ability that his scoring rate has barely changed.[2] This is in line with our intuition (well my intuition anyway) that Costa is the better player.

But Emerson tore his ACL on the last day of the season – we would have to look elsewhere. Andy Robertson was also 23. He had looked excellent over 1,500 minutes in Hull's 2014/15 Premier League relegation season, then had been the standout young full-back in the Championship in 2015/16 – we rated him as performing to an average Premier League standard and he started nearly every game as Hull were promoted. But in 2016/17 Hull conceded 80 goals in the Premier League, with Robertson (and future England and Manchester United defender Harry Maguire) starting the majority of games in defence, and were relegated again. Robertson's defensive ratings suffered. It was difficult to analyse him: Hull had changed manager and tactical style upon promotion, and did so again halfway through the season.

Robertson was always great in attack – the Possession Value he added through dribbling and passing was consistently way above average. But his 2016/17 defending concerned me: Moreno was another full-back whose attacking abilities exceeded his defensive ones and he'd lost his place in our team because of it. Again, Jürgen proved critical. When warned of our uncertainty about Robertson's defending, he replied that he didn't care if he could defend or not; he needed his left-back to attack. He could solve any defensive problems by giving Robertson more cover. I was impressed by Jürgen's practical approach. Rather than demanding the perfect player, he was willing to find creative solutions to maximise each player's strengths and minimise their weaknesses. He often talked of his preference for players with one or two 'extreme characteristics' – game-changers. If and when those game-changers had weaknesses, he was willing to use other players to compensate for them. This philosophy was exactly in line with my beliefs about squad building.

It didn't start well for Robertson at Liverpool. He had started only two Premier League games by the beginning of December and Moreno had regained his position at left-back. But Moreno suffered an injury and Robertson immediately took his chance. His attacking was everything we hoped it would be, and he was given licence to bomb forward by Jürgen. But his defence improved beyond our expectations, to the point where he became one of the best all-round left-backs in the Premier League. Robertson was also an excellent value signing – Emerson and Mendy's transfer fees and wages were much, much higher. But if it wasn't for Manchester City's pursuit of Mendy and Emerson's injury, Robertson may never have ended up at Liverpool. For there to be three excellent young left-backs available was unusual, and in retrospect we ended up with by far the best one.

A Chance to Rebalance

We started well in the Champions League and the Premier League. Manchester City were running away with the league, but we were only three points behind second place at the turn of the year, and had qualified for the knockout stage of the Champions League. We were playing brilliant attacking football. Salah had been as successful an addition as Mané and Firmino, and Coutinho was playing as well as ever. With those four players, we had one of the best attacks in Europe. Our defence, however, was not among the best in Europe. We were about to get an opportunity to change things.

In summer 2017, Barcelona had seemingly been taken by surprise by Paris Saint-Germain paying the buyout clause of €222 million for their star Brazilian striker Neymar. They scrambled to placate their angry fans, signing Ousmane Dembélé from Dortmund for €135 million, and they also attempted to sign Philippe Coutinho from us. Coutinho had just signed a new contract and we were under no pressure to entertain Barcelona's overtures. Eddy's opinion is that you shouldn't sell your best players, and Coutinho was certainly one of our best players.

Asked again and again about a potential transfer fee, Eddy refused to even suggest a number. Many of his contemporaries in the Premier League thought he was crazy to not even consider what would certainly be a high fee but he was adamant. The summer window closed, but Barcelona kept asking and Coutinho himself agitated for a move. In January 2018, it was finally agreed that Barcelona would sign Coutinho by paying Liverpool a fee of £105 million up front, plus £37 million in easily achievable bonuses. The old adage says you should always sell when someone offers you more than something is worth, and Coutinho's contract was simply not worth £142 million.

In summer 2017 we had been annoying Southampton in much the same way that Barcelona were annoying us. We wanted to sign their central defender Virgil van Dijk. He was the best young defender in Europe, and somehow he wasn't already playing for a European giant. Van Dijk looked brilliant in our analysis, but you didn't need fancy analysis to see that: his brilliance was obvious to everyone. Unfortunately, we'd signed Mané, Lallana, Lambert, Lovren and Nathaniel Clyne from Southampton in the past few seasons. To say our approach for Van Dijk was unwelcome is an understatement.

After Coutinho's departure, we had money to spend and could finally pay the price that Southampton felt compensated for the loss of Van Dijk – a then world-record for a centre-back of £70 million plus £4 million in add-ons. We had lost one of the best attacking midfielders in the world but had gained the best young centre-back and, as with Mané and Salah, Jürgen, Scouting and Data Analysis were unanimous that Van Dijk was the best option for Liverpool. As a bonus we still had plenty of money left over.

The 2017/18 season ended poorly. We reached the Champions League final in Kyiv, but lost 3–1 to Real Madrid, with Mo Salah substituted off injured after 30 minutes and a goalkeeping error helping

Madrid to victory. But despite the disappointment of Kyiv, the future was bright. Player recruitment, driven by Jürgen's ability to attract talent, was working very well and we were confident we could improve the team with more signings.

Success at Last

Summer 2018. Funded by the Coutinho money, we signed Alisson Becker from Roma for a world-record fee for a goalkeeper, until Chelsea smashed the record a few weeks later. Alisson was another star whose quality was already clear, hence the high transfer fee. Alisson is one of the few players that Eddy watched live before signing. He decided to do that because he freely admits he is no expert on goalkeepers. And after watching Alisson play, he still wasn't sure, so relied even more than usual on data analysis and on our goalkeeping consultant Hans Leitert (yet another signing from the Red Bull group). Data analysis showed that Alisson and Jan Oblak at Atlético Madrid were the best goalkeepers in Europe, and Hans agreed. Jürgen wanted a goalkeeper used to playing with his feet as well as making saves, and that made Alisson the preferred choice.

Fabinho also joined from Monaco. A defensive midfielder who could also play as right-back, he had been weirdly overlooked by the European giants in 2017 when they had raided Monaco's title-winning team. He was another slightly awkward looking player, but his passing in possession and his breaking up of opposition attacks rated very highly in our model. His versatility could also be useful: if players can play different positions then fewer specialist back-ups in every position are needed, meaning that funds do not have to be spread thinly across a large squad. Fabinho had played for three seasons as a right-back for Monaco before moving to central midfield, and had been a Liverpool target before. In 2016 Jürgen was keen to upgrade our options at right-back so we analysed every promising young right-back in Europe. Me and Daf were really excited that we might sign Fabinho, who at only 22 looked like one of the standout young right-backs in our Possession Value model, and the Scouting department agreed he would be an excellent signing. But all our hard work was wasted. After training one day, Jürgen walked into Eddy's office and told him: 'We don't need a young right-back any more. Trent Alexander-Arnold looks fantastic!'

The player I was really excited by was Naby Keïta. He inherited Steven Gerrard's number 8 shirt and I thought he was a worthy successor to it. He had been brilliant at Red Bull Salzburg as a defensive midfielder. We tried to sign him in 2016 but instead he joined Salzburg's sister club Red Bull Leipzig. There he played as an attacking midfielder and was immediately a Bundesliga star. His passing and dribbling were outstanding and he was still only 23. I was more excited about Keïta's arrival than I had been about any other player, including Mo Salah. Unfortunately, Keïta was not the star I hoped he'd be at Liverpool. He suffered a series of injuries, and his buccaneering style was never really trusted. Keïta was happy to risk losing possession in order to create a scoring chance, but our coaches prioritised the midfield's defensive contributions over their attacking ones. When he played, Keïta played to the level that I hoped he would. He just didn't play very much.

We started the 2018/19 season brilliantly, but in contrast to 2017/18 we continued playing brilliantly. We won 97 points in the Premier League, the third highest total ever, and the highest total ever by a team not called Manchester City. Before 2019, winning 90 points had always resulted in a Premier League title, but we had the misfortune of competing against Manchester City, who had become the best Premier League team ever under the leadership of Pep Guardiola. The title race went down to the final day and we were beaten by a single point.

Still, at least we had qualified for the Champions League final, thanks to that unlikely turnaround against Barcelona that caused me to lose my voice. I almost missed the game in Madrid – the bus I took to the ground with some colleagues and some VIPs got stuck in a traffic jam. An hour before kick-off, and with no sign of the jam clearing, we decided to walk to the stadium. A few Liverpool fans outside the stadium spotted us coming and started asking Kenny Dalglish if he had any tickets going spare (he didn't). Me and my colleague Woody became Kenny's impromptu bodyguards. Woody used to be in the Navy and performed the job admirably, but I am the most ineffective bodyguard anyone could imagine. We just about made it into the stadium a few minutes before kick-off, and I watched one of the worst games of football I'd ever seen. It didn't matter – we beat Tottenham Hotspur 2–0 and won the European Cup. The thing that really sticks in my mind is the bus parade through Liverpool the next day. Among the hundreds of thousands of fans cheering the team through the city were a few holding up photos of loved ones who hadn't got to see Liverpool win the European Cup again. Arrigo Sacchi said it best: of all the unimportant things, football is by far the most important.

The following season, we took advantage of a rare slip by Manchester City, and Liverpool won the Premier League for the first time, winning 99 points on our way to the title. It was our first league title for 30 years. The squad that won the title was almost identical to the 2018/19 squad, although Alisson was injured in the first game of the season and the new back-up keeper Adrián played in 11 Premier League games, and in the European Super Cup victory against Chelsea.

We won 26 of the first 27 Premier League games we played that season, drawing the other away to Manchester United. It was the best start to a Premier League season in history. Our amazing start was certainly helped by scoring first in the vast majority of games. We only went behind in five of those first 27 games, and came back to win four of them, including a memorable last-minute winner by Andy Robertson against Aston Villa. In all we'd spent more than half of the time in the lead in those first 27 games, and less than 10% of the time in a losing position. To put that in context, Manchester City led for about 42% of the time in that period. In terms of goalscoring, City dominated the league, scoring 102 goals to our 85. As usual, they often blew opponents out of the water, winning 14 games by a three-goal margin or better. By contrast, we only won seven games by such a large margin. Defensively, we did match City, thanks to Alisson and to our defence encouraging the opposition to take very low-quality shots against us.

The quality of the players at a team's disposal fundamentally dictates their chances of success. And the players who contributed most to our title win were nearly all recent arrivals. New signing Adrián made nine starts. The 2018 signings Van Dijk, Alisson, Fabinho and Keïta made 38, 29, 22 and nine starts, with Van Dijk playing every minute. The 2017 signings Robertson, Salah and Alex Oxlade-Chamberlain made 35, 33 and 17 starts. The 2016 arrivals Wijnaldum, Mané and Matip started 35, 31 and eight times. And the 2015 signings Firmino, Joe Gomez, Milner and Origi made 34, 22, nine and seven starts.

The only other regular starters that season were 2010 signing Jordan Henderson with 26 starts and Academy product Trent Alexander-Arnold with 35. The team was unrecognisable from the one that was ridiculed in our disastrous 2014/15 season. Since then, nearly every new signing had met with the approval of our data analysis, of Eddy's new scouting process, and of the manager. We'd finally demonstrated that our approach to squad building worked, and we'd achieved it with a net transfer spend much lower than most of our big six rivals.

We ended up experiencing Liverpool's greatest period of success since the 1980s. In addition to the Champions League and the Premier League, we won the Uefa Super Cup and Fifa World Club Cup in 2019, and the FA Cup and League Cup in 2022.

Between 2019 and 2022, Liverpool achieved the three highest league points totals in its history: 92, 97 and 99 points. These were the eighth-, fourth- and second-best seasons in Premier League history. We are the only team to have failed to win the title with more than 90 points – and we did so twice.

Data analysis played an important part in our success. But its success was dependent on working in harmony with Scouting and with the manager. Mike Gordon, the president of FSG, often reflected on how difficult it was to assign credit to different areas of our football operations because each was totally dependent on the others working properly. Under Mike's leadership, FSG invested in the playing squad, in Jürgen, in a new stand at Anfield and in a new training ground, and laid the foundations for success. Eddy took notice of our data analysis, and based lots of decisions on it, but the really difficult part was completing the deals to sign and sell player contracts, which he did expertly. The deep market knowledge of Dave Fallows and Barry Hunter, and their leadership of their department, ensured Liverpool had one of the most effective traditional scouting departments in Europe. Most important of all was Jürgen: his charisma and exciting attacking style made it easy to attract players to the club. Best of all, he usually liked the same players as Eddy and FSG. And when he preferred a different player, as was the case initially with Salah, he was open to persuasion. All of these things were necessary for success.

The Measure of Success

Success should not be judged on trophies. A little more luck and we might have won three Premier League titles and three Champions Leagues. A little less and we may have won nothing. As a data analyst I understand success in a different way, by looking at the underlying improvements in our team.

First, the signings. Jürgen had integrated three signings per season into the squad: Firmino, Milner and Clyne in 2015/16; Mané, Matip and Wijnaldum in 2016/17; Salah, Robertson and Van Dijk in 2017/18; and Alisson, Fabinho and Keïta in 2018/19. In our 2018/19 season, 83% of our Premier League starts were made by players who were not playing for Liverpool in May 2015. Add in the integration of Academy product Trent Alexander-Arnold and it's 90%. The identification and integration of new players, nearly all of whom were successes, progressed at a very rapid pace. Of teams continuously in the Premier League over the period, only Everton integrated more starters than us between May 2015 and May 2019, but their performance on the field did not improve like Liverpool's (to put it mildly).

Next, the improvement in our team's performances. Between 2012/13 and 2015/16 we won 1.76 points per game, the worst performance of the big six, though we did slightly underperform in Expected Goals, which ranked us fourth. But in the 2016/17 to 2019/20 period we achieved 2.28 points per game, only just behind Manchester City (2.35) and way head of Chelsea in third (1.98). The half a point per game improvement was easily the best in the league, and our improvement in Expected Goal Difference over that period was second only to Manchester City's.

One of my department's jobs was to make league forecasts, and to do this we rated teams' strength based on past performances. At the start of 2015/16, we rated ourselves as the fifth best Premier League team, 25% better than the average Premier League team. Back then we rated Manchester City as the best team, 92% better than average. By the end of 2019/20 we rated ourselves as the second best team, more than twice as good as the average team. Manchester City were running away from the rest of the league at an alarming pace – they had become two and a half times better than the average team. And we had not only kept up with them, we'd got much closer in quality to them.

In terms of financial performance, we punched above our weight. We averaged 87 points per season from 2016/17 to 2019/20, second only to Manchester City, who gained 89 points. But our net transfer spend over that period was less than half of theirs. At least Manchester City achieved success with their heavy spending; Manchester United spent nearly as much in the transfer market but only achieved 71 points per season. Chelsea (75 points) and Arsenal (66 points) also spent more than us. The only team who achieved a similar result to us was none other than Tottenham Hotspur, spending far less than the rest of the big six, and averaging 73 points over the four seasons.

Wage bills are the biggest component of expenditure for Premier League teams, and these have historically correlated more strongly with success than transfer spending. Our wage bill increased commensurate to our success – elements of player contracts were performance-based so our wage bill was high partly *because* we were successful. Our successful stars also signed contract extensions on higher wages. But our wage bill was still lower than both Manchester clubs and less than 10% higher than Chelsea's.

Our total expenditure on the squad, wages and net transfer fees was about 30% lower than both Manchester clubs, about equal to Chelsea, and about 10% higher than Arsenal. But our performance on the pitch almost matched Manchester City's and was far ahead of every other team. Tottenham, still working with Decision Technology, also managed to extract a high level of performance per pound spent. Manchester United and Chelsea did not use data analysis at the time. Manchester City had an in-house data and insights team, but I don't believe that data analysis had much effect on the club's decision-making in recruitment. Arsenal had a brilliant data department – in 2012 the club had bought an analytics company called StatDNA. Very smart people like Jaeson Rosenfeld and Sarah Rudd started working full-time for Arsenal. But the impact of data in decision-making at Arsenal was unclear: Sarah has said that Arsène Wenger was the sole decision-maker at Arsenal.[3] He would listen to everybody but the data analysts were always unsure how much weight he placed on data, how much on scouting, and how much on his personal opinion. This is in contrast to Liverpool post-2015, where the general rule was 'if the data says no, the player is not signed'.

The quality and success of our signings, our real improvement in team strength, and our financial effectiveness were more important for the club's long-term prospects than the trophies we won. These accomplishments would have been true whether we'd won nothing or whether we'd won much more. John Henry, Mike Gordon and the rest of FSG felt the same way: the recruitment process implemented by Eddy was valued over results, even when results were at their worst.

What We Learned

Using data analysis to do player recruitment was an untried strategy in 2012. We had had some success with Spurs, especially with Van der Vaart and Bale, but data was only a component of Spurs' recruitment – it was not central. So at Liverpool we had to learn as we went along.

As the seasons passed, we received feedback on the signings that we made. It eventually became clear that our 2013 signings Iago Aspas and Luis Alberto were very good players. Our data analysis and scouting work was correct to highlight them as talents, but our squad had so much attacking talent that they were surplus to requirements, and they were not fully trusted by the manager. The lesson? Being a good player may be a necessary condition for success, but it is not a sufficient one. Manager buy-in is essential, and we received further lessons on this point through the failed Balotelli transfer, and the initially unsuccessful Firmino one.

Constantly questioning ourselves was very tedious. But we always tried to interrogate our decisions to understand if our processes were sound. The failed Marković transfer led Eddy to add a layer of detailed video work to every shortlisted player. The Benteke debacle showed us that we were correct to pay lots of attention to team style and player style, and discount some players as unsuitable. The presence of Premier League buyers for Benteke confirmed that the 'Premier League premium' applies to sales as well as purchases, and it limited the financial downside of the deal. It seems a little strange to talk about failures more than successes, but the reality is we learned more from the failures.

We learned from successes too: Firmino's flexibility was a strength not a weakness, though his true potential was only unlocked when Jürgen changed formation to put him in the 'false 9' role that made best use of his versatility. Mané was a lesson that character references are sometimes not to be trusted. Salah taught us that the football world's concept of 'failure' is often wrong.

And Robertson showed that good players can play for relegated teams.

We always tried to follow evidence and avoid biases. Eddy would not read scouting reports and he would even try to avoid conversations about potential signings because he wanted to avoid biasing himself towards or against a player before he watched them play. This is not because Eddy is easily swayed by other people's opinions, it is because he knows that *everyone* is subconsciously biased by others' opinions. But most sporting directors are not so careful about subconsciously infecting their judgements through exposure to other opinions or reading newspapers before forming their views. This problem is well-known in other fields: crime witnesses are not allowed to talk to each other, because they influence each other's recollection of events after sharing their experiences.[4]

I also learned about luck. As a statistician I already knew that luck is baked into football. I experienced it during that semi-final win over Barcelona, and when 97 points failed to win the Premier League. Luck is also baked into squad building. If Blackpool hadn't changed the terms of Tom Ince's transfer, Coutinho wouldn't have arrived. If Barcelona had not been distressed buyers, Coutinho's outsized transfer fee would not have paid for the signings of Van Dijk and Alisson. If Salah hadn't 'failed' at Chelsea his obviously super performances for Roma would have put him outside Liverpool's financial range. We also experienced bad luck with recruitment, such as failing to sign Salah in 2014. Every team has its share of good and bad luck. The difference at Liverpool was the data-driven process Eddy and Mike Gordon put in place allowed us to capitalise on our good luck and minimise the impact of our bad luck.

The most important lesson was teamwork. Football is a team game. Running football operations is also a team game. In *The Signal and the Noise*, Nate Silver discusses how in baseball, data seemed to have lost its edge over scouting.[5] One reason was that the scouts had started using statistics: scouts plus data beats either on its own. The reason our signings from 2016 were successful is that every one of them was approved by every aspect of football operations: if Data said yes, and Scouting said yes, and Video Analysis said yes, and Financial Analysis said yes, and (most importantly) if the manager said yes, then Eddy would sign the player, confident that they would be a success. Few players passed all these tests, and often some compromise was needed for everyone to agree, but the same committee-based system that had been a laughing stock in 2015 finally yielded results. We had changed football by demonstrating that a diligent, evidence-based approach to player and manager recruitment could dramatically turn around the fortunes of a team.

PART TWO

How Football Works

6.

Gambling on Data

Have you tried the simplest thing that might possibly work?

Kent Beck

A Betting Revolution

The data revolution inside football clubs followed directly from a similar data revolution in gambling. As football data began to become available online, a group of obscure academics wondered if it might be useful in predicting the results of games. The work they did to find out would have huge ramifications for two English clubs.

Goals are rare events. In the 29 Premier League seasons from 1995/96 to 2023/24[1] there have been 29,706 goals. There have been 1024.3 goals per season, or 2.70 per game; 7.8% of games resulted in zero goals and 5.9% produced six or more goals. This scarcity of goals makes data analysis challenging in football: the very thing you are trying to measure happens rarely and is often subject to some uncontrollable or unrepeatable circumstances – a lucky deflection, or a mishit cross. However, this seeming weakness can be considered a strength if you understand probability theory.

The Poisson distribution, also known as the 'Law of Small Numbers', governs the statistics of rare events. The law claims that if you know the average rate at which an event happens, then you know how likely it is that you will see a given number of events. It doesn't matter what you are measuring – the number of winning lottery tickets in any given week, or the number of mutations in a strand of DNA. If the events happen at a fixed rate and independently of one another, they will follow the Poisson distribution. And it turns out that a football team's chance of scoring a given number of goals is pretty close to the prediction given by this law. To be clear, in football, goals are *not* independent of one another – teams who are leading often become more defensive, which lowers their scoring rate. But the approximation of the Poisson distribution is good enough to be useful in predicting a team's performance.

Here's a real-life example of the Poisson distribution. Imagine you work in a shop and customers arrive at random times. On average, five customers arrive per hour, but that doesn't mean exactly five arrive every hour. Some hours will be busy and some will be quiet, just through chance. The most likely number of customers to come through your door is four or five, but there will sometimes be seven and sometimes two. In any particular hour, the Poisson distribution tells us there's a 7% chance of seeing nine or more customers and a 12% chance of seeing three or fewer.

People tend to have a psychological blind spot when it comes to the Poisson distribution: they grossly underestimate the natural variability in outcomes. For example, if a team averages 1.5 goals per game playing at home against average opposition, the Poisson distribution predicts there will be a 22% chance of them scoring exactly zero goals against average opposition. If the team ends up scoring zero goals, it is tempting to think they are truly a bad team. But there was an appreciable chance – 22% – that they would score zero. This is usually a case of mistaking luck for performance, or noise for signal. When information is limited, we should be wary about drawing conclusions from our observations.

Back in 2011, I had the opportunity to test the predictions made by the Poisson distribution. The first 99 games of the Premier League season had produced 295 goals, at a rate of nearly three goals per game. There followed many articles in the UK football press discussing this 'goal glut'.[2] Was it caused by the amount of money recently spent on strikers, or dreadful defensive mistakes?

Experts were assembled to give their view. Ray Houghton, a marauding midfielder and a Liverpool legend of the 1980s, was quick to blame defenders: 'This goal glut is down to dreadful defending, simple as that. I've felt for ages that the art of defending has gone.'

Nigel Winterburn, the former Arsenal full-back, was more charitable: 'Teams appear to be playing in a more adventurous style, and that not only increases the amount of goals they score but also the amount they concede, as defences become more vulnerable to the counterattack the higher up the pitch they go.'

Using the power of the Poisson distribution, I had come to a very different conclusion. It was simple for me to perform a computer simulation of the first 99 games of the 2011/12 season using a method that has become known in football data analysis circles as 'Dixon-Coles'.

In 1997, Mark Dixon and Stuart Coles – two academics working at the University of Lancaster – published a paper in the *Journal of the Royal Statistical Society: Series C (Applied Statistics)*.[3] The journal was not much read by football club owners or managers but when, on a rainy London day in late 2005, my old boss Henry Stott showed me their work, I was captivated. Sat in Decision Technology's cramped offices, just off the Euston Road, I read about how Dixon and Coles had modelled each team's individual propensity to score and concede goals using the Poisson distribution.[4] The resulting estimates of teams' scoring and conceding abilities were then used to predict how many goals a team would score and concede on average in each specific game.

Once we have a prediction of the average number of goals scored by each team, the Poisson distribution does the rest: plug in the averages and it spits out the chance of any particular outcome happening. If we expect the home team to score 1.5 goals on average, Poisson says we have a 22% chance of observing zero goals, a 33% chance of one goal, a 25% chance of two goals and so on.

My Dixon-Coles inspired analysis showed that, when the season kicked off, the first 99 games had been predicted to produce 279 goals. The actual number scored – 295 – was more than expected, but was it really high enough to have produced all those claims of a goal glut? Again, the Poisson distribution made it trivial to calculate the answer: if 279 goals were expected, then there was a 17% chance 295 or more goals would be observed.[5] About a one-in-six chance.

All the articles written about expensive strikers and defensive blunders, all the expert testimony lamenting the death of defending, or identifying new attacking tactics, were explaining something that needed no more explanation than rolling a six with a dice. This overreaction to short-term, unrepeatable fluctuations (or 'luck', to put it more succinctly) is the bane of football. Managers sacked because of a few losses, or strikers lauded as the next big thing because of a scoring streak, are often just experiencing the vagaries of the Poisson distribution.

The 'goal glut' non-story was particularly interesting because everyone had missed the *real* story – since 2006 goal-scoring in the Premier League *had* significantly increased. In 2006/07, 295 goals in the first 99 games *would* have been a truly surprising event,[6] but by 2011/12 it was not at all unexpected. The real story of gradually increasing goals had been missed until a not-unexpected fluctuation drew everyone's attention to it, well after the underlying change had happened. The reason behind this gradual increase in goal-scoring came from the bigger teams: Spurs, Everton and Manchester City had increased their scoring ability, with little change in their defensive ability. Arsenal and Chelsea had increased both their scoring and conceding rates. Meanwhile, Liverpool, Newcastle, Bolton and Blackburn were rated as more liable to concede goals in 2011 than in 2006.

These changes happened gradually over a five-year period. Some of the changes had obvious explanations. For example, Manchester City had invested more heavily in attackers – Tevez, Adebayor, Džeko, Agüero – than defenders. Defensive managers such as Mourinho, Benítez and Allardyce had left their clubs. But in each case the propensity to score and/or concede more had incrementally changed over a five-year period, not all of a sudden in 2011/12.

One of the features of Dixon-Coles is that it allows for team strengths to change in time. This makes sense because players arrive and leave, get injured and return to fitness. How quickly team strengths update can be calculated using Bayes' theorem. As mentioned earlier when analysing players who have had only limited game-time, Bayes' theorem is used to formulate predictions about the future by taking both prior beliefs and recent evidence into consideration. For example, if you believe someone is a good driver, you would predict a low probability of them crashing their car in the next year. But if you learn that they have had three crashes in the last year, you will update your belief about how good a driver they are. And your revised belief will lead you to estimate a higher probability of them having another crash in the future.

When it comes to football teams, the number of goals scored and conceded in one game constitutes rather weak evidence of their abilities, with the result that team strengths change on a slow time-scale (if goals is all the evidence we have to go on). Our analysis led to this rule of thumb: 'Your team's strength tomorrow is a mix of about 98% of your team's strength yesterday, and 2% of how well you did compared to expectations in today's game.' The reason is the Poisson distribution: if 1.5 goals are expected, then it is not unlikely to observe zero or three goals by chance, so we *cannot* pay too much attention to the last result. If we have more information (about the number and quality of chances created, for example) then we can pay more attention to the recent evidence and less attention to our prior beliefs.

This slow updating of team strength goes against psychological instinct. Daniel Kahneman gives an example by asking you to imagine a game between two teams with identical records.[7] One team thrashes the other – in your revised model of the world the winning team is much stronger than the loser, certainly more than 2% stronger. And further, your view of the past may incorrectly change: in hindsight, it feels like it was always clear that the winner was the stronger team.

I published my analysis on Decision Technology's blog, with the

title 'Premier League Goal Glut – What Goal Glut?!'[8] I was confident that my analysis was correct, but I was a little nervous: what if
I had missed some vital factor? There *had* been some very odd
results in those first 99 games, including Manchester United beating
Arsenal 8–2, and losing at home to Manchester City 6–1. Arsenal
themselves won 5–3 away to Chelsea. As the season progressed, my
worries rapidly evaporated. The 2011/12 season ended with 1,066
goals, which was a Premier League record, but only by three goals:
1,063 had been scored in 2010/11.

A Mug's Game

Dixon and Coles had a stronger motive behind their seminal work
than disproving the goal glut sensationalism of the football press.
The title of their paper was 'Modelling Association Football Scores
and Inefficiencies in the Football Betting Market'. Once they had
their estimates of team scoring and conceding and made their predictions, they compared them to bookmaker odds, to see if there
was money to be made. Bookmaker odds contain an implicit prediction of the outcome of a game. For example, if a bookmaker was
to take bets on rolling a six with a dice, the fair odds would be 5/1.
Five times out of six, I'd lose my bet (losing my stake of, say, £1),
and one time out of six I'd win £5. In the long run, I'd win as much
as I'd lose because the odds offered accurately reflect the chance of
rolling a six.

Now bookmakers do *not* offer fair odds, which is why betting is a
mug's game. A bookmaker might offer odds of only 9/2 on rolling
a six, and you'd win only £4.50 for every £5 lost. Most bets offered
at casinos and on sports events have a negative expected return. A
game between two evenly matched football teams might have odds
of 5/4 home win, 12/5 draw, 21/10 away win. Like in the dice
example, if the odds are fair they represent the number of losses
expected per win. So 5/4 implies that the chance of a home win is
$4/(4+5) = 44.4\%$. The same calculation gives a prediction of 29.4%

for the draw and 32.2% for the away win. These predictions are a bit fishy: they add up to more than 100% – 106% in this case. This extra 6% is the bookmaker's 'overround'. The overround is proportional to the bookmaker's expected profit margin on each bet, also known as the 'juice', the 'vigorish', the 'cut' or the 'edge' in the colourful language of the turf accountant. The margin is the bookmaker's expected profit, gained by offering worse-than-fair odds.[9]

It is an extremely difficult task to make a profit when the expected return is minus 6%. Back in 1997, bookmaker margins were 11%, and it was in theory even more difficult to make a profit. Dixon and Coles analysed the games where their predictions were out of line with the bookmakers. For example, if the bookmakers gave odds of 5/1 on the away team but their model predicted a more than one-in-six chance of the away team winning, the bet in theory had a positive expected return. Their analysis showed that they theoretically made a positive (but not quite significantly positive[10]) return when their expected return was at least 15%.

This obscure academic work attracted the interest of two men working in the betting industry – Tony Bloom and Matthew Benham.

In the mid-2000s Bloom and Benham were interested in betting markets more exotic than the traditional win, draw or lose bets on offer at British high street bookmakers. These exotic markets were traded at huge volumes in the Far East. One of the markets was called 'Asian Handicap', because of its popularity in the Far East. An Asian handicap adjusts the winning margin required for a bet to win. For example, Manchester United at home to Luton Town may have a handicap of –1.5 goals. If Manchester United win by more than 1.5 goals the bet wins, otherwise it loses. The other exotic market was 'Over-Under', which was a bet on the total number of goals. For example, a bet on over 2.5 goals would win if 3 or more goals were scored in the game.

One of the strengths of the Dixon-Coles model is that it gives a probability for every possible scoreline, making it trivial to calculate the fair odds for these bets. If the Asian Handicap is –1.5, simply add up all the probabilities for the scorelines where the home team wins by at least 2 goals. For over 2.5 goals, simply add up all the probabilities for the scorelines with at least 3 total goals.

Bloom, working for the bookmaker Victor Chandler, introduced Asian Handicap betting to the UK.[11] When he had investigated the Asian Handicap market, he found that the odds offered in the Far East were often wrong. Far East bookmakers also operated at a much lower margin than their UK counterparts and allowed much larger bets to be placed. Bloom and Benham quickly and quietly made a killing. The market slowly became more efficient, but an edge remained: Bloom had founded a company called Starlizard that used data analysis to predict the fair odds for each market and identify discrepancies. Benham did much the same, founding a company called Smartodds.

Goals Change Games

In addition to the Asian Handicap and Over-Under markets, 'in-running' or 'in-play' markets were also gaining in popularity. In these markets, the odds update second by second, reflecting the fact that the chance of each scoreline changes depending on the current scoreline and the time remaining in the game. These markets offered further opportunity for mispricing by the bookmakers, or overreaction by the bettors. For example, if bettors overreact to a goal being scored by betting heavily on the leading team bookmakers will shorten their odds, meaning that the current losing team may have a greater chance of winning than implied by the odds.

In 1998 Mark Dixon, this time working with Michael Robinson, updated Dixon-Coles so that they could predict the final scoreline at any point during the game.[12] This allowed anyone who could program such a model to predict how odds should change second by second. Their paper, 'A Birth Process Model for Association Football

Matches', revealed how the dynamics of the game change as it gets closer to the final whistle. Some of their insights were in line with experts' understanding of in-game strategy, while others confounded intuition.

Dixon and Robinson showed that goal rates generally increase over the course of the game. And they showed that when the home team is leading 1–0, their rate of goal-scoring decreases while the opposition's rate of scoring increases. This also agrees with intuition: the home team often tries to defend a lead, with the result that their scoring rate decreases. If the away team is leading, things are slightly different: both the home scoring and the away scoring rate increase. Finally, they found that scoring rates generally increase after the first goal has been scored. In summary: 'goals change games'.

They also tested out the adage that 'the most dangerous time for conceding a goal is immediately after you have scored' – the so-called 'strike-back effect'. They found this was not true, with goal conceding being *less* likely in the two minutes following scoring, perhaps due to the amount of time it takes to restart a game. Conceding was also no more likely after scoring than in other situations in the five-minute period following scoring. The authors commented that the strike-back effect was probably suggested because people have a tendency to overestimate the frequency of surprising events.

The Information Game

To keep their edge, Bloom and Benham, now working with Dixon and Coles respectively, had to continue innovating. Bookmakers are not stupid, and they really hate to lose money. The smarter ones implemented their own versions of Dixon-Coles and Dixon-Robinson to check that their odds were not out of line with reality.

In the never-ending quest to stay ahead, Bloom and Benham began to use information that traditional bookmakers also rely on to adjust their odds: injury news, motivation, weather and so on. The difference was they used the information in an analytical rather than an intuitive way. Bookmakers used to rely on intuition to decide whether to shift the odds slightly if a player is injured, or how aggressively to update the in-running odds if one team is dominating. Bloom and Benham combined their judgements with data analysis.

The only way to really know whether the market overreacted or underreacted to information such as a team dominating a game was by analysing the in-game data. The problem was the data didn't exist. So Starlizard and Smartodds also employed hordes of collectors to systematically gather information during each game. Each chance in the game was given a rating to reflect the collector's belief in the quality of the opportunity. A speculative long-range shot would receive a low rating while a tap-in would receive a high rating. And the collectors were not restricted to collecting shots: a good chance that a striker just fails to connect with still received a rating. As one insider put it: 'It's a very expensive and labour-intensive way of codifying a team's performance levels, but it's still better than xG [Expected Goals] now because trained people see the game and can take into account situations that don't result in a shot, which xG is blind to.'[13]

This chance quality data, collected over thousands of games, allowed Bloom and Benham to understand whether the market's reactions to the dynamics of the game were rational, but it had also inadvertently generated the first ever Expected Goals databases. The data was qualitative rather than quantitative, but it was very valuable. It would take until the late 2000s before quantitative data was generally available to purchase even in the biggest leagues. Benham and Bloom had collected a wealth of performance data for every game it was possible to bet a sizeable sum on. It had made them a fortune in the world of gambling, and they were about to turn their gambling edge into an edge for two football clubs.

Brentford and Brighton

Tony Bloom is a lifelong Brighton & Hove Albion fan and bought the club in 2009, while they were in League One. Fourteen years later they were playing in a new stadium and finishing sixth in the Premier League. Matthew Benham is a lifelong Brentford fan, and bought the club in 2012, while they were in League One. Eleven years later they were playing in a new stadium and finishing ninth in the Premier League. Brighton and Brentford have massively overachieved expectations, while keeping wage bills and transfer spends low. And they have done it because their owners implemented an evidence-based, decision-making process for running their clubs.

Being a professional gambler is a very risky business, one in which it is lethal to mistake signal for noise by overreacting to short-term fluctuations in a team's form or to irrelevant information. Nate Silver said: 'Our brains, wired to detect patterns, are always looking for a signal, when instead we should appreciate how noisy the data is.'[14] Bloom and Benham have taken the lessons about signal and noise, skill and luck, that they learned in the brutal world of sports betting and applied them to running their clubs. Tellingly, Benham has observed: 'People say that good luck and bad luck evens out over the course of the season, and that the table never lies. But that's simply not true.'[15] These are unusual and perceptive words for a football club owner.

Brighton and Brentford use the services of Starlizard and Smartodds respectively to analyse their performances using data, and to help scout players across the world for recruitment. In the betting world, the professional gambler bets on an outcome when the bookmaker offers a better price than they should. The equivalent idea in player recruitment is to sell a player's contract whenever the transfer fee offered is worth more to the club than the player's performance, and buy a player's contract whenever the cost is lower than the value the player's performance brings to the team.

Brentford

Buying and selling player contracts rationally takes a huge amount of discipline, but Brentford have followed this principle brilliantly. They are traditionally a small club: when Benham took over in 2012 they had not been in the top division of English football since 1947 and their stadium, Griffin Park, was tiny – its capacity was only 12,300.[16] Brentford's small revenues meant that they competed at a financial disadvantage, even while in League One and the Championship. After promotion to the Championship in 2014/15, they were in the bottom half of the table when it came to wage bills. Over five Championship seasons they maintained one of the lowest wage bills in the league while average Championship wages skyrocketed. Brentford did not spend on transfers either. The Championship is a league where teams tend to break even or make a profit on transfers: lots of clubs spend all their revenue on wages and are often forced to sell players in order to balance the books. Brentford profited much more from transfers than the average team in the Championship. This was a necessary evil – being a small market team with a small stadium limited their income: low wages and transfer profits were necessary to keep the club financially viable.

Despite the low wages and high sales, results on the pitch were impressive: they finished their first Championship season fifth and then finished ninth, 10th, ninth, 11th, third and third before finally winning promotion to the Premier League by beating Swansea City in the 2020/21 play-off final. In their worst Championship season, 2018/19, their new head coach Thomas Frank lost eight of his first 10 games. Other owners may have considered a change, but ideas like Dixon-Coles and Expected Goals allowed Brentford to look beyond outcomes. Frank was still head coach when Brentford were promoted and is still head coach today.[17] Benham told Christoph Biermann in *Football Hackers*: 'Results are not completely irrelevant. But they are mostly noise.'[18]

How did they achieve success? Their strategy can be summarised as: 'sell your best players'. Season after season, Brentford sold at least one, and more often two or three, of their most important players for a profit.

The sales process started as soon as promotion to the Championship was achieved. In summer 2012 Brentford signed Adam Forshaw on a free transfer after a six-month loan. Forshaw, a former Everton youth player who had failed to break into Everton's first team, was a regular starter in Brentford's final two seasons in League One. It didn't matter that he'd been part of their successful promotion campaign, he was signed by Wigan for approximately £2.5 million. Forshaw became Brentford's biggest sale since 1999. Some of the transfer income was used to sign Moses Odubajo and Andre Gray, who started nearly every game for Brentford in 2014/15, their first Championship season, with Gray scoring 17 goals. These two successful signings left after just one season – Odubajo joined Hull City for £3.5 million while Gray moved to Burnley for £6 million. The same season, James Tarkowski, who had stayed at Brentford for two seasons, joined Burnley for £3.6 million.

This cycle of selling and replacing successful players for a profit continued. In 2016/17 Scott Hogan, signed from Rochdale for about £750,000, was sold to Aston Villa for a fee believed to be an initial £9 million. Hogan was replaced in 2017/18 by Ollie Watkins, a young striker playing for Exeter City in League Two, for an initial £2 million. Watkins was unusual: he stayed at the club for three successful seasons before Aston Villa paid about £28 million for him. Watkins' career has flourished (he is now an England international) and Brentford saw his quality before anyone else. Again and again, the pattern repeated. Chris Mepham, a graduate from the B team, played for the first team for only one and a half seasons before joining Bournemouth. Saïd Benrahma and Neal Maupay stayed for only two years before joining West Ham United and Brighton respectively. Ezri Konsa was a Brentford player for only one year before joining Aston Villa. Brentford made a large profit on all these players.

Clubs do not usually prosper when selling their best players.

Spurs struggled after selling Gareth Bale, and Liverpool felt the effect of selling Luis Suárez and Raheem Sterling because the transfer profit was not reinvested wisely. Brentford prospered because they used data analysis to guide their process. They signed players from unfashionable lower league clubs like Leyton Orient, Luton Town, Oldham, Rochdale and Exeter City. Two of their biggest successes – Maupay and Benrahma – were contracted to the big French clubs Saint-Etienne and Nice, but neither had been successful. They spent most of their time away on loan at smaller clubs like Ajaccio, Châteauroux and Stade Brestois.

Smartodds, like Liverpool, had models inspired by Dixon-Coles to allow them to benchmark these teams' abilities against the abilities of Championship teams. European games in the Champions League and Europa League allow us to gauge how top-flight French sides perform against top-flight English sides, and promotion, relegation and cup games mean that we know how strong the second and third divisions are compared to the first in each country. A Dixon-Coles model operating on all games across Europe therefore allows player performances to be adjusted upwards or downwards based on the strength of their opponents compared to Championship opponents. This is a quantitative way of understanding whether a player playing well in League Two in England or Ligue 2 in France can survive and prosper in the Championship. Smartodds also had a wealth of proprietary performance data – their own version of Expected Goals – with which to inform recruitment. It is no surprise that some of their biggest successes – Gray, Maupay and Watkins – were strikers. Tools like these, together with traditional scouting, helped Brentford identify undervalued talent, and it was wildly successful.

The players who arrived were not only ready-made replacements for departing stars, they were also young. In their first Championship season Brentford had the youngest squad in the league, with an average age of 24.8, a full two years younger than the average Championship squad's age. During their seven-year stay in the division, they never ranked lower than third for youngest average age, and their oldest season was their promotion season, with an average

age of 25.2. It's easy to infer that their focus on youth was data-driven. Transfer fees peak on average in a player's mid-twenties, and performance peaks in a player's mid-to-late twenties. In order to transfer players out for a profit, Brentford had to buy young. All of Brentford's most successful sales were signed between the ages of 19 and 23.

At Liverpool, we followed a similar strategy. Between 2014/15 and 2017/18, we were always among the three youngest teams in the league, and were the youngest in 2017/18, a season in which we reached the Champions League final. There was an informal ban on signing players older than 24. Occasionally, the rule was relaxed: James Milner was 29 when he signed for Liverpool but was a free transfer, massively experienced, very good, could play just about any outfield position, and the manager wanted to sign him. Our motivations for signing young players were much the same as Brentford's: performances and potential transfer fees increase as a player moves towards his mid-twenties. Every successful signing would either attract a transfer fee or, even better, improve and help us compete for titles.

At Liverpool, once we were successful, we had the option of keeping our star players instead of cashing in on a transfer fee. Brentford, after promotion in 2021, have found that the increased revenue of Premier League football has allowed them to do the same. Since promotion they have not had to sell their stars, and their net transfer spend has been mid-table among Premier League clubs though to their great credit they have maintained the lowest wage bill in the league. They have continued to spend wisely but have not had to repeat their remarkable six-year Championship trick of selling their best players and improving their performances season on season. I think they more than deserve this luxury.

Brighton & Hove Albion

Brighton have also had a period of remarkable success under the guidance of Tony Bloom. They followed a slightly more conventional path than Brentford. By the time Brighton were promoted to the

Championship in 2011 they had moved into their new Falmer Stadium, with a capacity of more than 30,000, having played in a temporary stadium for more than a decade. In the Championship, Brighton were a mid-table team in terms of finances, paying average Championship salaries.

The club typically overperformed their wage bill in the Championship, finishing 10th, fourth, sixth, 20th,[19] and third before gaining automatic promotion by finishing second in 2017. Brighton's transfer strategy varied. In their first season in the Championship, they spent a lot on transfers. But in the following seasons they posted transfer profits that more than made up for their previous spending. The sale of future Premier League winner Leonardo Ulloa to Leicester City realised a large profit. And Will Buckley and Liam Bridcutt followed Gus Poyet, their old manager at Brighton, to Premier League Sunderland. In a familiar tale, Buckley and Bridcutt had been regular starters under Poyet at Brighton, but Brighton were happy to sell for a profit and both players struggled in the Premier League. Buckley made only nine Premier League starts and Bridcutt 19. Brighton certainly knew how to profit from a manager's preference for his old players. Brighton ended their Championship stay by spending heavily but effectively, with their more expensive signings – Shane Duffy, Glenn Murray and Anthony Knockaert – proving to be important players in their promotion season.

In the Premier League, Brighton, like Brentford, took advantage of their increased revenue and began to spend in the transfer market. Their net spend for their first three Premier League seasons was above the league average, but the situation has rapidly reversed in recent seasons. In summer 2021, Arsenal paid £50 million for Ben White's services. Then Chelsea started signing Brighton players and staff. Marc Cucurella, Robert Sânchez and Moisés Caicedo all joined Chelsea, each realising huge transfer profits for Brighton. Their manager Graham Potter and his coaching staff were also hired by Chelsea, with Brighton receiving £21.5 million in compensation. Chelsea did not get much value for money: Potter only managed Chelsea for 31 games before being sacked.

On top of the recent transfer profits, Brighton have kept their wage bill below the Premier League average and have transitioned from being one of the oldest squads in the league to being slightly younger than average. As with Brentford, Brighton are not exclusively data-driven. Some of their recent transfer successes had not played a huge amount of senior football before joining, so traditional scouting would have been needed alongside data analysis in order to be confident of their investment in a young player. But crucially, data is at the heart of their decision-making process.

Beating the Market

Brentford and Brighton have achieved success because their owners understand the relationship between risk and reward. Both teams were happy to sign 'risky' players from lower division clubs, and happily pursued the 'risky' strategy of allowing their best players and their managers to leave, if the price was right. These decisions *were* risky, but the clubs calculated that the potential rewards outweighed the risks. This approach to risk versus reward was made clear to me in a brief conversation I had with Matthew Benham a few years ago. We are both advocates of attacking football – mathematically, it is clear that a draw is an unfavourable result unless you are a significantly worse team than your opponent. Benham told me that his instructions to the Brentford manager were to attack, regardless of the opponent and the situation in the game. In minute one, Brentford must attack. In minute 90, leading one goal to nil, and down to 10 men, Brentford must attack. I thought the approach was brilliant but gave my opinion that I would be happy for my team to defend a lead, if they were a man down in the final minute away to Real Madrid. Benham's reply was that there is so much risk aversion in football that you have to demand extreme behaviour to have any hope of getting a manager to be anywhere near as attack-minded as is optimal.

Another skill of the professional gambler is to appreciate when markets change, and to be alive to the possibility of an edge disappearing, or a new edge appearing. Looking from the outside, it has been interesting to see Brentford adopt a more defensive approach in the Premier League. 'Just attack' may be a great heuristic for a better-than-average Championship club, but it may not be for a new Premier League club playing against some of the world's best attackers.

At Liverpool we admired both Brentford and Brighton's signings, though we never told them that. Me and my colleague Daf Steele used to keep lists of players who looked outstanding in their domestic leagues but were either not quite good enough for Liverpool or played in a style that didn't fit ours. The centre-backs Pontus Jansson at Leeds and Zanka at Copenhagen rated as Premier League standard players, but weren't really suited to playing in Liverpool's high line. Both moved to Brentford. Frank Onyeka was the best young midfielder in Denmark. He played for FC Midtjylland, another club owned by Benham, and soon joined Brentford. Yoane Wissa had been brilliant in Ligue 2 then in Ligue 1 for years – in 2012 he would have been on Liverpool's shortlist but by 2019, when he moved to Brentford, we had the luxury of shopping in more expensive markets.

Brighton also signed players on our radar. Pascal Gross performed at an above-average Premier League level while playing in the second division of the Bundesliga, and has played at that level for years for Brighton. Enock Mwepu was the best young midfielder in Austria. Kaoru Mitoma was the best player in Japan, rating above the Premier League average. It was very rare for us to rate a player in Japan anywhere near Premier League level, and it's still a source of regret to me that I didn't insist that Mitoma be more seriously considered as a potential Liverpool signing. Marc Cucurella was easily a Premier League level player while playing in Spain, and when Chelsea paid a barely credible £62 million to sign him, Brighton immediately replaced him with the only young full-back in Spain who we rated at a similar level, Pervis Estupiñán.

Both Brighton and Brentford have been success stories in this

'Moneyball Derby', though arguably to different extents. Both are successful Premier League clubs today, and both were in League One when Bloom and Benham took control. A natural way for gamblers to measure success is with money. In his brilliant book *The Price of Football*, Kieran Maguire notes that in 2019 Brighton's holding company owed Bloom £271 million in interest-free loans. I looked up Brighton's latest accounts – in 2023, Brighton owed Bloom £373 million.[20] Success has certainly come at a price, despite Brighton's modest wage bill and recent transfer profits. Brentford also paid a price for their success. Their 2023 accounts show that they owe Benham a mere £104.4 million in equity and loans.[21]

While looking through Brentford's accounts I noticed two of their key performance indicators: they list their league position (ninth in their second Premier League season), and then they list their 'xG league position' (seventh). Brentford's commitment to a data-led approach goes as far as demonstrating in their annual financial statement that their performances on the pitch were better than their results, and they used Expected Goals to do so.

Alcohol, Tobacco, Firearms and Gambling

One of my favourite Panini stickers is from 1977. West Germany World Cup winner Paul Breitner played for Eintracht Braunschweig, and they were sponsored by the German liqueur brand Jägermeister. The photo could only have been taken in the seventies: Breitner sports a glorious horseshoe moustache and 'Jägermeister' is emblazoned across his bright yellow shirt in a magnificent gothic font. The days of alcohol brands advertising on football shirts are over. The days of bookmakers advertising on shirts will soon be over too.[22] Gambling is like strong drink – it may be fun in moderation but it is addictive and damaging.

The story of Tony Bloom and Matthew Benham may paint the picture that it's possible to beat the market. But for every success story there are thousands of failures and bankruptcies. Every pound won by Starlizard and Smartodds is a pound lost by someone else, and the bookmakers also take their cut. Starlizard and Smartodds keep their edge by paying millions for detailed data to be collected on every game, and millions more for Ph.D. statisticians to analyse that data. The average punter does not stand a chance. Even without 'smart money' in the market, betting has a negative expected return, and if you are lucky enough to start winning, bookmakers will soon limit the amount you can bet. And if you keep winning, they will soon turn down your business. Like drinking, betting may be fun, but it is rarely profitable.

7.

What to Expect if You're Expecting Goals

There are only five probabilities the average human can handle: 99 percent, one percent, 100 percent, zero, and 50-50. That's it.

Richard Thaler

Shoot! Don't Shoot!

Philippe Coutinho is a classic 'number 10', an attacking midfielder playing just behind the strikers. He can thread accurate through balls and make dangerous runs with the ball. He is also quite good at shooting. I remember being at Anfield for his Liverpool debut – a dreadful loss to Roy Hodgson's West Bromwich Albion. The game was notable only for a missed Steven Gerrard penalty and a master-class in time-wasting from West Brom's goalkeeper Ben Foster. As injury-time ticked down, Coutinho took a shot from about 20 yards out. It was blocked by a defender. It didn't really matter as Liverpool were 2–0 down but this first long-range shot was a sign of things to come.

During his time at Liverpool Coutinho built a reputation as the Premier League's best long-range shooter. He scored 14 goals from open play with shots from outside the box – more than any other player in that period. The only other players to hit double figures were Sergio Agüero, Harry Kane and Yaya Touré. More than 60% of Coutinho's shots were taken from outside the box. One year after his debut, in the middle of our 2013/14 title challenge, we played away against Fulham. The game started badly with a calamitous

Kolo Touré own goal. After 71 minutes, Liverpool were still 2–1 down when Coutinho shaped to shoot from 20 yards out. Watching the game on TV, I shouted 'Don't shoot!' but Coutinho felt otherwise and scored a brilliant equaliser. Gerrard scored an injury-time winner to keep our title challenge alive.

I was delighted with the result but I was concerned about Coutinho's propensity to shoot from distance. Over the course of his Liverpool career, it seemed that Coutinho's best-in-class haul of outside-the-box goals proved me wrong, but I stand by my opinion: in order to score those 14 goals, Coutinho attempted 281 shots. The 14 goals he scored were certainly valuable, but there were also 267 attempts that did not lead to a goal. One-third of his attempts were off target and more than a third were blocked. Only 80 shots tested the goalkeeper, and 66 of them were saved. Were all these wasted opportunities really worth the occasional wonderful goal?

A Shot of Optimism

That less than 5% of Coutinho's outside-the-box shots converted into goals should not have been a surprise even in 2014, when the concept of Expected Goals had barely entered public perception. An investigation into how shots convert into goals was published as early as 1962 by the psychologists John Cohen and E. J. Dearnaley.[1] I was made aware of their work when I read Ken Bray's excellent book *How to Score* in 2006. Cohen and Dearnaley had asked 33 players, including 20 professionals from West Bromwich Albion and Manchester United, the distance at which they thought they had a 1% chance of scoring with only the goalkeeper on his line to beat. The players estimated that they could score one goal for every 100 attempts at about 32 yards from the goal-line. They were then asked about the distance from which they would score with 20% of their shots, then 40%, 60%, 80%, and finally the distance from which they would be confident they could score every time.

The distance at which they guessed a 20% chance of scoring was

21 yards – well outside the box. The second part of Cohen and Dearnaley's experiment was to get the players to actually take shots from their estimated positions. The players did not perform as well as they had estimated – from 21 yards only 15% of their shots were successfully converted. They were overly optimistic in all their estimates.

This bias towards optimism is well known in behavioural psychology and was documented by Daniel Kahneman in *Thinking, Fast and Slow*. When asked to provide estimates of the cost of a project, the time it will take or its chances of success, people tend to be much too optimistic. It seemed the same was true of footballers.

In Cohen and Dearnaley's experiment, the players would have considered their own skill, and the relative ease of scoring – the ball is not moving, and there are no defenders challenging for the ball. They may have underestimated that the goalkeeper also has a relatively easy task – he knows that a shot is imminent and where it will be taken from, a luxury he does not have in a real game – leading them to an overly optimistic view of their chances of success.

Despite their over-optimism, the footballers were pretty good at estimating their chances. In absolute terms their estimates were always within about 5% of the observed success rate, which is a very mild case of optimism bias.

This experiment is, as far as I'm aware, the first demonstration of Expected Goals in football. The essence of Expected Goals is to attach a probability to each shot – its chance of converting into a goal. This is exactly Cohen and Dearnaley's experiment, and they revealed the first truth of Expected Goals: your chances of scoring from a shot rapidly diminish as distance from goal increases.

Slowly Catching Up with Reep

I made my first attempt at an Expected Goals model in 2006. I had read about the work of Cohen and Dearnaley but was unaware of Pollard and Reep's 1997 paper that introduced Expected Goals.[2]

I would discover Pollard and Reep's work in 2007 but in 2006 I was ignorant of it and keen to find some data to corroborate or challenge the old conclusions of Cohen and Dearnaley.

At that time a significant amount of my week was spent dreaming up ideas for Danny Finkelstein's weekly 'Fink Tank' column in *The Times*. I thought Cohen and Dearnaley's work would make a great article but Danny demanded that we say something about how modern-day Premier League teams fared when it came to shooting – there was no guarantee that results from 1962 obtained in a fairly artificial situation would hold in top-flight football nearly 50 years later.

Thanks to our relationship with *The Times*, we received something called 'manager reports' from the data supplier Opta. These reports consisted of tables of statistics for each player. Luckily for me, the shots were separated into different categories: six-yard box, inside box, outside box, free-kick and penalty. It wasn't perfect but I had some data that I could use to bring the insights of Cohen and Dearnaley up to date.

The results were as extreme as Cohen and Dearnaley had led me to believe. One-third of shots from inside the six-yard box converted into goals. That dropped to 14% from inside the box (but outside the six-yard box) and crashed to only 4% for shots from outside the box. We also had results for direct free-kicks and penalties. Direct free-kicks had a conversion rate of 8.4%, more than twice as high as other shots from outside the box. Penalties were converted 77% of the time.

This stark difference in conversion rates – especially for penalties – had a profound effect on me. I became ambivalent towards long-range goals – one of the most joyous events in a football game – and began to re-evaluate some of my favourite players. This was heresy among my Liverpool supporting friends – Steven Gerrard loved a long-range shot and had scored famous and vital goals from distance. I also began to feel sympathy for players who were denied penalties by the referee. The intuitive calculation that players must make when they are fouled in the penalty area is to compare the chance of winning a penalty to the chance of scoring in the current situation. Penalties represent a *huge* scoring chance – their 77% conversion chance was nearly two and a half times greater than a typical shot from within the six-yard box! If a player has been fouled in the box, and thinks that it's 50-50 that the referee will award a penalty, the expectation of a goal is 50% times 77%: 37.5%. That's a very valuable chance: according to Expected Goals, fewer than one in 20 shots taken in the Premier League have a conversion rate as high as 37.5%.

Even though shots from the six-yard box were high-quality in terms of conversion, they were also rare: only 1.5 of them happened per game, compared to 11 from inside the box and eight from outside the box. Direct free-kicks (one per game) and penalties (one every five games) were rarer still.

I assembled these results into a model that I christened 'iBob' – the 'in-box-outside-box' model. The iPod Nano had recently been released, and I thought a similar name would somehow capture the zeitgeist. Each team's propensity to create and convert shots could now be split into shots of different quality. If a team created relatively more shots from inside the box they would look superior in the iBob model than they would in a model that treated all shots equally.

In 2012, just after I joined Liverpool, Eddy asked me to introduce myself to my new colleagues in Melwood. Space was at a premium: the number of staff had increased since FSG's takeover, and we were quickly outgrowing the building that was completed back in 2001, when Gérard Houllier was manager. I managed to book the press room for a Thursday morning. The cavernous room had plenty of space to accommodate the world's press and it felt faintly ridiculous to be showing my slides on an enormous screen to an audience of only four: our Video Analysis department plus the only other member of the Research department at the time, Tim Waskett. I explained the relative value of penalties, and another piece of analysis I had done on red cards. If it is late in the game, your team is winning by one goal, and you can prevent a 50% chance of the opposition scoring by committing a foul worthy of a sending off, you should do it: the statistics say that you have more chance of holding on to the current one-goal lead with 10 men than if you allow the dangerous opposition chance.

The video analysts intuitively understood these arguments but had not seen them explained using numbers before. Despite their general agreement with my conclusions, one analyst labelled me 'the most cynical man in football'. I felt this was a little unfair. Football fans shouldn't hate the statistician. They should hate the game that weights penalties so extremely, and whose goals are so rare that it is sometimes better to be sent off than allow a chance of conceding one.

Another example of the value of penalties and the capricious nature of football occurred in 2011. The Ivory Coast winger Gervinho was signed from Lille by Arsenal. I had analysed the player for Spurs back in summer 2010. I remember Eddy asking me to break down why we had rated him so highly. As it turns out, he had won many penalties, and penalties are highly valued. Eddy was quite rightly dubious about a player's ability to *repeat* penalty-winning, and was also unsure whether it could translate to the Premier League. Arsenal presumably did not share Eddy's doubts and Gervinho started in their first game of 2011 / 12, away to Newcastle United. After 75 minutes, Gervinho dribbled into the box and went down under a challenge from Cheick Tioté. I leapt off my seat – Gervinho had won a penalty in his first Premier League game! As I was dialling Eddy's number to gloat, I looked up at the screen to see the referee sending off Gervinho for slapping Joey Barton. The referee had not awarded a penalty, and Barton had begun an earnest, though aggressive, discussion with Gervinho, presumably informing the Ivorian of his lofty ideals regarding sportsmanship in the Premier League. Maybe penalty-winning was not so easy to translate between leagues after all.

Weighted Shots, Expected Goals

In 2007, I stumbled across Pollard and Reep's paper on Expected Goals while I was developing the 'Castrol Index', a statistical rating of players for the European Championship and the World Cup that would make use of the detailed data now available.

I was keen to extend the iBob model to take advantage of the new shot-by-shot information. Inspired by Cohen and Dearnaley, I had begun to model the effect of distance on shot conversion when I read the paper describing Pollard and Reep's 'Weighted Shots' model. I could not believe what I was reading – a decade before me, in 1997, they had built a model similar to the one I was now creating. Their work contained several ideas that I hadn't considered, and I gratefully incorporated them into my model.

Reep had collected detailed data on 489 shots taken in the 1986 World Cup in Mexico. It included information on the distance and angle of the shot from goal, whether the shot was the player's first touch, whether there was a defender within one yard of the player when the shot was taken, and whether the possession originated from open play or a set play. All these factors, except 'first touch', were found to improve the prediction of whether a shot would become a goal. Increasing distance, tighter angles and close defenders were bad news. Open-play shots were likelier to be converted than shots originating from corners, all else being equal.

Opta's new event data included details of each individual shot: the location from which the shot was taken, the situation of the shot (from open play, a corner situation, a counter-attack and so on), the identity of the shooter, and whether the shot was headed, kicked or 'othered' (an attempt at goal coming off a shoulder or backside). My results were similar to Pollard and Reep's, with the chance of scoring decreasing rapidly as distance increases and angle tightens.

I was able to replicate Pollard and Reep's finding that shots from set-pieces have a lower conversion chance than equivalent shots from open play. Knowledge of whether a shot was taken in a counter-attacking situation revealed that these opportunities were much more valuable than shots from general open play.

The pattern for all situations was clear: conversion chance

rapidly decreases as the distance from goal increases. Headers are lower quality chances than kicked shots: it is more difficult to generate power and accuracy with a header than with a kick, and all headed shots are one-touch attempts, while the taker of a kicked shot can often choose whether to try a one-touch finish or attempt to control the ball first. Dead-ball situations – penalties and direct free-kicks – are usually preferable to open-play situations. This may seem strange when you consider that only about 8% of direct free-kicks are converted, but the shots they should be compared to are outside-the-box shots, which have an even lower conversion rate.

The reasons for the relative difference in conversion chance between set-piece, open play and counter-attack are clear: in set-piece situations, the box is usually littered with defenders, while in counter-attacks there are few defenders between the shooter and the goalkeeper, improving the odds of the striker scoring.

I hope that my lack of enthusiasm for Coutinho's long-range shooting is becoming clear. The average conversion chance our Expected Goals model assigned to his outside-the-box shots was only 3%. Coutinho's conversion was much better than expected at nearly 5%, which showed that he was very skilled at converting long-range shots. His success rate from outside the box was more than 60% higher than the model predicted but even so his prospects for success were low.

When Do You Press Pause?

The Expected Goals model I have described considers all shots, but does not consider how well the shot was struck. Imagine watching the highlights of a game. The striker shapes to shoot. Now press pause. This is the point at which most publicly advertised Expected Goals models make their calculations. At Liverpool, we called this the 'Pre-Strike' model: we know that a shot will happen in the next moment but that is all we know. We don't know if it will be drilled into the top corner of the goal, if it will be aimed straight at the goalkeeper, or if it will be sliced over the crossbar.

Pausing the video just before the shot is struck causes a problem: we can't say anything about goalkeeper performance. If a shot with a high conversion chance according to Expected Goals ends up going off target, the goalkeeper should probably not be rewarded for the lack of a goal – all he had to do was stand and watch while the shot sailed over the bar.

We also can't say anything about the finishing ability of players, that is whether they can outperform their Expected Goals. We can start to answer this question by asking whether players who shoot often are better at converting their chances than players who rarely shoot. If we add 'shooting experience' to a Pre-Strike Expected Goals model, we find that experienced shooters – those with hundreds of Premier League shots to their name – outperform players who rarely shoot. The shot-shy players are often defenders or defensive midfielders who unexpectedly find themselves with a chance of scoring. It should be no surprise that specialist strikers are better at shooting.

The solution to this problem of measuring goalkeeper performance and finishing ability is to press the pause button at a slightly later time. Rewind the highlights video and watch the shot again. The striker shapes to shoot. Don't press pause yet. The striker takes his shot and the ball is just about to fly off his boot. Now press pause. This is what we called the Post-Strike Expected Goals at Liverpool.

With this Post-Strike Expected Goals we can see the trajectory of the shot. We *know* whether it is drilled into the top corner, or hit straight at the keeper. Something quite extreme happens when we add trajectory information to Expected Goals: two-thirds of all shots get assigned with a 0% conversion chance. If a shot is off target, as more than a third of Premier League shots are, there is no way it can be a goal. The same is true of the 2% of shots that hit the post or crossbar, although in that case the striker might be labelled 'unlucky'. More than a quarter of shots are blocked by defenders before their trajectory can be estimated and so they too must be excluded from the Post-Strike model.

Shots are converted into goals about 10% of the time. If a shot is on target, the conversion chance leaps to about 30%. This tells us two important things. First, on average, a striker converts a 10% chance into either 0% if it goes off target, or 30% if it is on target. Second, the average conversion chance of a shot that the goalkeeper faces is 30%.

The Post-Strike Expected Goals model that I developed considered the distance of each shot from the centre of the goalmouth as it crossed the line. The trajectory has a huge influence on conversion chance. Consider a shot from open play taken from the penalty spot: if it is hit into the middle of the goal, its conversion chance is only about 15%; if it is hit into the top corner, the conversion chance rockets to about 90%. This intuitive result should also make clear the problems with measuring goalkeeper performance using save percentage: a goalkeeper facing many shots directed into the middle of the goal should be expected to save many more of them than a goalkeeper facing many shots requiring acrobatic saves.

My colleague Daf Steele pointed out a weakness in this model. If the goalkeeper has already been beaten and the striker can simply tap the ball into the net, surely it would make sense to kick the ball into the middle of the goal rather than the corner. My model could perversely incentivise strikers to aim for the corner of the goal when there was no need. Daf showed how we could use the goalkeeper's position to improve our Post-Strike model. Instead of looking at how far away from the centre of the goal the trajectory was, we could look at how far away from the *goalkeeper* it was.

Daf's new model depended on the idea of *interception distance*. This is the length of the shortest path the goalkeeper can take to intercept the shot, and using interception distance improved our model. In this new model, it was sometimes better not to aim for the corner, if the goalkeeper was in a poor position.

We had a long-running project at Liverpool with my friend

(and Liverpool's goalkeeper consultant) Hans Leitert. Hans was a goalkeeper for Austria Vienna and Austria's under-21 national team before an injury brought his playing career to a premature end. When I first met him, he was Red Bull's global head of goalkeeping. It was a sunny summer day, but we were cooped up in Decision Technology's offices discussing American goalkeepers – Red Bull had a club in New York. When the meeting was over we were both keen to continue the conversation so headed into the London sunshine to find some lunch. Several hours later, in a now empty restaurant on Charlotte Street, Hans was waving away the waiting staff and explaining the finer details of his theory of goalkeeper performance to me. I thought to myself: this is not a typical goalkeeper coach. Hans has a very clinical approach to understanding player performance. If you ask his opinion on a goalkeeper, his answer will usually be: 'I cannot say anything about him! I have not studied him in detail yet.'

Our project with Hans was to systematise his video analysis of goalkeepers, so we could collect data that wasn't available from Opta. Hans noted actions about the goalkeeper's position, whether he was still, moving or prone (both before the shot and when the shot happened), the striker's movement before the shot, the goalkeeper's movement after the shot, and whether the goalkeeper was under pressure from opponents. In addition to all this objective detail, Hans made a judgement of the difficulty of the situation and whether the goalkeeper had made a slight mistake. This extra data gave a huge insight on goalkeeper performance and allowed us to compare our Post-Strike model to Hans' expert view.

The results were illuminating. Daf's model allowed us to say something about goalkeeper positioning: would we have estimated a lower conversion chance if the goalkeeper's position had been slightly different? Shots for which we'd concluded the goalkeeper was not in an optimal position usually coincided with comments in Hans' analysis like 'Why coming so far off line???' and 'Not a logical positioning'. Combining data with expert opinion had illuminated and validated the results of the new Post-Strike model.

Adding Context

Whenever I stood up while watching a game at Anfield to yell 'Don't shoot!' at Coutinho (usually as a response to the rest of the crowd shouting 'Shoot!') I could see the exact situation that the player found himself in. Was a defender right in front of him? Was the goalkeeper off his line? Did he have an open team-mate to pass to instead?

The Opta data that we used in our Pre-Strike model saw none of this. If Coutinho was central and 25 yards from goal, the model would say the conversion chance was 3%. Goalkeeper off his line? 3%. Under no pressure or extreme pressure from an opponent? It didn't matter, the model would always just say 3%. There was a huge amount of context in each shot that was unknown. For this reason we knew that we couldn't give feedback about individual shots.

As ever, the answer to these problems came from better data. Since 2015, the Premier League had provided tracking data, where the players' positions are recorded every 40 milliseconds. This allowed us to see all the things missing from Opta's data, but its use was limited: we only had access to Premier League games so couldn't use it to help scout players outside the Premier League.

In 2017 a new data supplier, StatsBomb, offered more granular shot data for any competition we wanted. Their collectors paused the video of each game every time a shot was taken, and noted the positions of all the players. We could finally distinguish between the previously 'identical' shots that any fan could tell had very different chances of success.

I decided to take inspiration from Daf's Post-Strike model and reuse the concept of interception distance. We have already seen that if the goalkeeper was far from the shot's trajectory, the interception distance is high and chance of scoring is (pretty obviously) much higher.

Now we could see the position of *all* the defenders, not just the goalkeeper, and for *all* the shots, not just shots on target. We could also add the interception distances of the defenders into the mix. We were also able to include much richer information about the shot – how many attackers and defenders were ahead of or behind the ball, how far off his line the goalkeeper was, how far away the defenders were, how much of the goalmouth the defenders and goalkeeper covered, and whether the goalkeeper was standing, moving or prone.

The extra context provided a significant boost to the predictiveness of our model – on average, the predictions from the new model were a few percentage points closer to reality than our old model. There was significantly more complexity in the new model, but it was a price worth paying to generate better estimates of shot conversion.

One outcome of all this extra information was that the shot situation – whether the shot occurred from open play, a set-piece or a counter-attack – had a vastly reduced importance. We knew that the 'set-piece' or 'counter-attack' labels that we'd previously used were only a proxy for things that *really* affect the conversion chance – how many defenders were behind the ball, and whether they were effectively covering the goalmouth. Now that we could see those things explicitly in the data, the labels lost much of their importance.

The new model made lots of other predictions that were instinctively understood by fans, but that Expected Goals models up to that point could not make. Defenders cause an 'Expected Goals Shadow' to be cast in front of them. This shadow is a region of low Expected Goals for shots taken from right in front of a defender – because the defender only has a chance to block a shot that is right in front of them.

We could also estimate for the first time the size of the impact an outfield defender can have: a shot from the penalty spot in open play, with the goalkeeper on the line and no defenders nearby, is, pre-strike, predicted to have a similar conversion chance to a penalty. But if the defender is in a position to block, the goal chance reduces to less than 30%.

The closest defender still casts a shadow even if he is further away from goal than the shooter – the shot's conversion chance is lower than it would be if he was not there. This may seem strange, because the defender cannot physically affect the shot. The defensive shadow in this case reflects an implicit pressure on the striker. If the defender is a few yards away, he can't influence the shot directly, but his presence means the striker only has a limited time in which to take his shot. He has to rush a little and so the conversion chance is smaller than if the closest defender was far away and the striker had more time to take his shot.

The Post-Strike Expected Goals model also improves when defender positions are taken into account, but their effect reverses: the defensive shadow becomes a defensive spotlight. If a shot makes it past a defender who might have blocked it but didn't, it has a *higher* conversion probability than if the defender had not been in front of the shot. The goalkeeper is unsighted for these shots and has less time to react. One of Coutinho's tricks was to draw a challenge from a defender and take a shot just as the defender attempted to block. If the block was unsuccessful, the goalkeeper's job was made a lot more difficult. However, 104 of the 281 shots Coutinho attempted from outside the box in open play were blocked – the defender failing to block was a pretty big 'if'.

Preventing Outcome Bias

Aside from recruitment, the main use of our Expected Goals models was to track Liverpool's performance game by game, compared to pre-season expectations and outcomes. A recurring theme of football analysis is outcome bias: the tendency to pay too much attention to the result of a game and not enough attention to the performance that led to the result.

With our Dixon-Coles inspired forecasting model, we knew what to expect from Liverpool and our opponents before each game. With our Expected Goals or 'fair score' models, we knew how the team had performed in each game. We compared each performance to our pre-game and pre-season forecasts to gauge whether the team was improving or declining. This focus on forecasts and performances rather than results allowed us to downplay a lucky run of good or bad results.

That is not to say we *ignored* the outcomes, but results in football tend to revert to underlying performance: good luck cannot continue for ever. This led to the Research department being emotionally out of sync with the rest of the training ground. The morning after a loss was usually accompanied by a funereal atmosphere at Melwood, but our analysis often showed that Liverpool could have (and sometimes *should* have) won the game. Consequently I, and the rest of the data team, often felt much more upbeat than our training ground colleagues. Conversely, we were fun sponges after a victory, reminding our colleagues that the goals we scored do not always get converted, and the clean sheet achieved might have owed something to luck.

In my first season at Liverpool in 2012/13 we finished seventh, behind even Everton. But our Pre-Strike and Post-Strike Expected Goals performances suggested a fairer finish would have been third or fourth. The following season we finished second, a huge difference in outcome. But our Pre-Strike and Post-Strike fair scores suggested second or third would be in line with performances – a much smaller difference in performance. The world had underrated us in 2012/13 then slightly overrated us in 2013/14.

We had hugely overperformed our goal-scoring expectations in 2013/14. Powered by Suárez, Sturridge, Sterling and Coutinho, we scored 101 goals. Our Pre-Strike model suggested 80 goals was a fair return, although our players had taken their shots very well, recording one of the best Post-Strike goals totals seen in the Premier League. I remember a conversation at Melwood with the Video Analysis department, who were new to data analysis in football. They questioned the validity of our model: 'Ian, how can I trust these fair scores when we always end up scoring more than the fair score?' In their shoes I would have asked exactly the same question.

Looking back over the past few seasons before 2013/14, I could see we were an outlier. Our Post-Strike Expected Goals was 20% higher than Pre-Strike, much higher than any other team had ever managed. This was partly due to the pinpoint accuracy of Suárez and Sturridge. The following season, with Suárez gone and Sturridge injured, we underperformed both Pre-Strike and Post-Strike Expected Goals. But even if we had retained Suárez and Sturridge had been fit, we would have been unlikely to repeat our extreme 2013/14 goal-scoring season.

In 2014/15 we lost Suárez to Barcelona and Sturridge to injury. Partly due to losing two elite finishers, and partly due to reversion to the mean, we plummeted from scoring 20 goals more than expected to 10 fewer. Again, the change in outcome, falling from second to sixth, was much bigger than the change in performance, from second or third to fourth or fifth. It is one thing to understand the concept of Expected Goals and understand that results will deviate from performances over the course of a season, but it is something else entirely to experience the roller coaster of brilliant outcomes one season to terrible outcomes the next, as we did in my early years at Liverpool.

Expected Goals Isn't Everything

I have argued that Expected Goals gives a better view of short-term performance than results. Over the longer term, comparing expected to actual goals, it turns out that better teams score more goals than expected and worse teams score fewer goals than expected. This is due partly to better teams having better strikers and goalkeepers, and partly to their ability to create advantageous situations that are not fully captured in Expected Goals models.

To truly understand the qualities of a player or a team we must pay attention to both process, or Expected Goals, and outcome, or actual goals.

Each step in the historical arc of Expected Goals, from my basic iBob model to Pollard and Reep's Weighted Shots to today's sophisticated models, has moved each shot away from the average conversion rate and closer to 0% for long-range efforts or 100% for penalties and tap-ins. The first step in this process was thanks to Charles Reep (again) and the statistician Bernard Benjamin, who published a paper in 1968 called 'Skill and Chance in Association Football'.[3] This was the first time that the average shot conversion rate of about 10% was reported. This can be seen as the extreme end of an Expected Goals spectrum, with every single shot assigned the same 10% conversion chance.

At the other end of this spectrum is the outcome. In this 'perfect hindsight' model, each goal is inevitably a goal, and each miss inevitably a miss. But the best measurement of performance is somewhere in between Expected Goals and actual goals.

Ben Torvaney has analysed the relative value of Expected Goals versus actual goals in his 'Stats and Snakeoil' blog.[4] He built two forecasting models, one using Expected Goals and one using actual goals. He then combined the models to see if they produced superior match forecasts to either individual model. They did: taking both expected and actual goals into account produced more accurate forecasts than either on its own. The optimal amount of attention to pay to Expected Goals was 70% compared to 30% for actual goals.

At Liverpool we hit on a different solution to the same problem. Each outfield player and each goalkeeper was given a conversion skill. Players that consistently overperformed the predictions of our Post-Strike model increased their skill rating and vice versa. The result was that elite finishers like Son Heung-min and elite shot-stoppers like Alisson Becker were expected to score and save more goals than the model estimated. A side effect was that making a save from a Son shot, or scoring past Alisson, was more highly rewarded than performing the same action against a lower rated player.

For post-match analysis, we didn't bother too much with conversion, which varies hugely on a game-by-game basis. My opinion is that it's better to underplay conversion given that people tend to be biased towards perfect hindsight.

The Game Is Changing

When asked about the impact of data analysis in the Premier League, people often cite the steadily declining distance from which the average shot is taken in the Premier League. The distance from which kicked open-play shots are taken has dropped nearly every year, from 21.7 yards in 2011/12 to 19.4 yards in 2022/23. This has resulted in conversion increasing from 8% to 10%, just as an Expected Goals model would predict. A 25% relative increase in shot conversion is a huge difference and is heralded as *the* triumph of data analysis in football.

I am very doubtful of this claim. Even today, most Premier League clubs do not take data analysis seriously, and its adoption has certainly not increased steadily like average shot distance has decreased. Data evangelists have also ignored the downside of closer range shots: the price teams pay for closer range shots is that fewer shots are taken.

In 2011/12 there were 18 open-play kicked shots per game. By 2022/23 that had decreased to 15, a decline of 17%. The extra efficiency in the conversion rate of shots has been mostly wiped out by the decreased number of shots.[5] The outcome is that today we see about 1.5 goals per game from kicked open-play shots, the same as we did a decade ago. However, there is an advantage to taking fewer shots from closer range. Each shot comes with a cost attached to it, a cost that is conveniently ignored in Expected Goals models. Most shots – even high-quality, short-range ones – usually do not get converted into goals and most of the unsuccessful attempts lead to a loss of possession. Given the choice between fewer high-quality shots and more lower quality shots, with the same total number of Expected Goals, I would choose fewer higher quality shots because it gives the opposition less opportunity to begin a possession of their own. Pep Guardiola has turned this idea into an art form at Manchester City, with his team endlessly moving the ball around to create a good scoring chance rather than being satisfied with a speculative shot and surrendering possession. This is ironic, because a speculative shot did for Liverpool's title hopes in 2018/19. Manchester City played Leicester City in their penultimate game of the season, needing a win to go above Liverpool ahead of the last round of fixtures. As usual, Manchester City had dominated the game but unusually they had failed to score. After 70 minutes, Vincent Kompany shot from more than 25 yards out. It thundered into the top corner, the only goal in a 1–0 victory. Manchester City beat Liverpool to the title by one point.

It is not only the elite teams who have been decreasing their shot distances. Since 2010, every Premier League team except Manchester United has decreased the distance from which they take shots. Arsenal and Manchester City always took short-range shots and the more analytically inclined clubs Liverpool, Tottenham Hotspur and Brighton have undergone the sharpest declines. But everyone in between, from Aston Villa to West Ham United, follows the same pattern. The exception, Manchester United, have hovered around the 20-yard mark. Shooting from 20 yards on average made them the second shortest distance team in the Premier League in 2010/11. They also shot from 20 yards out in 2022/23 but this was the fifth *longest range* shooting. This has been driven in recent years by their high-volume shooter Bruno Fernandes taking many a long-range shot, as Coutinho did. Coincidentally, Bruno's Pre-Strike and Post-Strike Expected Goal conversion rate for shots outside the box is nearly identical to Liverpool-era Coutinho's, though his actual goal conversion is lower.

In the early days of Jürgen Klopp's management, Liverpool's excellent Expected Goals numbers allowed us to understand that the team's underlying performances – the quality and quantity of chances created and conceded – was very good. We knew that we were a brilliant team long before the rest of the world did, and we knew we should not pay attention to a few bad results.

8

The Value of Possession

*The process of rating players can be compared to the measurement of
the position of a cork bobbing up and down on the surface of agitated water
with a yard stick tied to a rope and which is swaying in the wind*

Arpad Elo

Death by Football

Brendan Rodgers had a plan: 'When you've got the ball 65-70% of
the time, it's a football death for the other team. It's death by football.'[1] This was the plan he had used at Swansea, and he wanted to
replicate it at Liverpool. It made a lot of sense: it's difficult to score
without the ball, and it's difficult to concede when you have it.

Although having the ball is important, what you do with it is critical. At Liverpool, our opponents were very happy to let us have the
ball in midfield, where we posed no immediate danger of scoring a
goal. To understand the difference between simply having the ball
and using it effectively, we developed a Possession Value model
(introduced in Chapter 2). We called it 'Goal Probability Added' but
it has since been popularised as 'Expected Threat'.

The basic idea is to estimate the chance a possession ends with a
goal from any given situation. The model allowed us to see that
Brendan's concept of dominating midfield possession was sterile: it
was not very effective at increasing our goal-scoring chances. To
get this point across I boiled down our Possession Value model
into a simple concept – 'Dangerous Possession'. There are two

complexities that make possession a flawed statistic for predicting wins. The first is location – some teams are happy to let you have the ball in your own half. The second is game state – some teams are happy to defend a lead without the ball, and wait for a counter-attacking opportunity.

Most elite teams like to dominate possession, and this leads to possession having a high correlation with goal difference. Back in 2013, when trying to market my Possession Value model to my colleagues, the Premier League looked similar to how it looks today. The teams with the highest goal difference – Manchester United, Chelsea, Arsenal, Manchester City, Liverpool and Spurs – all dominated possession. And the less successful teams by goal difference were dominated in terms of possession. But there were two outliers: Roberto Martínez's Wigan Athletic, and Swansea City, who were still playing a similar style of football as they had under Brendan the previous season. Both teams were possession-heavy like the big teams but both had a negative goal difference. For them, possession dominance did not pay off.

One of the insights from our Possession Value model was that possession in the attacking third of the pitch was much more valuable than possession in the other two thirds of the pitch. I calculated 'Dangerous Possession Dominance' as an easily understood substitute for Possession Value. Dangerous Possession Dominance is simply the difference in possession in each team's attacking third. Possession in the other two thirds of the pitch is just ignored. Looking at dangerous rather than overall possession dominance dramatically increased the correlation between possession and success. Wigan and Swansea had plenty of possession, but not where it hurt the opposition. Neither team had more possession than the opposition in the attacking third, and their lack of Dangerous Possession Dominance was in line with their negative goal difference. Conversely, when looking at 'Safe Possession' Dominance – ignoring the attacking third – the correlation with goal difference becomes much smaller.

In England in 2012/13 no Premier League team had less than 50%

of possession *and* a positive goal difference. But in Spain there was an outlier. The polar opposite of Roberto Martínez's 'lots of possession but negative goal difference' approach was Diego Simeone. He had just completed his first full season at Atlético Madrid. Atlético had 5% *less* possession than their opponents, but their goal difference was +34, easily the third best in La Liga. Looking at Dangerous Possession, Atlético had 3% *more* than their opponents – only Real Madrid and Barcelona dominated the attacking third more. Simeone's team did not care about having the ball in general. But they did care about having possession in the opposition's attacking third, and they cared about the opposition not having possession in Atlético's defensive third. This is not to advocate Simeone's style of play (which can be very difficult to watch), but to demonstrate that *where* you have the ball matters more than just having the ball.

Goals Change Games Again

Possession also depends on game state. Liverpool's two games against Newcastle United in the 2012/13 season demonstrated this perfectly. In the home game, we dominated both possession and final-third possession, but the game finished 1–1. Newcastle were happy with an away draw and ceded possession to us. When they went ahead they were even happier to sit back and defend. The away game finished 6–0 to Liverpool but Newcastle had more possession *and* more final-third possession than us. Even possession-heavy Liverpool were happy to sit and counter-attack once we'd established a big lead.

The relationship between possession and game state was consistent for all teams. It didn't matter if you were the best or worst team in the league, you saw more of the ball when behind and less of it when ahead. On average across the league, teams had 4% more possession than their opponent when losing and 4% less when winning – an 8% swing. For Liverpool there was no relationship between possession dominance in a particular game and success in a particular game. Better teams tend to have more possession, and of course better teams win more. But increased possession for a *given* team in a game did not correlate very strongly with increased success.

Do Counts Count?

The reason that possession was a simple route into explaining Possession Value is that until the mid-2000s, it was one of the few statistics about general play that was commonly available. All of the statistics – shots, passes, fouls – were only available in aggregate. And this fundamentally limited the usefulness of data analysis. To understand why, consider the iconic theme tune to the football highlights show *Match of the Day*. The notes played in its first four bars comprise one A, one B, eight C sharps, two Ds and three Es. This is factual data, but in this aggregate form it doesn't really convey much useful information about the tune.

Understanding football by analysing aggregate statistics is similar to trying to understand music by analysing the number of times each note is played. There are certainly correlations, like the one between possession and goal difference, but the mechanisms that give rise to them are unclear. The advent of event data, where each on-ball action is seen in sequence, changed everything. You can see each event in its proper context: what had just happened and what happened next. And like with music, what happens next in the sequence is crucial.

It is remarkable how quickly the idea of Possession Value is hit upon when the right data becomes available. Within weeks of seeing Opta's event data in 2007 I was analysing how the ball transitioned around the pitch and giving a value to each location. Richard Pollard and Charles Reep introduced Possession Value as 'Goal Yield' in the same 1997 paper that introduced Expected Goals.[2] I had discovered their paper while developing my own version, and as with Expected Goals, I was impressed that they'd invented the idea a decade before anyone else. Their work was only possible because

Charles Reep had painstakingly collected the data himself. In 2011, a company called StatDNA made some event data available for a research competition. The competition was won by Sarah Rudd, who independently invented her own Possession Value model. StatDNA hired Rudd, and the company was bought by Arsenal in 2012, as they embarked on their own data analysis journey.[3] Karun Singh created a similar model called 'Expected Threat'. Karun has since left his engineering job at Facebook to join Arsenal.

When I arrived at Liverpool, my first task was to build a new Possession Value model, improving on what I'd built before. It was brilliant to be working at Melwood, but we didn't have any office space. An old bedroom block, commissioned by Rafa Benítez but hardly ever used, would take nine months to convert into our office. So me and my colleague Tim would use the boardroom, spending hours sketching out how the new Possession Value model would work on a flip chart. When the boardroom was needed for meetings we set up camp in Eddy's small office. Tim would bring in a chair and set up his laptop on the edge of Eddy's desk, and I would place my laptop on top of the filing cabinet and work standing up. Despite the interruptions we made good progress and the new model was ready within a few months.

Possession Value Models

Most Possession Value models are built using the Markov chain assumption,[4] which is a fancy way of saying 'assume the current state of affairs is independent of the past'.

A good way to understand a Markov chain is by using an example from gambling. Imagine you have £2 in your pocket and I offer a £1 bet that the flip of a fair coin will come up heads. Your aim is to win £4 before you go bust. What are your chances? You have a 50% chance of losing your first bet and a 50% chance of winning it. After two bets, you have a 25% chance of having lost both and gone bust. There's a 25% chance you are £2 up. The other 50% of the time, you win one and lose one (or vice versa), and end up back where you started.

After three bets, you could be bust, down £1, up £1 or up £3. And we can work out the chance of each scenario because we know the chances of each outcome after two bets. And we can keep on applying the same calculation to find out what happens in the long run.

After four bets, you might have achieved your aim of winning £4 by flipping four heads in a row – the chance of four heads in a row is 6.25%. But most likely you'll still be playing. After 25 bets, you've probably gone bust (65% chance) or won £4 (32% chance), but you may still be playing (3% chance). Eventually you'll either go bust (67%) or hit your goal of £4 (33%).

The reason we can do these calculations is that the amount of money in your pocket at any one time does not depend on the path that took you to that amount of money. If, after 10 bets, you are back where you started with £2, your chance of going bust is the same as it was before you started betting: the future is independent of the past.

What does this have to do with football? We can make a similar Markov chain analysis to understand the value of a possession. In football, the present does depend on the past, but it is a useful approximation to pretend it doesn't. We take each game situation, action by action, and assign it to a 'game state'. The game state depends on the location of the ball, and what kind of possession the team has – normal, defensive, set-piece or counter-attack. One example of a game state might be 'we have the ball in the centre circle, in normal possession'. Another example is 'we have the ball in the opposition corner, in set-piece possession'. We then use data from past games to estimate the chance of moving from any game state to every other possible game state. For example, transitioning from 'centre circle normal possession' into 'central just outside opposition box' is reasonably likely, while transitioning to 'ball in own box, defensive possession' is very unlikely. We end up with a table of numbers detailing the chance of transitioning from any game state to any other game state.

We now have the ingredients needed to calculate the chance of scoring a goal (winning £4) or losing possession (going bust) from any particular game state (amount of money in our pocket). Just like the gambler, we can compute our long-term goal-scoring chance on a possession by applying the same calculation again and again. Our table of transitions told us where we might be after one step in the possession. The same table allows us to calculate where we might be after two, three, four steps and so on.

The outcome of all this work is a goal-scoring chance attached to each game state. In normal possession, in your own box, you have about a 0.2% chance of eventually scoring before losing possession. In midfield that increases, but only to about 0.5%. As you approach the opposition box, the chance of scoring (that is, scoring before losing possession) rapidly increases, to about 1.5% just outside the box, then to about 10% as you reach the penalty spot. Possession in central areas tends to be more valuable than possession on the wings. If possession is 'defensive' – with the ball pinging around after a tackle – it is less valuable. This is not surprising as the ball is not fully in anyone's control. Far from goal, set-piece possession is more valuable than normal possession because you get a free attempt to move the ball into a more valuable state. But inside the box it's less valuable than normal possession because the opposition have usually packed the box with defenders.

Teams have a greater chance of scoring a goal if they have possession further up the pitch, or in a more favourable situation like a counter-attack. It may be surprising that having possession in midfield is 'only' worth 0.5% of a goal, but there are hundreds of possessions per game, and only 2.70 goals on average.

From Possession Value to Player Rating

Armed with the concept that different game states have different goal-scoring chances, we can start to understand the impact each player's actions have. Imagine you are an attacking midfielder who attempts to thread a pass from an attacking midfield position to the edge of the box. We can look up the scoring chance of each game state in our table of goal probabilities to see the impact of such a pass. We might rate the team's current position in attacking midfield as having a 1% chance of scoring before losing possession. The edge of the box is more valuable with, say, a 5% chance. If you complete the pass, then you have increased your team's chance of scoring on this possession by 4%. If you fail to complete the pass then you have decreased your team's chance of scoring by 1%. This is the basis by which we rated a player's impact on the game.

Football is not only about goal-scoring, we also have to pay attention to goal-conceding. If your pass is unsuccessful you not only decrease your team's chance of scoring to zero, you also allow the opposition to gain possession, giving them a chance to score. Attacking midfield for us is defensive midfield for the opposition, so that unsuccessful pass has also increased our chance of conceding from 0% (we don't usually concede if we have possession) to about 0.3%. As a player your critical decision is whether the reward of a successful pass is worth the risk of losing possession. In our example the rewards are big – 4% of a goal – but the cost of a failed pass is 1% of a goal scored plus 0.3% of a goal conceded.

We can use these ideas to calculate an adjusted pass completion percentage, in the same way that Post-Strike Expected Goals allows us to calculate an adjusted save percentage for goalkeepers. Imagine that you attempt 100 of those passes from attacking midfield to the edge of the box, and complete 25 of them. The 25 completed passes add 4% of a goal each: 100% of a goal in total. It doesn't matter how many goals were *actually* scored from these possessions. In our model 100 of these passes add 100% of a goal, so we reward the player with 100% of a goal.

Most of the passes were not successful. The 75 unsuccessful passes *cost* 1.3% of a goal each: 97.5% of a goal in total. Overall your 100 passes have added 2.5% net goals to our chances. If you'd completed only 24, your passes would have cost your team goals instead of gaining them. For this particular pass then, a success rate of only 25% increases net goals. A player with a 50% success rate for this classic number 10's pass is a very good player.

Conversely, a player passing only short and backwards has to achieve a completion rate of close to 100% to break even. These passes usually mean little for a team's prospects of scoring, but there is always a price to pay should possession be lost. This is what we saw with Joe Allen. He had a brilliant pass completion percentage and added value with his passing, but his success rate *needed* to be brilliant for him to break even in terms of adding goal-scoring value. Players who attempt dangerous passes can get away with a lower completion rate: fortune favours the brave.

Back in that 2011/12 season when I was extolling the virtues of Steven Gerrard and Lucas Leiva, Gerrard's completion percentage was only 80% compared to Allen's 91%. There were certainly players who risked the ball less than Gerrard *and* added comparable value – Michael Carrick, Mikel Arteta, Gareth Barry and Paul Scholes. Others lost the ball much more but we rated them as very effective passers – Alex Song, James Milner, Danny Murphy and Yohan Cabaye. Joe Allen was a combination of higher pass completion but lower value added, like his team-mate Leon Britton, Sandro at Spurs, and the Wigan midfielders James McCarthy and James McArthur.

Measuring a player's passing impact in terms of goals scored and conceded is only the first step to understanding whether they can improve your team's chances of success. The midfielders at Swansea and Wigan were following their managers' tactical instructions, which were – presumably – to concentrate on safe midfield possession. Maybe these players *could* play like Gerrard if given the opportunity. But we had seen no evidence that they could, while many other players had demonstrated an appetite for risky but rewarding passing. When signing players who have played lots of senior football, a good rule of thumb is 'what you've seen is what you'll get'.

The Ridgewell Problem

Liam Ridgewell was a very good footballer. He was a regular starter for West Bromwich Albion and Birmingham City in the Premier League. He won the League Cup with Birmingham City and the MLS Cup with Portland Timbers. But for all his qualities few would have rated him as one of Europe's best defenders in 2007/08. He had started 33 games in the Premier League for Birmingham, and they had been relegated, in 19th place, with the second worst Expected Goals Conceded in the league.[5]

When I met Damien Comolli at Spurs Lodge near the end of the 2007/08 season, in the same meeting where he became convinced of the value of our model, he commented that my list of the best defenders in Europe wasn't nearly as convincing as the list of attackers. Ridgewell looked outstanding. How could this be if he'd started for one of the worst defensive teams in the league? Defensive actions were recorded, and were measured by the Possession Value model, but most defensive actions were positive in their outcome. Opta recorded some defensive failures, like a subjective 'error' or a 'challenge lost', when an opponent dribbled past a defender. But the bulk of defensive actions were tackles, interceptions, blocks and clearances. And these were usually associated with winning possession, which according to Possession Value has a positive defensive value. All those actions help to stop a goal from being conceded.

Ridgewell had been particularly active at intercepting and clearing, especially in his own box where the danger was high, and he'd been richly rewarded for doing so. He'd also blocked shots: his goal-line clearances converted opposition Expected Goals into zero actual goals conceded. But Birmingham's defence could by no means be considered good by Premier League standards and Ridgewell played in the middle of that defence.

In common with other team sports, football has always found it most difficult to measure and analyse defensive ability. The problem we had was that we were unsure of the defenders' positions when tackles *didn't* happen and a dangerous chance was conceded. Even at Liverpool, Eddy paid relatively more attention to video analysis and the opinion of scouts when judging defensive performance.

Trying to measure defensive performance with event data is difficult. Defenders who made no active intervention were often critical for allowing or preventing dangerous situations. Ridgewell, by contrast, was all-action, due to a malfunctioning defence for which he was partly responsible.

Given that we didn't usually know where the defenders were, we had to make an approximation. Whenever the opposition took a shot or moved the ball to a more dangerous location, we made an educated guess about which defenders were responsible. We knew where each player usually was positioned in relation to their teammates because we could see the location of their on-ball actions. So when the opponents made an attacking move, we knew which defenders were typically nearby. When a shot is conceded centrally, the centre-backs take more responsibility. If a cross is conceded from the left, the left-back takes more responsibility for it than the right-back. This concept of defensive responsibility allowed us to assign defensive debits for allowing opposition chances as well as credits for stopping them.

In Ridgewell's case, he racked up a lot of credit for heroic goal-line clearances and blocked shots, but this was balanced by sharing responsibility for the many chances that Birmingham conceded. Ridgewell wasn't the only Birmingham player responsible for allowing these chances, and he averted more than his fair share of danger. But, after accounting for his defensive responsibility, we no longer rated him as one of the best defenders in Europe, although he was still the best at Birmingham City.

The new defensive ratings were still imperfect. For any particular opposition chance, we could only assign responsibility based on average defensive positions. This meant that a few defenders usually took a share of the blame. Often this was fine, but occasionally there was a clear positional error from one of the defenders that any fan could point out. And sometimes a player was unfairly blamed. I remember a game against West Ham United where Michail Antonio tackled Liverpool's left-back Alberto Moreno on the West Ham goal-line, leaving him in a heap on the ground. A few seconds later West Ham crossed the ball from Liverpool's left for Antonio to score. Moreno took some responsibility for that cross, because it came from the left. But in this particular case it really wasn't his fault. By the time the cross came in, he had only just managed to run back into defence.

It was approximations such as these that led our defensive ratings to be a little less accurate than our attacking ones, even after fixing the 'Ridgewell Problem'. Despite this, the ratings worked well for understanding defensive performance, and recommended the signings of Virgil van Dijk, Joël Matip and Mamadou Sakho. It would take the advent of tracking data to truly understand defensive ability.

There Is Only One Ball

Johan Cruyff said: 'There is only one ball, so you need to have it.' In the world of Possession Value, having the ball brings with it a great responsibility. You are responsible for your team's current goal-scoring potential. What you do with the ball changes that goal-scoring chance, and your decision may even end your team's goal-scoring chance.

When I was developing the Possession Value model, I was inspired by Dean Oliver's book *Basketball on Paper*.[6] Oliver was using statistical techniques to rate basketball players, which is exactly what I was trying to do for football. In his book, Oliver introduced the idea of 'usage' – how many of your team's possessions end with you either losing possession, shooting or even scoring.

When players end a possession, they effectively end their team's current chance of scoring. Ending a possession is typically bad news. But if a player has ended a possession by taking a shot, the Expected Goals value he creates often outweighs the cost of losing possession, even if a goal is not scored. There is another price to pay when taking a shot: shots are taken at the expense of your team-mates – your usage of the possession stops other players using it.

Analysing usage allowed us to see the impact of different types of attacker. High-volume, high-quality shooters like Mohamed Salah or Robert Lewandowski are huge assets to a team, but they use up possessions with their shots. And this tendency means other players get less opportunity to shoot. There are diminishing returns to high-volume shooters: going from zero to one has a bigger impact on a team than going from one to two, because the second shooter takes away some of the opportunities the first might have had were the second not on the pitch or less inclined to shoot.

This idea of usage led us to question whether attackers were adding value by using up possessions or by keeping them going. Our favourite type of striker was the 'triple threat' – a player who could add value through shooting, passing and dribbling. These players are difficult to defend against – they can choose to pass or dribble instead of shoot. And they use up fewer possessions than players whose only skill is shooting. At Liverpool we had the luxury of three triple threats in Roberto Firmino, Sadio Mané and Mo Salah. Even so, Salah was the highest volume shooter, and benefited from the passing ability of Firmino. Separating players' contributions into different types of action – passing, shooting and dribbling – allowed us to begin to understand teamwork. Too many shooters and the ball does not get passed into dangerous locations. Too many passers and the ball does not get shot into the opponent's goal. Like-wise, Salah's presence increased Firmino's impact on the team.

Speaking for the Numbers

The Possession Value model was the workhorse of our player ana-lysis for many years at Liverpool. It contained lots of approximations and assumptions but was very effective. We used it to filter thou-sands of players down to the dozen or so who could make a difference to our team. This focus on a few relevant players allowed our Scouting department to do comprehensive video analysis on each and fill in the gaps that the data couldn't see. For each short-listed player, 20–30 games were analysed in depth on video, a level of detail difficult to achieve for more than a few players. Nine of the starters in the Champions League final win against Spurs in 2019 were signed with the help of the Possession Value model. The only exceptions were the Academy prodigy Trent Alexander-Arnold and captain Jordan Henderson, who was signed by Damien Comolli in Liverpool's pre-data era.

We learned through experience which of our model's assumptions were reasonable and which had to be changed. In today's world there is a temptation to just 'follow the numbers', but I agree with Nate Silver's opinion: 'The numbers have no way of speaking for themselves. We speak for them. We imbue them with meaning.' If we had just followed the first numbers the model produced instead of critically evaluating them, the Ridgewell Problem would not have been solved and we would have signed active defenders instead of effective ones. If we had simply totalled players' Expected Goals we would not have understood the interplay between creators and shooters. We may have made the mistake of loading our team with shooters instead of trying to find attackers whose skills complement each other.

Another way we 'speak for the numbers' is through the hundreds of tiny decisions and assumptions we make when creating a model of how football works. All data-driven models reflect the beliefs and decisions of their creators – they are not as objective as we like to believe. The big assumption in Possession Value models is the Markov assumption – that the present does not depend on the past. This is clearly untrue – if the ball is quickly passed from one side of the pitch to the other then back again, the defence may be dragged out of shape. We could invent a more complicated model that allows the Possession Value to change based on the last few game states.[7] This sounds like a good idea but causes some problems. Stronger teams tend to have more possession, but we know that the relationship between possession and success is complicated. While working for StatsBomb, Dinesh Vatvani pointed out that using information about the past to calculate Possession Value may cause goal-scoring chances to look higher in long chains of possession, simply because stronger teams have longer chains of possession. This is an example of 'information leak', when a model learns things we don't want it to learn.

With the Markov assumption, attacking midfield possession is worth about 1% of a goal. If the goal-scoring chance is allowed to change based on the last few ball touches, attacking midfield possession after a long chain of possession might be valued higher than 1%. The question is whether those extra touches really increase our scoring chances. Or does the fact that we've been in possession for a while simply give our algorithm a clue that the possession belongs to a team like Manchester City or Barcelona, who are more likely to score than the average team?

Possession Value also depends on the player. In attacking midfield we might say that the goal-scoring chance is 1%, but if your name is Lionel Messi it is much more than 1%. The average goal-scoring chances are only a benchmark by which to compare players. Messi's contributions in attacking midfield usually end with the game in a state of play that has much more than a 1% goal-scoring chance. His ability to consistently outperform our benchmark is how he achieves an excellent rating.

An important piece of work was to combine Possession Value with our Dixon-Coles inspired team strength model. Adjusting player ratings for strength of opposition allowed us to compare the goal-scoring chance created by a midfielder in Germany or Greece with that of a midfielder in the Premier League. When I say things like 'the chance of scoring on this possession from the corner of the pitch is 1%', I am referring to the average Premier League team playing against average Premier League opposition. If you play against Bayern Munich, the scoring chance is lower, and if you play against Hamilton Academical the scoring chance is higher. The Greek Super League is nowhere near as strong as the Premier

League, and while playing there Kostas Tsimikas had the luxury of not having to play against the strongest team, because he already played for Olympiacos. The relatively low quality of many of the teams he faced led us to downgrade his Possession Value rating significantly, but he still rated as above Premier League average, and we were happy to sign him as back-up to Andy Robertson.

The most important advantage of Possession Value is that it converts all of a player's actions into one currency: goals. Whether you tackled, passed, shot or fouled, everything is measured by the difference between the team's chance of scoring (and conceding) before and after your intervention. This simplifies analysis. We can concentrate on one metric by which to measure players. Today, hundreds of metrics are available for players, and it is unclear to the untrained eye which are important and which are trivial. By asking only one question – 'How much does this player increase his team's goal-scoring chance?' – our analysis becomes much clearer. The weak point of Possession Value was measuring defensive quality. The problem of measuring defence would begin to be solved once a new data source became available, a source where you could see for yourself where all the defenders were.

9.

Track Your Man

In football, time and space are the same thing

Graham Taylor

Seventy-seven Metres

The directors' box at Anfield is usually a more sedate place to watch the game than the main stand. I experienced only one occasion in the box when everyone went wild: the 2018 Merseyside derby. With the game still tied in injury-time, Everton's fans were lighting blue flares to celebrate their 0–0 victory. But in the last few seconds, an error from the Everton goalkeeper allowed Divock Origi to score the winner. It wasn't only the prawn sandwich brigade (myself included) who allowed their emotions to get the better of them, Jürgen Klopp was also euphoric and ran on to the pitch to celebrate with our goalkeeper Alisson in the centre circle. It was an expensive run – he was later fined £8,000 by the Football Association for misconduct.

After every game, we calculate the physical statistics of each player – how far they ran, how many sprints they made and so on. But after the Everton game, there was an extra name on the team sheet: Jürgen Klopp. In his celebration, he ran 77 metres, 8 of them at sprinting speed. He reached a top speed of 26 kilometres per hour, faster than Alisson's top speed in the game. Our midfielders had each covered more than 11 kilometres in the game, and our forwards had reached speeds above 32kph. But Jürgen's physical output was admirable for a 51-year-old.

The data had been collected with a video camera rig high in the gantry of the Sir Kenny Dalglish Stand. The cameras are situated high enough to capture the whole pitch at once. The video they record is fed into an algorithm that converts it into 'Optical Tracking Data': 'optical' because the source is video, and 'tracking' because the data tracks the locations of the players. The locations of all 22 players and the ball are recorded every 40 milliseconds. The name given to this kind of technology is computer vision. Similar algorithms detect faces and foreign text for translation on your smartphone. It's not an easy task to convert video to data – the algorithm needs to work out where the white lines of the pitch are, detect where the players are, and identify which player is which. Sometimes, manual intervention is needed to clean up the data – for example, if a substitute is warming up close to the touchline he may accidentally be recorded as an extra player. The same goes for a manager who has run on to the pitch before the end of the game. The effort expended in creating the technology and algorithms necessary for Tracking Data was worthwhile: it has led to a dramatic improvement in how we analyse the game.

Has Anyone Told the Clubs?

In 2013, I received a call from David Woodfine – Woody – who at the time was head of performance analysis at West Ham. He asked if I'd heard about the Premier League tracking data deal. I had not. He, like performance analysts at many other clubs, was frustrated with the tracking data that was available to clubs. Every club had to individually source their own supplier and would only receive data about their own games. Data was only available for away games if the same supplier had cameras installed at the away stadium. The biggest supplier was a company called Prozone, which had been around since the 1990s and had given many of today's football executives their first job. By 2013, many clubs were dissatisfied with Prozone's services – prices kept increasing, only aggregate summary statistics were made available, and the raw positional data was not shared.

Usually, club employees would just grumble among themselves about the poor data provision. But Woody had met the Premier League's head of information, Paul Gornall, and told him about the clubs' dissatisfaction. Paul surprised Woody by telling him the Premier League were already investigating the idea of collecting tracking data for the whole league and were about to sign up with a supplier, ChyronHego. This was great news but Woody was a bit confused – how come the Premier League hadn't told the clubs about their plans for data collection? The league had seen the commercial possibilities of tracking data, but the impact it may have on clubs had been overlooked.

Woody began a lobbying campaign to make tracking data available to clubs, and I was his first recruit. Having free tracking data would have a big impact on every club's performance analysis budget, so there was no shortage of analysts happy to join Woody's campaign. For my part, I insisted that access to raw data should be included in the league's deal. Prozone had been the gatekeepers of tracking data for many years and were loath to share it with anyone. The data revolution in football could have happened years earlier if it wasn't for Prozone's protectionism. Bill James had warned me and Eddy about gatekeepers – in baseball in the 1980s, a similar monopoly existed, and the company that had the monopoly worked hard to keep their data secret. Bill said that one of the most important things he did was to break that monopoly, which was a barrier to progress. If the Premier League would give clubs the raw tracking data, it would shatter Prozone's monopoly.

Woody assembled a like-minded set of performance analysts from Liverpool, Everton, Aston Villa, Chelsea, Manchester City and Arsenal. The Premier League agreed that the clubs could have access to the tracking data but in its first season, 2014/15, each club could only access its own games. I was interested in seeing the rest of the league's data – without that, data from our own was not very useful for anything except analysing our players' physical exertions.

Tactically, we could analyse our own performances, but our performance depends on the opposition's. And we couldn't say much about the opposition without seeing how they performed in other games.

The clubs involved in Woody's crusade agreed with the principle of sharing and lobbied the league again. The Premier League had convened an analysts meeting for the first time, partly to discuss plans for the new tracking data. It was held at the Sherlock Holmes Hotel on Baker Street one afternoon. The meeting room was in the basement, and the air conditioning was either malfunctioning or non-existent. In the stuffy atmosphere I raised the idea of data sharing. There was a lot of resistance – mostly from the smaller clubs. Their reasoning seemed to be that they didn't have the ability to make use of the data themselves. They said they had nothing to gain from sharing, while the more forward-thinking clubs did.

Eventually the league agreed that the seven clubs who wanted data sharing could share between them all the games involving one of the seven. This was the key to getting full data sharing to happen. In the next meeting we pointed out that the seven sharing clubs had 14 games of data for every Premier League team, and all 38 games of the sharing group. Meanwhile, the non-sharers could only see their own games. The non-sharers relented and we finally agreed in 2016 that every team would be able to access the data from all 380 Premier League games.

Player Swap Deals

The official Premier League tracking data did not get off to the best start. To investigate the data, my colleague Tim Waskett developed a program to visualise it. On the computer screen we could see a bird's-eye animation of all the players moving around the pitch, like in the old Football Manager video games. Occasionally, the players would appear in strange positions, with a defender where you might expect a striker to be and vice versa. The problem was that player identities were being swapped. When players crossed each other's path the computer vision algorithm would sometimes get confused about who was who. The confusion was worst at events like corners, where many players were in close proximity to one another. We also received tracking data for all Uefa games, but until 2021 Uefa did not exercise any quality control over it, so we could not trust it. Players would occasionally blink out of existence for half a second before magically reappearing. In one game James Milner took a corner and, if the data was to be believed, got stuck on the corner flag for the next seven minutes.

We could check the quality of the tracking data because we also had on-ball event data. Tim had synchronised the on-ball events with the tracking data. If the on-ball data said that Fabinho was making a pass in central midfield, but the tracking data said that Fabinho was in the left-back position, then someone had made a mistake. The synchronisation was a challenge for Tim because the timing of the event data was only accurate to a couple of seconds and the location was only accurate to within a couple of metres. Another problem was the tracking data itself didn't contain any 'events', only the locations of the players and the ball. We had to come up with a method of working out whether an event had happened. To do this, Tim reduced the game of football to a set of velocities and accelerations. If the ball rapidly accelerated away from a player a pass had probably been made. If the ball rapidly decelerated next to a player, that was probably a pass reception. If the ball suddenly changed direction, it was a header or a one-touch pass. Some events were more difficult to detect: fouls and tackles did not always have tell-tale ball movements associated with them. Even so, Tim was eventually able to match the vast majority of on-ball events to the exact moment they happened in the tracking data.

Gee, I Could Have Thought of That

The really important aspect of tracking data is tactical: we can see the off-ball movement of the players. Our Possession Value model had worked well, but we knew that the goal probabilities we attached to various game states were only approximations. Having the ball in attacking midfield against a set defence is very different to having the ball in the same location with a striker making a run into a big gap between two defenders. With tracking data, we could increase the accuracy of our goal probability estimates. But the new data was a curse as well as a blessing. It was unwieldy,[1] difficult to manage, and difficult to extract insights from. A more sophisticated model was needed, and it would take a lot of work to create one.

The Opta Forum was the first regular football analytics conference in the UK. It began in 2014 in a dusty lecture theatre in the basement of Birkbeck university, in the Bloomsbury area of London. The idea behind the conference was to give data to anyone with a good enough idea for analysing it. By 2017 the forum had grown exponentially. Birkbeck was no longer big enough and we moved to a flashy venue just opposite Euston Station. I sat down next to Liverpool's chief scout, Barry Hunter, to listen to a presentation called 'Physics-Based Modelling of Pass Probabilities in Soccer', given by an American called Will Spearman. Will began to explain his approach for calculating the chance of a successful pass. The player must be able to intercept the ball's trajectory, and he needs time to control the ball – the faster the ball is moving, the lower the chance that the player will be able to control it. The talk was a little too heavy on mathematics for a football crowd. After 10 minutes Barry leaned over to me and whispered: 'I think he's losing the audience.' I replied: 'I don't care about the audience. I think it's brilliant.'

Will's 2017 presentation, and one he gave in 2016, were the first times I'd seen anyone doing anything sensible with tracking data. His approach was football from first principles: he used ideas of players controlling space, and of the time needed to make and receive a pass in a way that spoke intuitively to how football worked. The opening line of one of his papers was: 'How can we quantify the value of a player standing, unmarked, at the far post waiting for a cross to come that never arrives?' This was exactly the sort of work that could harness the power of tracking data. I hired Will in 2018 to build for Liverpool a new tracking data powered version of Possession Value.

Pitch Control

The basic idea behind Will's work was a concept called 'Pitch Control'. It's a laughably simple idea that can be summarised as: 'If you can reach a given location on the pitch before anyone else, then you control it.' This already says a lot about football. Think about a game with only two players, each in his own half on the edge of the centre circle. In this situation each player controls his own half, because he is closer to every point in his own half than his opponent. But as Graham Taylor said: 'In football, time and space are the same thing.' We should care about who can get to the ball *quickest*, not who is closest to the ball. In our one-a-side game, if one of the players can accelerate faster than his opponent, he will be able to get to the halfway line quicker and so controls a little bit of the opposition half. Pitch Control naturally incorporates the physical abilities of players: the faster you are, the more of the pitch you control.

You don't even need to be faster to control more of the pitch, you just have to be in motion. If you are the same distance away from the ball as your opponent, and you have the same physical ability as him, you will get there first if you are already running towards the ball but he is stationary. Being the first to make a run gives you a little more Pitch Control. Conversely if you happened to be running *away* from the ball instead of towards it and had to slow down, turn around and start running towards it, you would not get there first.

The basic implications of Pitch Control allowed us to mathematically understand the game in the same way that professional footballers intuitively understand it. A striker making a run in behind between two stationary defenders temporarily controls some of the space behind the defensive line. If the space between the two defenders is too large, the striker may control some of the space behind them even without making a forward run. Just as players control more space in front of them while making a run, they control *less* of the space behind them. Lionel Messi is a master of stealing space behind defenders. During a quick attack, defenders rush back towards their own goal to cover the dangerous space near the goalmouth. Messi, off the ball, often follows a few yards behind the defenders, but stops before the defenders do. The defenders have just vacated the position where Messi now stands, in plenty of space to receive a pass. Deceleration can be as important as acceleration.

Another important ingredient in Pitch Control is uncertainty. The first component of uncertainty is time: a long ball punted down the field takes time to reach its destination. By the time the ball lands, many players may have had enough time to converge on it. Often after longer passes neither team is fully in control. Instead they are competing for control. Pitch Control is now uncertain, with each team's chance of controlling the ball weighted by how many players can reach its destination in time. The second component of uncertainty is ball control. It is one thing to be able to reach a given location first, but it is another thing to *control* a pass heading to that location. After the ball is passed, the receiver's chance of being able to bring it under control depends on how quickly the ball is moving and how quickly the receiver needs to move to control it. Players need a little time to bring the ball under control, so for quick passes or players stretching to get on the end of the pass it is uncertain whether they'll be able to control it.

And there is a third component of uncertainty: ignorance. With tracking data, it is tempting to think we know everything there is to know about the state of the game. After all, we can see every player's location every 40 milliseconds. But there is still plenty that we are ignorant of. A player may be fatigued or injured or just not trying very hard – he might not be in control of as much of the pitch as we think he is. A player may not be facing the ball – it could take him a second or two to realise a pass has been made. Or a player may just be a little slow to react to a changing game situation, or be lying injured on the floor and unable to run anywhere. There is also ignorance of tactics. A full-back who in principle can get on the end of a pass to the right wing might not dare to venture beyond the halfway line if he plays for a defensive coach like Tony Pulis. This ignorance is reflected in Pitch Control being probabilistic rather than deterministic. If a player can in principle get to the ball half a second quicker than his opponent, Pitch Control will not predict he will definitely control the ball. Instead, it may predict a 70% likelihood that he will control the ball. The other 30% of the time, one of the many factors that we are ignorant of may lead to an opponent controlling it.

All of these uncertainties needed to be accounted for as we built our Pitch Control model. Each element adds complexity to the model, and we need to be confident that the extra complexity is worth it – the more complicated the model the better its predictions need to be. The beauty of Pitch Control is that every extra element of complexity that we add has an explanation that is intuitive in footballing terms.

Including individual player top speeds and accelerations in our Pitch Control model adds complexity, but it is intuitive that if you can outrun your opponent you'll control more of the pitch than him. Adding the ball's time of flight leads to less certain Pitch Control, or in other words more 50-50 situations for long passes. This neatly describes the long-ball game. You can move the ball up the pitch more quickly with a long aerial pass, but the price you usually pay for it is less control. However, long aerial passes do not always mean less control. In a counter-attack situation with our players sprinting up the pitch and the opposition stranded in our half, we can have the best of both worlds: the ball quickly moved to the opposition half and under our control.

Adding the complexity of 'ball control' highlights the concept of 'touch'. A player with good touch needs less time and space to control the ball than the average player. Another way of putting it is that players with good touch have a little force field of greater Pitch

Control around them. Ball control also highlights the difference between attack and defence. Defenders often don't care about bringing the ball under control – any touch that takes the ball away from the opposition is a good touch. In congested areas, defenders have a little more Pitch Control than attackers because they don't need to take care of the ball in the same way. When fans think of the best players, they tend to think of 'touch' players – Pelé, Cruyff, Maradona, Messi. Touch players also tend to be very expensive. If you have a limited budget, you probably can't afford them. Your tactics when playing against them might concentrate on limiting their impact. And the easiest way to do this may be to create a lot of situations with contested control – one reason why lower budget teams sometimes decide to play the long-ball game.

Goal-scoring Probability

Just like in our original Possession Value model, *where* you have the ball counts for a lot. In the original model, location on the pitch and phase of possession were the only two ingredients that went into the calculation of goal-scoring probability. This is akin to viewing the game like table football. In table football, the players' positions are severely limited – they can only move across the pitch, not up and down it. In the original Possession Value model it's a similar situation: goal probabilities are averaged over many individual situations, with the result that we only see the average impact of a pass from position A to position B.

With tracking data, we can add a huge amount of context. The goal-scoring probability can now include defensive pressure on the player with the ball because we know how close the defenders are. We can control for the number of defenders and attackers ahead of the ball and behind the ball. This knowledge means we no longer need labels like 'counter-attack' or 'set-piece'. The useful information that was contained in those labels is now explicitly seen through the positions of the players. Counter-attack possession is valuable because few defenders are behind the ball. If we can directly see the defenders, we don't need the label.

A counter-attack opportunity is easily spoiled through a poor touch or an inaccurate pass that slows down play and gives defenders time to get back. And when you have tracking data, the goal-scoring probability can dynamically change to reflect this. With the Pitch Control approach, an accurate pass that keeps momentum going and fewer defenders between the ball and the goal is rewarded much more highly than a slightly inaccurate one that requires the receiver to slow down to control it and gives the defence a chance to regroup.

Intercepting Passes

It's important to control the pitch, and it's important to control it in the areas that matter. But it's also important that the ball is able to get to an area of the pitch that matters. A striker's run is for nothing if the ball can't be passed to him. This is closely related to the idea of ball control. Consider a pass that an attacking midfielder tries to thread between two centre-backs for the striker. The closer the ball is played to the centre-backs, and the slower the ball is played, the more likely it is the centre-backs will be able to intercept it. The pass needs to be drilled quickly into the forward. But a quick pass is more difficult for the striker to control. He might only just get his toe to it and see it dribble through to the goalkeeper.

We can factor in these complexities by analysing the speed and the trajectory of the ball and the player. Data from hundreds of thousands of passes is used to calculate how passing speed and accuracy affects players' abilities to receive or intercept the ball. If a ball passes near an opponent, the chance a team-mate receives it will be low, because the opponent has a high chance of intercepting the ball. These passes have a low probability of success.

Analysing passes in this way lets us ask questions related to passing ability. For example, each pass has a difficulty associated with it – its probability of being received by a team-mate. We can ask how the receiving probability changes if the ball had been passed at a slightly different angle or a slightly different speed. This tells us something about the skill with which a player executed a pass. If we test out a range of slightly different passes the player might have made and find that they all have a lower probability of being received than the pass that actually happened, that tells us the player executed the pass well. If the pass was inaccurately hit towards a defender, many of the slightly adjusted hypothetical passes will have a greater chance of being received – that is a badly executed pass.

Putting it All Together

We can calculate a superior Possession Value with these ingredients. For an action to be valuable, it needs to move the ball to a location on the pitch where our team has a high level of Pitch Control. But Pitch Control is not sufficient: the ball needs to be moved to a location where there is a higher goal-scoring probability – further up the pitch and with fewer defenders behind the ball. This is still not sufficient: the ball also has to have a high likelihood of reaching its destination, and a low chance of being intercepted by a defender.

A moment from Liverpool's 2019 home game against Porto in the Champions League illustrates these ideas. Naby Keïta had the ball in midfield and some time to pick his pass. Mo Salah made a run from the right, dragging the left-back out of position. And Jordan Henderson was running into the space vacated by the left-back. Because Mo is fast, he partially controlled a bit of space centrally behind the defensive line, even though two defenders were right on top of him. There were no Porto players on the right wing so Henderson completely controlled that space. Liverpool's central defenders were completely in control of their own half. A pass back to defence had a very high chance of success. It would have had to be very badly hit to be intercepted by a Porto player. But the goal-scoring probability would have been very low if the ball had gone backwards – this was a low-risk, very low reward option.

Mo's run in behind put him in a very valuable space. Liverpool would have had a 10% chance of scoring if Keïta managed to get the ball to him. But in addition to the two defenders tracking Salah's run, the attempted pass would have had to get past two other Porto players – we rated it as only a 10% chance of a successful pass – a high-reward but very high-risk option.

Henderson was in an acre of space on the right wing – a 5% goal-scoring chance should the pass succeed. The pass was by no means easy to make. There were two defenders who could intercept if the pass was inaccurately hit. We rated it as about a 60% chance of Henderson receiving. This is a moderate-risk, high-reward situation, and the optimum one to make according to the model. Keïta turned down the sure-thing pass to Van Dijk that created no value, and turned down the small chance of successfully passing to Salah, who was in a very valuable location. Keïta's chosen pass to Henderson created 5% of a goal, for which Keïta was rewarded. The same pass would not have been rewarded as highly if the pass to Salah was on, because Salah's location was more valuable. But it was not on, and Keïta made the right choice.

A perfect example of the superiority of tracking data came in a game against Tottenham in March 2019. A Tottenham counter-attack left Virgil van Dijk isolated in his own half against Spurs players Moussa Sissoko and Son Heung-min. Sissoko ran with the ball towards goal. Van Dijk had to impede Sissoko's progress but also had to prevent an easy pass to Son, a far more deadly striker. With the passing lane cut off and under pressure from Van Dijk, Sissoko elected to shoot from 16 yards out but blasted the ball over the crossbar. Without touching the ball, Van Dijk made a crucial and skilful defensive intervention: finally, with knowledge of the off-ball player positions, we were able to fully understand the impact Virgil made on the game. In the old world of event data, all we would have seen was an off-target shot from Sissoko, for which the defenders would have shared some blame.

Tracking data allowed us to attach more confidence to our statistical ratings of defenders, especially centre-backs. Retrospectively, Van Dijk at Southampton had been even more outstanding in our tracking data model than he had looked in our event data model. In 2021 Liverpool were in the market for another centre-back, and Eddy was a big fan of Ibrahima Konaté at Red Bull Leipzig. Konaté looked relatively much, much better in our tracking data model than in our event data model. The reason was Red Bull's kamikaze approach to attacking. When a Red Bull team wins possession, they flood forward to make the most of the opportunity. This has been a successful approach but it often leaves their defenders in trouble. Should possession be lost, Red Bull are often open to a counter-attack and the one or two defenders who didn't join in the attack often have a huge amount of space to cover trying to firefight the counter-attack.

The event data could not see how much trouble Konaté found himself in, through no fault of his own. But the tracking model, with its knowledge of everyone's position, blamed Konaté much less for failures in 1-on-1 or 2-on-2 situations, because they are very difficult to defend. And conversely he was rewarded more for the occasions when he successfully defended these difficult situations. Our tracking data analysis indicated Konaté was an ideal signing, and he has prospered while having to defend huge amounts of space at Liverpool.

The Next Frontier

Until about 2018, football teams were only able to access tracking data from the league they played in. That changed with the advent of 'broadcast tracking'. This technology does not require multiple cameras in the stadium to create tracking data, only a TV broadcast of the game. This is thanks to the massive increase in computing power and artificial intelligence technology in the past few years.

Tracking data collected from a TV show has its own problems.

For one thing, not all of the players are on the camera at the same time. On top of this, there are reverse angle replays, advert breaks and close-ups of the managers to contend with, which can cause severe data quality problems. Even so, the promise of tracking data for any number of leagues is very attractive for player recruitment. Liverpool, being one of the few clubs with an in-house Research department, was the first club to start using broadcast tracking data. As more clubs started investigating tracking data, they called us up to ask our opinion of it. I was surprised to discover that most clubs were interested in it for the physical aspect – getting an estimate of how far and fast players ran. At other clubs, it was the fitness departments as much as the scouting departments that were interested in the new data source. The idea seemed to be that the Premier League was a more physical league than others in Europe. I agree with this idea, but the physicality is as much about being kicked and being pushed off the ball more than in other leagues, and how far you can run in a game has little to do with that. In our tracking data model, a player's speed and acceleration is important, but only as far as it affects his ability to control the pitch or get on the end of a pass.

The next two frontiers in tracking data are 'pose data' and artificial intelligence. Pose data is currently provided for Champions League games. Instead of containing one location per player every 40 milliseconds, pose data contains 29 locations per player: the location of a player's feet, ankles, knees, hips, shoulders, elbows, hands, eyes and ears are collected.[2] This is a brilliant data set but it is a challenge to analyse. The avalanche of raw data is difficult to ingest and store and at Liverpool I hired a software developer, Ian Jenkins, to help us to deal with it. The new data can tell you things that traditional tracking data can't – which way a player is facing, which way a player is *looking*, whether he is jumping or making a kicking action. This data will allow us to say a lot more about a player's decision-making and skill execution, but it will take an order of magnitude more work to create insightful models. One obvious application is reducing our ignorance: if players are lying on the ground injured or mid-air in a jump we know they will not be able to accelerate towards the ball, and our calculation of Pitch Control will be more accurate.

The other frontier is artificial intelligence. Our approach to analysing data at Liverpool was to create models based on simple principles like Pitch Control. The strength of this approach is that simple modelling concepts can be explained to people who aren't data science specialists. And in order to convince a sporting director or a manager of the value of our analysis, it needs to be explained in football terms. Another approach to analysing data is artificial intelligence. This consists of throwing all your data into an extremely complicated model and allowing the AI algorithm of your choice to make predictions from it. AI is extremely powerful and AI models usually have greater predictive power than simpler handmade models like the ones we typically used at Liverpool. But there is a price to pay: you don't really know the reason *why* the AI model is making the predictions it does. In other words these models are often not intuitive and not very interpretable, even by data analysts.

With tracking data, though, there are various applications where we may not care about interpretability, and AI models can be incredibly useful in these cases. At Liverpool, we collaborated with the AI company DeepMind to see 'what AI can do for football, and what football can do for AI'.

This collaboration gave us the ability to 'hallucinate' player trajectories.[3] In broadcast tracking data, we don't know where the players are when they are off-camera, so we have to estimate. All we care about is that the estimates are accurate – this is an ideal application of AI. This idea also opened up the possibility of predicting future player trajectories. We can press pause on a game, and then ask the computer to forecast the next 10 seconds of the game, telling us where the players are likely to run.[4] This has exciting possibilities. The AI algorithm can repeatedly suggest many ways the game might have gone – sometimes the full-back decides to push up and sometimes he decides to stay at home. We can compare these hallucinated possibilities to what actually happened in order to say something about the effectiveness of the move that actually happened compared to the thousands of moves that might have happened but didn't. We also analysed corners by building an AI model to examine the attacking and defensive set-up at corners and suggest adjustments to player positions and runs in order to increase the chances of scoring.[5] The model was impressive – experts could not tell the difference between real corner situations and situations that had been invented by AI.

The advent of AI applications and pose data will help us better analyse player performances and may even enable us to start exploring different tactical schemes for playing the game. As with the first iteration of tracking data, the new data is both a blessing and a curse. It will take a lot of work to extract insight from it. But the rewards are high, like the rewards we received for being the first club to wring insight out of the original tracking data.

10

Paying for Performance

I've never seen a bag of money score a goal

Johan Cruyff

Football Finance

Bags of money may not be able to directly score goals for your club, but they help enormously in attracting players who *can* score goals. In the Premier League in 2021/22, £3.6 billion was spent in wages[1] and £1.85 billion on transfer fees.[2]

It's one thing to identify a player who can improve a team's performance, but it is quite another to understand whether that player represents value for money. After all, the principle behind *Moneyball* is not to improve performance, it's to maximise improvement in performance while minimising cost. Of Premier League teams' revenue, 65% is spent on wages and 25% is spent on transfer fees. For example, Southampton in 2021/22 earned £151 million, spent £113 million on wages, £51 million on incoming transfers and earned £31 million on outgoing transfers. The denominator in *Moneyball* is money. And 90% of money is spent on players. If we want to achieve a bigger bang for our buck we have to spend money effectively.

Liverpool are one of the highest revenue clubs on the planet, but we could only spend what we earned, and we were competing against higher revenue clubs such as Manchester United and Gulf-owned clubs such as Manchester City. Our task was to use the club's revenue responsibly. We had to understand what aspects of a player's performance the transfer market paid for in terms of fees, and what aspects were rewarded with higher wages. We also had to understand our financial performance compared to the rest of the league: were we spending more or less of our revenue than our rivals on wages and transfer fees? And were we achieving better performances for our level of spending?

In *The Price of Football*, Kieran Maguire uses Arsenal as an example to demonstrate how the Premier League's revenues and costs have grown since its inception in 1992/93. Arsenal's revenue increased by 2,671% between 1993 and 2019, or 13% per year. But their wage bill increased by 3,169%, or 14% per year. Few clubs in England make consistent profits because most of their revenue is spent on transferring and paying players. An alternative way to view a football club is as a very complicated mechanism for distributing money to players. Across all leagues, wages are by far the biggest cost centre for every club. Wages account for about 65% of club revenues in the Premier League. If that seems high, consider that in the Championship the majority of clubs spend more than 100% of revenue on wages, as their owners gamble on Premier League promotion.

Increases in revenue have been driven by TV broadcast deals. In 2021/22 the Premier League TV broadcast deal accounted for £2.5 billion of revenue. The biggest beneficiaries were Manchester City, who received £153 million. Norwich City received the least money – £100 million. For Premier League teams competing in the Champions League there is £80–£120 million extra broadcast revenue to be made. Larger clubs also make significant sums of money from commercial activities such as selling sponsorship rights and shirts and, on matchdays, selling tickets. On average in the Premier League, about 15% of revenue comes from matchday activities and 30% from commercial activities. But for smaller clubs like Burnley and Brentford, about 80% of revenue comes from TV broadcast payments.

There is another source of income for teams: transfer fees gained by selling players. These are not usually included as revenue in clubs' financial accounts, because they tend to be one-off, difficult to repeat windfalls. Outside the Premier League, transfer revenue is a real source of income. In the Championship, for example, clubs on average receive more than they spend in transfer fees. But in the Premier League, transfer income is sooner or later exceeded by transfer spending.

What Clubs Pay Players For

Premier League

Liverpool had been historically bad at achieving value for money with player wages and transfer fees. When I arrived in 2012, generating a good level of performance for our level of wages and fees was a priority. In the words of W. Edwards Deming, we needed to 'measure what we were doing, analyse what we were doing, and then improve it'.

The first step is to measure – we needed to collect data. We had detailed data on what we were paying our own players, but we needed to compare ourselves to our competitors. We embarked on a mission to find out what other teams paid. The information was not easy to find, but through informal conversations with agents, players and managers we were able to estimate how much players in different teams earned. At the time, the Premier League told its clubs how much each had spent on player wages,[3] so we could compare the individual salaries to the team totals and check the salary information we'd collected was grounded in reality. Knowing what teams paid in total wages also told us something about the salaries of the players we *didn't* have information for. If we know all but one of a squad's salaries and the total wage bill, then we can easily calculate how much the missing player earns.

All in all, we were able to collect estimates for about 30% of the players over four Premier League seasons. With the data assembled, we could analyse how wages are correlated with performance data. I used six different kinds of data to predict wages and gave the data the acronym 'praise'. 'P' was for position: players in different positions earn different amounts of money. 'R' was for ratings: stronger teams tend to pay higher wages, and I could also find out whether players who rated better in our Possession Value model had higher wages. 'A' was for age: very old and very young players tend to earn less. 'I' was for inflation: as we have seen, wages follow revenue in the Premier League and over the years revenue and wages have both increased. 'S' was for how a team had signed a player: a transfer, a loan, or was the player home grown? Finally, 'E' was for experience: we might expect regular starters to command higher wages than bench-warmers. I looked at different types of experience too: experience in internationals, top leagues and second divisions might have different effects on salary.

Nearly every piece of data that I'd collected had a significant correlation with salary. The positional variables were most important. In our Possession Value model, having possession further up the pitch and central is more valuable than in defence and on the wings. The salary model mirrored this pattern: strikers, wide forwards and attacking midfielders are paid the most, all else being equal.[4] It was interesting to find that target man type strikers were paid less than other kinds of forward. Midfielders were paid less, and defenders less still. The lowest paid position was goalkeeper. One aspect of our Player Classification model measured what proportion of a team's free-kicks and corners a player took. I found that players who took a lot of set-pieces were paid relatively more than players who did not. This is perhaps not surprising, as it is usually the most skilled passer or shooter of the ball who is allowed by his team-mates to take set-pieces.

The strength of the team also impacted player salaries. If a player has transferred in from a stronger team, his salary will tend to be higher. The only way to attract a player already at a strong team (and already being paid a lot) is to offer him even more money to join your team. Finally, our Possession Value rating of the player's performance was also correlated with higher wages, although the effect of a good player rating was much smaller than the effect of a strong team. Another way of saying this is that an average player on a strong team may earn more than a good player on an average team.

The other variables were intuitive. Players earn less when they are young and less when they are old. Earnings increased from age 18 and peaked around age 29, before tailing off. Wage inflation was about 10% per season between 2009 and 2013, and your wage also depended on how you arrived at the club. Transfers in earned more than loan players[5] and free transfers in. Academy products earned less than transfers, but the effect reversed if the Academy product had been at the club a long time. 'Club legends' earned even more than players transferred in.

Serie A

When I'd finished building the salary model, Eddy started using it as a frame of reference for negotiations with agents. His feedback was that agents seemed to hold an intuitive version of a similar model in their heads. Good agents instinctively knew what wage their player could command at a Premier League club. Obviously the agents would always start negotiations high – maybe an 80th or 90th percentile wage according to our model – but their wage demands across different players varied in exactly the way our model predicted.

Eddy pointed out that the Italian newspaper *La Gazzetta dello Sport* published the salaries of Serie A players, and these were rumoured to be quite accurate. It would be a very interesting exercise to see if the salaries paid by Italian clubs varied in a similar way to their English counterparts. It became an annual tradition for me to copy 500 names – Acquafresca to Zúñiga – and salaries into a spreadsheet, though sometimes I roped my partner into helping.

I found that, though salaries are lower in Serie A than the Premier League, the Italian teams paid their players in a remarkably similar way to teams in England. In Italy, as in England, wages decreased for player roles further back on the pitch. There were some differences – Serie A is a league with old players, and it pays older players relatively better than the Premier League. And the impact of playing for a stronger team was much greater in Italy than in the

Premier League – likely due to club revenues in Italy being heavily weighted in favour of the big clubs. The Premier League's more even distribution of TV broadcast money means that their smaller clubs earn relatively much more than smaller clubs in other leagues.

What Clubs Pay Other Clubs For

We also wanted to benchmark what a 'fair' transfer fee would be and see if the transfer market worked in a similar way to the player wages market. Liverpool had overpaid for players like Alberto Aquilani and Andy Carroll in the past, though the Carroll overpayment was offset by Chelsea overpaying for Fernando Torres. We were keen to stop overpaying and the only way to do this was to find out what represented an overpayment.

Transfer fees are difficult to find accurate information for. The numbers reported in the press are not always accurate – they often report what clubs want the public to think about the fee rather than the real fee. Centre International d'Etude du Sport has estimated that transfer fees reported by the media are about 10% less than reality.[6] Some publicly listed clubs do publish information about transfer fees, but few clubs are publicly listed. A popular source of transfer fee information is the German website Transfermarkt. Data published there is not always accurate, but it is usually close to reality and was good enough to use for our model of transfer fees.

I added extra variables to the 'praise' model that I'd used to predict player wages. In addition to estimated transfer fees, Transfermarkt also publishes 'market values', which is a crowd-sourced opinion of a player, represented in euros. These market values represent the public's opinion of a player and have historically correlated quite well with transfer fees. I also looked at how close to expiry a player's contract was and which countries the transfer was between. The differences in fees across countries were large. In 2016, the Chinese football bubble was in full swing, and Chinese clubs paid very high fees – money was no object to them at the time. We also found a

'Premier League premium': if there were two identical players, each transferred from the same club but one going to the Premier League and the other to the Bundesliga, the one going to the Premier League might command a transfer fee 40% higher.

The results were very similar to the player wage model, and in addition we found that the 'market value' of a player was correlated with transfer fee. We also found that players with more years left on their contracts have higher transfer fees, all else being equal. This represents the selling club being under no pressure to sell – they have the option of receiving another season of performances from the player and selling the following year.

There was one interesting difference between the patterns we saw in wages and those in transfer fees: the effect of age. With wages, salaries increase with age, then decrease, all else being equal. But transfer fees only decline with age. This may seem counter-intuitive as the highest transfer fees tend to be paid for players in their mid-twenties. But the statistical approach I used attempted to isolate the effect of each different aspect of a player's data. Players in their mid-twenties usually have more experience, start more regularly, and are more likely to start for their national teams – these are all things that are positively correlated with transfer fee. And it's the reason fees look higher for players in their mid-twenties. But if we take two players who are identical in every aspect except their age, the younger one should command the higher transfer fee. For example, Barcelona paid only 18% more for 25-year-old Philippe Coutinho than they did for 20-year-old Ousmane Dembélé, despite Coutinho having vastly more experience.

When we compared the reported transfer fees to our model's estimates they made a lot of sense. Among the most expensive transfers of the 2015/16 season, our opinion was that Manchester United had drastically overpaid for both Angel di María and Anthony Martial. At Liverpool, we couldn't be too smug – we'd overpaid for Christian Benteke. Conversely, Chelsea had secured a huge bargain with Diego Costa.

There was one player who looked even better value than Costa:

Mario Balotelli. After I built the model I was surprised to find that back in 2014 we had apparently secured the bargain of the year. Balotelli was a player who would naturally be associated with a high transfer fee: he came from a strong club – AC Milan – was young, and had regularly played and scored in the Premier League, Serie A and the Champions League. He also had started regularly for Italy. Balotelli's high estimated fee was a case of incomplete knowledge. All the data pointed to a very high transfer fee. But some of the data not included in my analysis gave a clue as to why AC Milan were willing to sell him for the same price they'd signed him for just 18 months before. In his career Balotelli had done many misguided things. He appeared on TV wearing an AC Milan shirt while playing for rivals Internazionale and he'd been fined for throwing darts at youth players. He set off fireworks in his bathroom, wrote off cars and racked up parking fines. The potential risk of the transfer was clear to us even if I didn't have columns in my spreadsheet for number of fireworks set off indoors, or total parking fines paid.

Since I built my transfer fee model there have been academic papers published showing similar results. The aforementioned study by the Centre International d'Etude du Sport mentioned two Liverpool signings. Their estimate was that Balotelli's fee was 64% less than expected, and they drily noted that the difference could be explained by the 'disciplinary concerns surrounding the player'. The other signing was Mohamed Salah, a 23% underpayment. In that case, Roma were a distressed seller who needed to make player sales to stay within Uefa's financial rules.

All of the data that helps to explain transfer fees and wages are just proxies. The only thing clubs should be interested in is whether a potential signing is a good player, whether they improve the club's performances, and whether there might be a transfer profit when the player leaves the club. Data like contract length, market value, previous fees and strength of previous clubs give us clues as to how good the player is. But it is important to remember they are just proxies: the fact that a player plays for a strong club is not a guarantee that he is a good player. We used the transfer fee model to understand that players like Sadio Mané and Mo Salah were under-valued, but by some of our own models we 'overpaid' for Roberto Firmino. Just before we signed him Dortmund bid €25 million, which was the 'correct' price as far as the transfer fee model was concerned. But the market really undervalued his robustness against injury, his flexibility and his ability to increase his team's goal probability. A better way to view our 'overpayment' is to say that we were happy to pay for important aspects of performance that the rest of the market was not happy to pay for.

Not Signing Players

The transfer market has become part of the spectacle of football. It reaches a crescendo on deadline day, with Sky Sports News presenters excitedly giving updates on transfer rumours from inside stadiums. Season after season, the received wisdom was that Liverpool had 'lost the transfer window'. In the season we signed Sadio Mané, Manchester United signed Paul Pogba. Salah's signing was overshadowed by the arrivals of Romelu Lukaku at Manchester United, Alvaro Morata at Chelsea, and Pierre-Emerick Aubameyang and Alexandre Lacazette at Arsenal. The season after we won the Champions League, our only signings were the young defender Sepp van den Berg and the free transfers of back-up goalkeepers Adrián and Andy Lonergan.

Some fans were frustrated by our lack of signings, but there are good reasons to enter the transfer market with caution. Lots of transfers fail and many clubs have found that participation in the transfer market is not a recipe for success. But there are financial reasons to shy away from the transfer market too. In the financial world, few active traders can beat the stock market. You are better off investing in a passive index tracker fund than with a trader who claims their skills and market knowledge can generate outsized returns. One of the reasons traders find it difficult to beat the market is transaction costs. For every stock bought and sold, the trader pays a small fee. Trading that stock might theoretically return a profit, but the profit is eaten up once those transaction costs are taken into account. There is a similar set of transaction costs associated with signing a player. The Premier League demands a 4% transfer tax on all fees paid. Agents need to be paid for their services and players often command hefty signing-on fees, especially in the case of a free transfer. Finally, a new player will demand to be paid by today's standards, in a world of high wage inflation.

These fees add up to transfers costing clubs much more than the headline fee. Stock market traders lose money through fees if they buy a stock then sell it for the same price. And clubs are in a similar situation. A club that 'breaks even' on transfer fee does not really break even. The levies, agents' fees and bonuses are not clawed back. At Liverpool we were happy to enter the transfer market when we were confident of success, but we knew there was a large price to pay for transfers that were deemed a failure.

Money and Success

There is a high correlation between wages and points. Simon Kuper and Stefan Szymanski point out in *Soccernomics* that the wage bill alone explains a large proportion of a club's finishing position. Over a 10-year period, wages explained more than 90% of the variation in league finishing position across the Premier League and Championship.[7] This is a big challenge to any team trying to achieve more performance for less money – it seems at first glance like there is no way to break the extremely strong relationship between wages and league finishing position.

But wages do not *cause* success. Doubling your current squad's salary is unlikely to bring about vastly improved performances. The mechanism by which wages improve your league position is by attracting better players to your club, as Kuper and Szymanski point out. But how do you find better players? They must either be produced by your Academy or transferred in. But there is much, much less correlation between net transfer spending and success: clubs seem to be unable to reliably spend money on transfers to achieve success.

How come wages are strongly linked with team performance but net transfer spend (with bigger transfer fees usually linked to higher wages) is not so correlated with success? The reality is that the link between wages and success cuts both ways. Highly paid players help to create success, but success also helps to create highly paid players. Consider teams like Norwich City, who bounce around between the Premier League and the Championship. Relegation and promotion clauses in player contracts mean that they get paid more in Premier League seasons and less in Championship seasons – the wage bill follows the success. A similar process exists at the top of the table, with most teams paying a bonus for Champions League qualification or winning a title. At Liverpool we incentivised contracts to align the player's financial rewards with the success of the club. In seasons where we qualified for the Champions League or won a title, players earned more. In Germany, the link between success and wages is even more concrete: players' contracts include a payment per point that the team achieves.[8] There is also a filtering effect at play. Players who transfer in to a club and are successful will be induced to stay, through higher pay. The unsuccessful players do not get offered a pay rise. If a club, through luck or judgement, have signed good players their wage bill must increase if they want to keep them at the club for the long term.

At Liverpool, it was clear that the malfunctioning transfer market was the place to improve our financial performance – that was where the relationship between money spent and success was weakest. Between 2012 and 2023, Manchester United's net transfer spending was over 2.5 times more than Liverpool's. Manchester City's was more than twice Liverpool's. We spent significantly less than Arsenal and Chelsea. We only spent 10% more over the period than Spurs and West Ham, and we only spent 25% more than Everton. With a transfer spend comparable to our rivals we won the Premier League and the Champions League, and the players we signed produced a sustained level of excellent performance.

Our gross spend was high, at a very similar level to Arsenal's, but we recouped much more of our gross spending through sales than Arsenal did. Some of these sales, like Luis Suárez and Raheem Sterling, were not of our own choosing, but transfers like Philippe Coutinho were exemplars of transfer income being spent effectively. Our Academy also became a source of revenue, with players such as Ryan Kent, Harry Wilson and Neco Williams attracting transfer fees and going on to have successful careers. Successful loans, orchestrated by Julian Ward and later by David Woodfine, helped give our young players experience in senior football and make them attractive to clubs in the transfer market.

We paid large salaries at Liverpool, but that was partly due to the success that we experienced. Between 2016/17 and 2020/21, when our transfer process began to work properly, we won on average 83 points per season, second only to Manchester City. We paid high wages, though lower than Manchester City and Manchester United paid, and only a little higher than Chelsea. The big difference was in transfer spend, where we spent less than the rest of the big six, except for Tottenham. It doesn't really matter *how* money gets spent, be it on wages or transfers. All that matters is your performance given your total expenditure. In total we spent more than 20% less on the first-team squad than Manchester City and Manchester United, and about 5% less than Chelsea. The worst performing big six team over the period was Arsenal, whose spending was about 85% of Liverpool's but for a return of only 65 points per season.

The other overperformer was Spurs, whose spending efficiency had started back in 2008. Over the period I consulted for Spurs, their transfer spending pattern was similar to Liverpool's under FSG. Between 2008 and 2012, their gross spend was large, but the spending was paid for by the sales of stars like Berbatov, Keane and Modrić. In that period, Aston Villa and Stoke City had a higher net spend than Spurs. The difference between Spurs and Liverpool is that Spurs have continued to pay lower wages – by far the lowest of the big six.

PART THREE

More than a Game

Schrödinger's Manager

I've said it many times: we, the managers, are overrated in our influence

Pep Guardiola

Longer-term Performance

The question that FSG asked me about Jürgen's 2014/15 nightmare in Dortmund had a very clear answer: there was nothing to worry about in terms of Dortmund's underlying performance. It was an easy question to answer because the question was very specific. But the usual question you get asked about managers is rarely so precise. The usual question is 'Are they any good?' And this question is far more difficult to answer.

Klopp had started his career at Mainz, in the Zweite Bundesliga, in the practically pre-historic year of 2001. Back in those days, detailed performance data was not available. The only data we had on Mainz in 2001 was the full-time score, the name of the referee, and, if we were lucky, the bookmaker odds.

By 2013 we had developed our team strength and game forecasting model, which was conceptually similar to Dixon-Coles. The model worked best if data on the shots generated and conceded by each team was included, but it could also work using only goals. Reforecasting the 2001/02 season revealed that Jürgen's Mainz had significantly outperformed expectations – by about 15 points. We couldn't say exactly how or why they had outperformed expectations, but they had. In 2002/03 they repeated the trick, outperforming expectations by about nine points.

Like Dixon-Coles, the forecasts produced by our model were probabilistic, forecasting the chance of a win, a draw or a loss. This means we can do more than say whether a team overperformed or underperformed; we can attach a probability to the overperformance, or in other words measure how surprised we were by the points the team actually achieved. In the 2002/03 season, the probability was about 90%. In other words, if our forecasts faithfully represented the real chance of each outcome in each game, Mainz would have achieved fewer points than they actually won 90% of the time.

The bookmakers agreed with our assessment. The odds they offered on Mainz games implied that they had overperformed to exactly the same degree that our model suggested. If the bookmakers' opinion of Mainz had been different, more investigation would have been warranted. The bookies may have shortened Mainz's odds if lots of expensive new players had been signed. But in this case, the bookmakers were as surprised by Mainz's achievements as we were.

By now, alarm bells should be ringing. I spent Chapter 4 telling you that Jürgen's 2014/15 Dortmund were the victims of bad luck, rather than bad performance. Could the opposite have happened at Mainz? Could they have been lucky, rather than good? The answer, of course, is yes. If we had had to rely on goals rather than Expected Goals when analysing Dortmund in 2014/15 we would have said their results were significantly worse than expected – which of course they were – but in that case we were able to explain why.

We did not have that luxury with Mainz in 2001/02. We had done all we could with the data available, and it is certainly possible that Mainz were lucky. Repeating the analysis over Jürgen's career gave some more insight: in the 14 seasons before he arrived at Liverpool, his teams had achieved a 90th percentile or better season four times, and a below 10th percentile season only once (you guessed it, Dortmund 2014/15). In 14 seasons we would expect to see 1.4 seasons above 90th percentile and 1.4 seasons below 10th percentile. Jürgen's teams usually outperformed our model.

Spreading the Points and the Love

It's worth thinking more deeply about that Mainz 2002/03 season. Gaining nine points more than expected is impressive, but we only rated it as a 90% achievement. What the 90% score was really saying was that there was a 10% chance that Mainz could have just been lucky. The typical range for uncertainty or 'luck' is measured by a statistical quantity called 'standard deviation'. In the Premier League, standard deviation is about 7.5 points per season. For leagues where team strengths are more evenly distributed, the standard deviation is even higher.

What this means is that an average Premier League team, expected to score about 52 points, will achieve a total within the range 44–60 points about 70% of the time; 15% of the time they'll achieve more than 60, and 15% of the time they'll achieve less than 44. These are serious differences in points, but a 60-point season or a 44-point season is probably not due to the team getting better or worse, or the manager discovering a novel tactic. It is probably due to the fundamental uncertainty in the outcome of each game.

This observation has interesting implications for the Premier League manager of the season award. In recent seasons, the only managers from smaller clubs who have won have been Harry Redknapp in 2009/10, Alan Pardew in 2011/12, Tony Pulis in 2013/14 and Claudio Ranieri in 2015/16. According to the bookmakers, these managers benefited from an excess of 'results going their way' in the seasons they won the award. Spurs in 2009/10 achieved 6.5 more points than the bookmakers expected (well within the range we'd expect) and finished with 70 points. Redknapp's manager of the season award was not a result of unusually lucky or unexpected results but instead in recognition of breaking into the top four for the first time.

The other managers experienced much bigger swings in fortune. Pardew's Newcastle in 2011/12 finished with 65 points – a whopping 15 more than bookmakers had forecast. Pardew was famously rewarded with an eight-year contract by Newcastle's owner Mike Ashley. The bookmakers hadn't been as impressed as Ashley and did not shorten their odds on Newcastle the following season. They finished 2012/13 with 41 points, which was below expectations, but only by six points. And we have seen that six points below expectations is far from a rare occurrence. The huge 24-point swing was caused by a very lucky 2011/12 and a quite unlucky but not at all unexpected 2012/13.

The biggest outlier in terms of results came from Claudio Ranieri's Leicester in 2015/16. In their title-winning season, they won 81 points, a massive 27 points more than expected. They suffered a 37-point swing and finished 2016/17 with 44 points. But, like Pardew's Newcastle, their 44-point total was not unlikely – it was only five points worse than the bookmakers forecast. In each of these cases our forecasting model was in agreement with bookmakers' odds – we had also been surprised by Leicester's success in 2015/16. In summer 2016, our model rated them as only the seventh strongest team in England despite having just won the title.

We can also investigate the Expected Goals stories of managers of the season, as we did with Jürgen's Dortmund disaster. In each case, the game outcomes exceeded the performances in each game, whether measured by Pre-Strike or Post-Strike Expected Goals. Newcastle in 2011/12 managed to finish fifth with a negative Expected Goal Difference.[1] Leicester in 2015/16 also massively outperformed their Expected Goal Difference, and in 2016/17 their actual goal difference reverted to being much more in line with Expected Goal Difference.

Manager of the season is a recurring lesson in reversion to the mean. Club owners and managers should always have in their mind the number 7.5, the typical variation in points from season to season. Differences between outcomes and expectations that are less than 7.5 points are well within expectations. And if the standard deviation is 7.5 points, this means that points totals are expected to be 15 points away from expectations about 5% of the time. On average, one Premier League club per season will gain or lose 15 points more than expected, but it's probably not due to the manager.

It's the Players, Stupid

Our goals and shots-based models, and the bookmakers, had all been surprised at Dortmund's overperformance season after season. Our models knew about the quantity and quality of chances that Dortmund and their opponents had produced. But fundamentally it was the players on Dortmund's team that created these performances. Was it due to the players that they were so good?

The short answer is yes. Lots of famous managers agree that the players are the most important factor in football. No less an authority than Johan Cruyff said: 'If your players are better than your opponents, 90 per cent of the time you will win.'

Pep Guardiola agrees: 'I said many times when we make the [analysis] videos and we pause it and say: "Look guys, the space is there" – this is fake. How you have to make the decision, how many times you do it: it only belongs to the players. I've said it many times: we, the managers, are overrated in our influence.' He expands on the topic: 'Do you know the secret of my success as a manager? I'm going to tell you. Barcelona, Bayern Munich, Man City. This is the success of Pep. Messi, Lewandowski, Haaland, Agüero. This is the success. I love my mum and my grandfather but with them I don't win the Champions League.'

Massimo Allegri thinks in a similar way: 'I have to put the other players in a position to get the ball to [the best players], and once they have the ball, they decide what to do with it, what the best decision is. My son is eight, and every now and then we go on YouTube and watch the great players, the amazing things they do in attack and defence, because football is art. In Italy, the tactics, the schemes, they're all bullshit. Football is art and the artists are the world-class players. You don't have to teach them anything, you just admire them. All you need to do is put them in the best condition to do well.'

The players are clearly essential to a team's success. It's often asked whether Lionel Messi could perform on a cold, wet Wednesday night at Stoke. I'm more interested in seeing whether Pep Guardiola could perform on a cold, wet Wednesday night *managing* Stoke. I suspect that Messi's performance would be closer to his Barcelona ones than Guardiola's. Given that players are important, it was essential we analysed the squads Jürgen had at his disposal at Dortmund and try to understand how much they contributed to his success.

In 2010/11, when Dortmund won their first title since 2002, they had the youngest squad in the Bundesliga. Of the 13 players to start more than five games that season, attacking midfielder Mario Götze was 18, six players were 21, two were 22, one was 24, two were 25 and the oldest – goalkeeper Roman Weidenfeller – was 29. The average age of the starters was a tender 22 years and nine months.

There were prodigies all over the field. The central defensive pairing of Mats Hummels and Neven Subotić – a position that tends to feature older players – were both 21 and started nearly every league game together.

Midfielders Kevin Großkreutz (22), Nuri Sahin (21) and Götze (18) provided goals and assists and all three started nearly every league game. Shinji Kagawa and Robert Lewandowski were valuable squad players. Both were 21 years old, and both scored eight goals that season. Today these players are famous, and deservedly so, but they were not famous in 2010. They were youngsters who until that point had only played in their native Japan and Poland. Jürgen gave them the opportunity to play, and they rewarded his faith with brilliant performances.

In European football one of the often unwanted side effects of success is that bigger clubs want to sign your players. The lure of Real Madrid proved too strong for Sahin, who had been important to Dortmund's 2010/11 success. Many clubs might have struggled to maintain their success after losing such an important player, but Dortmund prospered. In 2011/12 striker Lewandowski, now 22, started every league game, scoring 22 goals and assisting eight. Attacking midfielder Kagawa also became a regular starter, scoring 13 goals and assisting eight. The replacement for Sahin was Ilkay Gündoğan – only 20 at the time, but a regular starter. A second title in two years was won.

A few years ago, I gave a talk about the challenge Jürgen faced in 2011, losing a very important player. A member of the audience commented that, of course, continued success was guaranteed: any team able to call on the services of Lewandowski and Kagawa obviously had a huge advantage over their opponents. Hindsight is a terrible force in football. In retrospect they are clearly brilliant players, but at the time they were not the Lewandowski and Kagawa the world knows today. They were unproven 22-year-olds.

They each had problems adapting to the Bundesliga. Lewandowski has said of Jürgen: 'He was the one who gave me belief . . . He also improved my finishing.' Kagawa was a new arrival from Japan. Slight of build, the received wisdom was that he would struggle in the Bundesliga. Jürgen credited his success partly to a change of balls.

Let me explain. I was not at Melwood very often – I was a hybrid worker long before the Covid pandemic popularised the idea. I kept odd hours and was having a late dinner in the canteen when Jürgen, always happy to talk to any member of staff, sat down next to me. For some reason we started talking about the relative merits of attack versus defence. If there were lots of goals in a particular league, did that mean the attackers were good or the defenders were rubbish?

It reminded me of a project I'd worked on in my previous job – rating players for the 2010 World Cup. Each position had a certain benchmark performance – strikers were expected to contribute a certain amount of Expected Goals and Possession Value and defenders were expected to prevent opportunities of a similar magnitude.

Over the group stage of the tournament very few goals were

scored, and very few Expected Goals were created. Strikers and midfielders were creating and taking fewer chances, and defenders were conceding fewer.

I told this story to Jürgen and said the conclusion must be the defenders were playing relatively better than the attackers. Jürgen pointed out that I'd neglected a different explanation – the ball. The 'Jabulani' ball used in World Cup 2010 had attracted a lot of criticism. Argentina's manager, Diego Maradona, said: 'We won't see any long passes in this World Cup because the ball doesn't fly straight.'

If midfielders cannot pass accurately then strikers cannot produce shots, and defenders will be rewarded for picking up possession from mishit passes. It was difficult to know whether the ball was really the cause of the strange ratings, but it was certainly a thought-provoking idea.

Jürgen's opinion was that Kagawa benefited from the Bundesliga's introduction of the 'Torfabrik' ball in 2010, effectively the same ball as the Jabulani. The lightweight ball was a much better fit for Kagawa's skills. Whether this was true or not, Kagawa became a very important player for Dortmund. Kagawa acknowledged Jürgen's influence on his career, saying: 'He's always thinking about his players, supporting them in important moments . . . I always felt there was nothing to fear as long as I followed his lead. That's the type of manager he was.'

The pattern of Dortmund's best players leaving, but the club still prospering, continued. Kagawa left for Manchester United and was replaced by Marco Reus, another brilliant young player. In 2013, Götze left for Bayern Munich and was replaced by Henrikh Mkhitaryan and Pierre-Emerick Aubameyang.

Jürgen achieved season after season of success with a young team, while losing some of his best players and having to replace them with other young talents. This was exactly the experience that was relevant to Liverpool. We'd been forced to sell our best players in 2013 and in 2014, and our squad had been the second youngest in the Premier League in 2014/15.

He looked like the ideal manager.

Another Option

Jürgen's successes, style of football and his willingness to play young players made him a natural choice for Liverpool, but we had to consider other candidates – there was no guarantee Jürgen would want the job, given that he was on a sabbatical. We also studied Carlo Ancelotti in detail.

Ancelotti had a very different background to Jürgen. Most of his previous clubs – AC Milan, Chelsea, Paris Saint-Germain and Real Madrid – spent very heavily on wages and had invested heavily in the transfer market each season, bringing star players to clubs where winning the title was the aim. His squads had historically been old – AC Milan and Chelsea in particular had among the oldest squads in their leagues when Ancelotti managed them.

Ancelotti's career performances up to the end of 2014/15 were much more in line with our expectations (and those of the book-makers) than Jürgen's. Over 14 seasons, his teams had realised 90th percentile or better results twice (Milan 2003/04 and 2005/06), and 10th percentile or worse results twice (Milan 2007/08 and Chelsea 2010/11). And over the 14 seasons, his teams had achieved only slightly more points than expected.

But Ancelotti's tasks had not been to take underachieving clubs like Liverpool or Dortmund and generate better results by developing young players. Expectations were already sky high at the giants he had managed. His job was to meet expectations and hope that titles arrived while meeting them. At each club he managed there was a plethora of stars. At Milan: Pirlo, Maldini, Shevchenko, Nesta, Cafu, Seedorf, Kaká.[2] At Chelsea: Terry, Lampard, Cech, Drogba, Ballack, Cole, Essien. At Paris Saint-Germain: Ibrahimović, Verratti, Thiago Silva. At Madrid: Benzema, Ramos, Cristiano Ronaldo, Marcelo, Bale, Alonso, Kroos.

Ancelotti's skill appeared to be in managing squads stuffed full of super players, who often come with super egos attached. If these players performed to expectations the teams would be successful, and Ancelotti had proven adept at keeping teams full of stars happy. Ashley Cole summed up Ancelotti's management skills eloquently: 'He managed the environment well, he made it fun. Everyone has respect for him because of what he [did] in the game as a player and as a manager. His mannerisms of how he treats people; always treats the person and not the player, which I think is really effective, especially when you've got a lot of egos. He engaged very well and everyone loved him.'

Ancelotti may well have been a success at Liverpool, but the challenge of coaching young and talented but relatively unproven players was not something he had much experience of. As talented a coach as Ancelotti is, Jürgen's CV was certainly more suited to the task at hand.

Coach Caution

Given everything I've said about Jürgen, you might think that it is possible to select a coach based entirely on data analysis. Unfortunately, this is not the reality. Few coaches can repeat success in different environments once you control for the quality of the players and the money available to spend. The data analysis we used for analysing managers was a tool for filtering, increasing bandwidth and gaining an unbiased overview of many managers. It is much more difficult to forecast future manager performance.

Robert McNamara was the United States' Secretary of Defense during the Vietnam War. He loved data, and thought that success in war could be precisely calculated. His idea was that in a war body count can be measured, and that the team with the highest body count is the loser. The US based its strategy on body count, with disastrous consequences.

Data analysis can lead to a distorted view of the world. We analysts measure what is easily measured and we tend to ignore what cannot be easily measured. However, if we make the mistake of thinking that which can't be easily measured is not important, then we'll make bad decisions.

The 'McNamara fallacy' summarises the problems with his approach. It goes like this.[3] First, measure whatever can be easily measured. Second, disregard that which can't be easily measured or give it an arbitrary quantitative value. Third, presume that what can't be measured easily really isn't important. Fourth, say that what can't be easily measured really doesn't exist.

An army general told McNamara that his body-count approach did not consider the feelings of the local population. McNamara replied he could not measure that, so it must not be important. Unfortunately for McNamara and the US the feelings of the local population *were* important and affected the war. As William Bruce Cameron put it: 'Not everything that counts can be counted, and not everything that can be counted counts.'

When analysing Ancelotti and Jürgen, I concentrated on things that are easily measured. As a data analyst, I need hard data to analyse. Studying a manager's results compared to pre-season expectations, how the results compared to Expected Goals, and reviewing the playing squads he has worked with is important. It gives valuable insight into the manager's past career. But those things must be weighed against what is not easily measured, and we should not pretend that those things are not important.

The things that are easy to measure – wage bills, transfer spends and league points – are things that managers cannot easily control. Factors that are difficult to measure – emotional tone, the ability to motivate players and the ability to attract new talent to the club – are things that managers can more easily control, and can bring huge benefits to teams, but only indirectly.

The maverick Argentinian manager and Leeds United legend Marcelo Bielsa is often caricatured as a tactics savant. But his understanding of a manager's role confirms that management is about much more than tactics. He lists the three responsibilities of a coach as: first, decide on the tactical approach; second, pick the players; third, set the emotional tone.

The tactical approach can be measured, but a good manager will adapt his tactical approach to maximise the talents of the players at his disposal. Do we prefer a pragmatist who will try to get the best results with what he has or a fundamentalist who insists on a style of play regardless of the suitability of the players? A tactical approach that is successful in one environment can fail badly in another. Roy Hodgson made a name for himself by overachieving at clubs of modest means – Fulham, West Brom and Crystal Palace. But when expectations were high, his approach was not successful, and his tenures at Liverpool, Internazionale and Blackburn were short and disastrous.[4]

Picking the best players is certainly among the most important responsibilities of a manager. We can tell to a certain extent if a manager is picking the players who *statistically* rate as the best, but there are many other aspects to picking a squad: psychology, fatigue and availability to name but three. I recently gave a talk to a group of former Premier League players and showed the season-by-season Possession Value ratings of one of them. The player pointed at the season that my model considered to be his worst and said: 'That's the season my son was born.' The manager's team selections must take into account many things that aren't easily seen in the data, not least a 3am feeding schedule.

Setting the emotional tone is something that is incredibly difficult to analyse using data. But it is something that is clearly very important. Ashley Cole's comments about Ancelotti reveal that he was excellent at setting the emotional tone in a team full of stars. But what works in a team full of stars may not work in a team full of nervous, unproven players. Lewandowski's comments about Jürgen hint at Jürgen's skill at giving young players confidence. On the other end of the spectrum José Mourinho's teams typically have a difficult third season, historically performing way below expectations despite having much the same squads as previous seasons. I have no idea whether the emotional tone that Mourinho set really was responsible for a decline in results, but he certainly seemed very unhappy in his press conferences in his final seasons at Chelsea, Manchester United, Real Madrid, Tottenham Hotspur and Roma.

There are many coaching qualities that are difficult to measure but important for success. Is a coach open-minded and reasonable? Is he able to attract players to the club through his style of play or his personality? Does he pick the best players available to him? And does he overreact to short-term noise or appreciate the underlying performances of his players?

Jürgen scores highly on all these qualities. His open-minded approach to transfer decisions was the key to Liverpool becoming successful. He was also key in attracting players to the club – players really wanted to play for him. One of the reasons was his style of play – players loved to watch Klopp teams – but another was his personality. As Lewandowski and Kagawa's comments show, he was able to build a strong personal relationship with his players.

We knew from his time at Dortmund that he picked the best players he had available, and he continued to do so at Liverpool – Firmino immediately became a starter as soon as Jürgen joined. And his focus on performance rather than outcome was admirable. After a loss, it takes a certain bloody-mindedness to say: 'The performance was good, we'll keep playing the same way,' but much of the time it is the correct approach.

The Bottom Line

There is some evidence that on the pitch, controlling for the quality of the players at his disposal, a good manager can add a few points per season. This is about the same value as a good player brings. This is in line with manager salaries – the best managers are paid a similar wage to the best players. If they reliably brought more value to teams than players bring, they should earn much more (although, as we have seen, the business of football is rarely rational). This conclusion may be in line with Pep Guardiola's thinking, but it is not in line with another manager I spoke to, who told me that '65% of success is down to the players, and 35% of success is down to the coaching environment. If you have good players but a bad manager, you have no chance of success.' A 35% increase in points would turn the average team into Champions League qualification contenders.

It may seem difficult to square the idea that managers don't matter *that* much for results with my opinion that Jürgen's appointment was absolutely vital for Liverpool's success. But the two concepts are not contradictory. Jürgen brought the best out of Liverpool's squad in 2015/16 by playing the best players in the best positions, having a clear tactical plan, and motivating our players. Even so, Premier League results were not very far above prior expectations in 2015/16. Results improved once players like Mané, Salah, Robertson, Van Dijk and Alisson joined. But it is uncertain whether they would have joined had Jürgen not been manager. And once they had joined, Jürgen played them in their best positions and motivated them to succeed.

Managers can improve players, but they do so mainly by putting players in systems that maximise their strengths and minimise their weaknesses. This is certainly one of Jürgen's skills: he often spoke of finding players with 'extreme characteristics' and working on tactical plans to cover up weaknesses in their game.

All players go through an 'ageing curve'. They improve in their teens and early twenties as they reach physical maturity and gain playing experience, reach a plateau in their late twenties, and gradually decline into their thirties, as their extra experience can no longer compensate for declining physical attributes. Those players who are able to play at the highest levels when young will make the most of their careers. By their mid-twenties they'll have much more experience than their peers. And managers like Jürgen who can find roles for young, improving players in their line-ups will reap rewards later on.

I will leave the final word on managers to two Premier League legends, who gave some insight into what it was like to work with two of the league's most successful managers. Roy Keane said of Alex Ferguson: 'Truthfully he didn't really give too much information. He never pulled me to the side or had any one-to-one chats. It was just a case of "Just get on with it." And what I learned, besides the manager and coaching staff, was I think I learned more from the lads I was playing with than any instructions I was getting from the manager.' Ashley Cole on Arsène Wenger: 'We didn't do much tactical work. Under Wenger, he just let you play, he let you play with that freedom, confidence, allowed you to make mistakes. We never done tactics, we just played.'

It's interesting that neither player cites tactics as important. The professional, competitive environment that Ferguson fostered was what Keane attached importance to. And Cole's insight shows that Wenger's strength was putting good players together on the pitch and allowing them to play. These factors were probably very important for the success of Manchester United and Arsenal. But they are factors that are very difficult to pin down and measure.

Schrödinger's cat is used to illustrate the nature of quantum mechanics. In Schrödinger's thought experiment, the fate of a cat in a box depends on radioactive decay, which is probabilistic. Because we don't know whether the decay has happened, we don't know if the cat is dead or alive. In a sense it is simultaneously dead *and* alive. Schrödinger's manager is like Schrödinger's cat. He may be the most important employee for the success of the team or he may not. He may be instrumental in attracting talent and motivating players, like Jürgen was at Liverpool, or he may not. We can't know if Schrödinger's cat is dead or alive unless we look inside the box. The difficulties in measuring manager impact are because we cannot know their true impact unless we can look inside the club.

12.

Goat War

Cristiano is so fast, so strong, so incredible,
but he has one problem: Leo Messi

Jürgen Klopp

The Fabric of Football

In late 2009, I was invited to the Royal Tapestry Factory in Madrid. Its original job back in 1720 was to supply tapestries to the court of Philip V, but in 2009 it would host the launch of a statistical ranking of football players – the 'Castrol Rankings'.[1] Castrol, a sponsor of Euro 2008, wanted to show that objective data could be used to rate players. The system I had devised for them was an early form of my Possession Value model. It was well enough received that Castrol now wanted me to publish a monthly ranking of players for the top five leagues in Europe and the Champions League.

Castrol enlisted the help of Cristiano Ronaldo. As their 'global brand ambassador' he would help publicise the rankings.

The press conference could not have come at a worse time. Two days before, 'Alcorconazo' happened. Alcorcón is a suburb of Madrid, home to a little-regarded team called Agrupación Deportiva Alcorcón S.A.D. At the time, they were playing in the third tier of Spanish football alongside Castilla, Real Madrid's reserve team, but two days before the press conference they had managed to beat

Real Madrid 4–0 in the Copa del Rey. Madrid had not played their strongest line-up against Alcorcón, but they did start with Raúl and Benzema up front, and Rafael van der Vaart in midfield,[2] and the loss was enough to incite panic among Madridistas.

The Tapestry Factory was packed with press and photographers – Ronaldo was already a superstar in 2009, having just become the world's most expensive transfer. The press conference started, and the first player to top the rankings was revealed to be . . . Barcelona's Thierry Henry. Ronaldo was third, just behind Lionel Messi in second place.

Questions from the press were taken. The first was about Alcorconazo. What did Ronaldo think of the disaster? The second question was also about the defeat, as was the third. The press were reminded that the questions should be about the rankings, not Alcorconazo. There seemed to be much less interest in the rankings than in Alcorconazo, but someone did ask Ronaldo what he thought about them. He thought they were absolute nonsense – probably not the response Castrol wanted from their global ambassador. Maybe in his view any system that didn't consider him to be the best player in the world was not a system that had any merit whatsoever. Ronaldo made it to the top of the rankings in December but the very next month was usurped by Messi, who remained its highest rated player for the following year.

One obvious application of data analysis is to answer the question of who is the greatest player of all time. In 2010, Messi was the best player in Europe, according to the Castrol Rankings. Today, in 2024, both players have finished their top-level club careers and are close to finishing as internationals too. Over the whole course of their careers, who was better – Messi or Ronaldo? And can one of them claim to be the Greatest of All Time? It is always possible to cherry-pick some piece of data if you want to show that Ronaldo is better than Messi, or vice versa, but if we are serious about deciding who is best, we must analyse all aspects of their game and put them into context before making our decision.

By the Basic Numbers

Unfortunately, data is not readily available for the giants of the past and we'll never be able to analyse legends such as Maradona and Pelé in depth. But even without detailed performance data on these players, it is easy to see their careers were much shorter-lived than Messi and Ronaldo's. The modern greats have been consistently brilliant for nearly 20 years. Pelé was denied a full competitive club career by Santos, who travelled the world playing glamorous friendlies. Maradona's brilliant club career in Europe lasted only 11 years.

Messi and Ronaldo have mind-boggling statistics. In his nine seasons at Real Madrid, Ronaldo scored 25 or more league goals every single season, and scored 40 in La Liga in 2010/11, 46 in 2011/12 and 48 in 2015/16. In each of his final 12 seasons for Barcelona, Messi scored at least 25 league goals, and managed 50 in 2011/12, motivated perhaps by a desire to outscore his Real Madrid rival.

The numbers behind these two incredible careers were explored by Simon Kuper and John Burn-Murdoch in the *Financial Times*[3] in June 2023 and they bear repeating. By May 2024, Ronaldo had scored 755 goals compared to Messi's 690 during their time in top-level football (the big five European leagues, Uefa competitions and competitive senior internationals).[4] But Messi scored these goals in far fewer minutes – 72,313 compared to Ronaldo's 81,594. In terms of goal-scoring *rate*, Messi is the better player, with 0.86 goals per 90 minutes compared to Ronaldo's 0.83.

Ronaldo has also benefited from taking and scoring more penalties than Messi. Penalties are extremely good scoring chances compared to most other situations, and the penalty winner is often not the penalty taker – there are good reasons to exclude penalties from our analysis. If we exclude penalties, Messi's goal rate drops to 0.74 per 90 minutes, but Ronaldo's drops to 0.68.

At first glance, Ronaldo and Messi look evenly matched. But

Chapter 8 showed us that there is more to football than goals. Chances must be created, and in chance creation Messi is by far the superior player. Messi has 339 top-level assists compared to Ronaldo's 272.[5] Messi assisted at a rate of 0.42 per 90 minutes, over 40% higher than Ronaldo's assist rate of 0.30 per 90 minutes. Another way of putting it is that over a 38-game season, Messi has averaged nearly 49 goals and assists per season, while Ronaldo has averaged 43 (which is also an outlandishly good return).

By these metrics, there is another player who almost bears comparison to Messi and Ronaldo: Robert Lewandowski, Jürgen's protégé at Borussia Dortmund. Lewandowski's 517 goals and 166 assists are less impressive totals than the usual contenders, but he produced them in far fewer minutes – 56,458 and counting. In terms of goals plus assists per 90 minutes, his rate of 1.09 is close to Ronaldo's 1.13. It is Ronaldo's longevity that gives him greater claim to GOAT status than Lewandowski. But Messi, with 1.28 goals and assists per 90 minutes, has produced goals and assists at a significantly higher rate than either. Cristiano Ronaldo and Robert Lewandowski do one job phenomenally: scoring goals. Lionel Messi does two jobs phenomenally, scoring goals and creating chances for his team-mates. By this measure, Messi is the true GOAT.

Other pretenders to the GOAT crown have similar raw goal and assist rates to Messi and Ronaldo, but applying some context allows us to discount them. Neymar and Kylian Mbappé have scored many of their goals in France for dominant Paris Saint-Germain. France is a weaker league than Spain, and Neymar and Mbappé do not have to play against the best team. Luis Suárez and Zlatan Ibrahimović have had incredible careers, but both stayed in the Dutch Eredivisie for a number of years, where goals are much easier to come by. Ronaldo Luís Nazário de Lima – the real Ronaldo – had a career cut short by injury and did not match the longevity of Messi and Ronaldo. Speaking of longevity, Erling Haaland is a true contender who is currently scoring at a higher rate than either Messi or Ronaldo, but he has to keep up the pace for another decade: it's a marathon not a sprint, Erling!

Messi and Ronaldo managed to rack up their staggering numbers through their availability. In top-level football Messi averaged more than 3,800 minutes per season and Ronaldo averaged nearly 3,900. Their career-long durability has been almost as astonishing as their performances. Lewandowski's availability was also excellent, playing more than 3,500 top-level minutes each season (and remember, German Bundesliga teams play four games fewer per season than La Liga teams). The newest claimant to the GOAT crown is Haaland. Only 24, he has already scored 193 goals and made 41 assists in top-level football, an incredible rate of 1.3 goals and assists per 90 minutes. But he is only five years into his career. His availability as much as his skill will determine whether he can challenge Messi's GOAT status over the next decade.

One of the challenges of incorporating a superstar into a team is that, as a general rule, they do not want to defend: their superior attacking talent allows them this luxury. Wayne Rooney – himself an incredible goal-scoring talent – has spoken about Ronaldo being allowed the luxury of not tracking back after Manchester United lost possession. Rooney did have to track back and, maybe surprisingly, was happy to do so, recognising that it was the best strategy for team success.

Something similar happened at Madrid: for all the attacking firepower in Ronaldo's Madrid – Bale, Benzema, Higuaín and Di María – they were always stocked with super defensive midfielders to carry the extra burden. Players like Alonso, Khedira, Essien and Casemiro stayed back and allowed the attackers to shine. And even stars like Modrić and Kroos, while not typical defensive midfielders, had to assume more defensive responsibility than they might have in a team without Ronaldo.

Madrid were a loose collection of superstars more than a team, but the collective always had super defensive talent to balance the attacking brilliance of Ronaldo, and his resultant (and deserved) lack of defensive responsibility. Paris Saint-Germain were another team stocked with formidable attacking talent – Messi, Neymar and

Mbappé – but unlike Madrid they have not prospered in the Champions League. When playing against opposition of comparable quality, three players who cannot or will not defend presents too much of a weakness. I bet that the coaches of Paris Saint-Germain were not as persuasive in getting Neymar et al to defend as Alex Ferguson was when he told Wayne Rooney he had to track back.

Taking Chances, Creating Chances

Over his career,[6] Ronaldo has been a far more prolific shooter in open play than Messi (who was also a very high-volume shooter). Ronaldo shot nearly five times per game, Messi just under four. But Messi's shooting was way more accurate than Ronaldo's: less than 40% of Ronaldo's shots tested the goalkeeper, compared to more than 46% of Messi's. This is also reflected in Expected Goals – Ronaldo's higher volume of shooting and lower accuracy is partly due to his penchant for a speculative shot. Ronaldo's Expected Goal conversion rate is about 11% while Messi's is much higher, at 14%.

This contrast in shooting tendencies continues when we look at Post-Strike Expected Goals. Messi's Expected Goal conversion rises significantly once shot trajectories are taken into account, while Ronaldo's does not. But in Ronaldo's defence, his *actual* goal conversion of 13% exceeds expectations, which may be a consequence of his ability to strike the ball hard. Messi actually converts more than 18% of his shots into goals, which also exceeds his Post-Strike Expected Goals conversion.

One area where Ronaldo does win is in variety of shooting: about one in six of his attempts on goal are taken using his head, compared to about one in 18 for Messi. And Ronaldo is more two-footed than Messi, with about a fifth of his kicked shots coming from his weaker left foot compared to about a sixth of Messi's shots coming from his weaker right.

We saw in Chapter 8 that there is a price to pay for taking a shot. A shot often relinquishes possession and denies a team-mate an opportunity to score. And while Messi and Ronaldo's goal rates are similar, Messi takes far fewer shots to score the same number of goals. In terms of Possession Value, Messi's shots are far more valuable, because they are much more efficient.

Both players are brilliant dribblers, but Messi adds about twice as much value through dribbling as Ronaldo. Messi manages this partly through sheer *quantity* of dribbling – he has remained a dribbler throughout his career, while Ronaldo's transition from tricky winger to centre-forward has naturally coincided with a decline in dribbling. Both players are world-class when it comes to dribbling, but Messi edges it in terms of adding Possession Value.

In terms of passing, Messi is the winner, though both players are very good passers. In his career Messi passes about 50% more in a game than Ronaldo, due to Barcelona's tiki-taka style. No forward playing regularly in the big five leagues and Champions League passes more than Messi, and he is among the best in the world at adding Possession Value with passing. Ronaldo is a superlative player in terms of taking shots and scoring goals. Messi is a master of shooting, but also creates much more for his team-mates than Ronaldo – he is the more impressive *team* player.

Set-piece Menu

The most skilful striker of the ball usually gets to take set-pieces, and it's no surprise that Messi and Ronaldo both take responsibility for direct free-kicks and penalties. When it comes to shots direct from free-kicks, each player's habits closely follow their open-play shooting habits. Ronaldo is happier to attempt a long-range shot direct from a free-kick: his Expected Goal conversion is about 4% compared to about 5% for Messi. And Messi shoots much more accurately than Ronaldo – 39% of his shots test the goalkeeper compared to 31% of Ronaldo's. Messi is a 'placement player' with a dead ball, as he is in open play, with his Expected Goals conversion post-strike much, much higher than pre-strike. Ronaldo, by contrast and as in open play, doesn't have particularly precise placement, but does convert goals at a higher rate than expected. Again this may be due to his ability to hit the ball very hard, or due to the unpredictable 'knuckleball' flight he sometimes attempts.

One area where Ronaldo is clearly superior is penalties, though he has padded his goal-scoring record with more easy-to-convert penalties than Messi has. Ronaldo's penalty conversion rate is about 3.5% higher than Messi's, and he hits slightly more of his penalties on target. Messi's special skills of judicious shot selection and accurate placement count for far less in penalty situations, when the goalkeeper knows the shot is coming and game theory is a much bigger factor in success.

School of Hard Knocks

Idiots often ask whether Messi could perform 'on a cold, wet Wednesday night at Stoke'. But it is true that Messi hasn't played at Stoke, while Ronaldo has (on a cold but sunny Boxing Day lunchtime rather than a cold, wet Wednesday night, but it still counts). A recurring theme of this book is context. We have to try to control for as many external factors as possible when making a judgement on a player, and Ronaldo's six Premier League seasons were a challenge that Messi didn't have to experience. Barcelona and Real Madrid dominated La Liga for years, with only Atlético Madrid later emerging as title rivals.[7] Meanwhile, the Premier League was very competitive when Ronaldo played there. Manchester United were often the best team, but they certainly did not dominate the Premier League in the way that Real Madrid and Barcelona dominated La Liga. Put another way, Messi often had only two *really* tough games per season in La Liga, but Ronaldo had six, and to make the challenge harder still, the middle classes of the Premier League were stronger than their La Liga equivalents.

The Premier League is also, frankly, a competition where players get kicked more. At Decision Technology we used to do a statistical review of the season for the Premier League. Part of the task was to compare the Premier League to other competitions. We noted, without comment, that the Premier League had fewer fouls and bookings than other leagues. The Premier League invariably added their own interpretation, lauding the 'fair play' that was on display in England compared to dastardly Continental Europe. My own interpretation is different. There are probably a similar number of contentious events in every league. The difference is that a slight kick or a shirt pull is more likely to be punished in other leagues but is often not given in the Premier League. Maybe this is a throwback to the game's origins in England as a form of muscular Christianity. Whatever the reason, the kicks that Ronaldo suffered in England (and theatrically brought to the referee's attention) were not rewarded with free-kicks as often as in Spain.

Ronaldo has also succeeded at three different clubs in three different leagues, playing in different positions, while the vast majority of Messi's career was spent at Barcelona. Ronaldo played mostly as a winger at Manchester United, and at the start of his Real Madrid career. He gradually switched to centre-forward and spent most of his time at Juventus playing up front. The formations and playing styles of the teams he played in also varied. Messi has moved between a right wide forward and a 'false 9' centre-forward role over his career, but played the vast majority of his games in Barcelona's famous 4–3–3 formation. The stability of club, formation and playing style that Messi enjoyed surely helped his performances. But Ronaldo managed to sustain a similar level of performance while having to adjust to a much greater variety of countries, formations and positions.

Looking at the way these two brilliant players interpreted their roles, this difference between them becomes even clearer. Messi is always just, well, Messi. Huge amounts of dribbling, huge amounts of creative link-up passing (more like an attacking midfielder than a forward) and lots of shooting. His consistency of style season to season has been remarkable. Meanwhile, Ronaldo has had various incarnations. In his first spell at Manchester United he was almost like a Messi who played wide – lots of dribbling, but crossing more and interchanging passes less. Season on season, Ronaldo reduced his dribbling, swapping it for more shooting. Then, as he moved to centre-forward, his link-up play and crossing were also sacrificed on the altar of shots. Ronaldo's career can be split into three eras – tricky winger, devastating wide forward and central shooting machine.

One place where Messi did have a harder time was in international football. In competitive internationals, Ronaldo's figures are far superior to Messi's: 0.75 goals and 0.26 assists per 90 minutes, compared to Messi's 0.48 goals and 0.33 assists per 90 minutes. Ronaldo has also played 20% more competitive international football than Messi. But Ronaldo has had one big advantage in amassing his international goals and assists: playing against rubbish defences.

Forty-seven of Ronaldo's goals and 13 of his assists for Portugal were scored against the footballing giants Liechtenstein, Andorra, Cyprus, Faroe Islands, Armenia, Latvia, Lithuania, Luxembourg, Kazakhstan, Estonia and Azerbaijan. Messi has not had the pleasure of playing against any of these teams. His easiest opponent was probably Bolivia, but playing against 'La Verde' in La Paz at an altitude of 3,637 metres should definitely not be categorised as 'easy'. Ronaldo has played the best European teams – Spain, France, Belgium, England – more often than Messi has. But Messi has also played against the cream of Europe, while Ronaldo has not played competitively against Colombia or Ecuador, and has played fewer games against Uruguay and Chile. Messi played eight competitive games against Brazil, while Ronaldo played only one (and neither scored). All in all, the brutal World Cup qualifying tournament in South America plus the Copa América makes for a more challenging set of opponents than the European qualifying tournaments and the Euros.[8] It is possible to adjust each player's scoring record for the quality of opposition, using a Dixon-Coles style model to discount a goal against Liechtenstein much more heavily than a goal against Spain. After adjustment, it turns out that the international contributions of Ronaldo and Messi, measured by opponent-adjusted goals and assists per 90 minutes, are about the same.

Messi Just Walks It In

Unfortunately tracking data was not available for the majority of their careers, so it's only possible to say something about the physical outputs of the players in their later years. In his second period at Manchester United, the 36-year-old Ronaldo did not cover much distance. His sprinting still matched that of much younger players but his physical performance was no outlier. I guess that in his younger years his top speed and sprinting workload would have been phenomenal but we don't have the evidence to know for sure.

There is even less evidence available regarding Messi's physical abilities. In recent Champions League seasons he has covered very low distances and has rarely sprinted. Most forwards who do not have to track back do not run as far as their team-mates, but most make up for it by sprinting a lot in counter-attack situations or when darting behind the opposition's defensive line. But not Messi. Messi doesn't run. Messi walks.

In Chapter 9 I mentioned Messi's deceleration – his ability to find space by slowing down quicker than defenders. Javier Fernández, a data scientist who worked at Barcelona, and Luke Bornn, a co-owner of RedBird Capital,[9] explored this idea in a 2018 paper called 'Wide Open Spaces: A Statistical Technique for Measuring Space Creation in Professional Soccer'.[10] They developed a concept of Pitch Control very similar to my old colleague Will Spearman's. Their idea was to use Pitch Control to explore the spaces created and used by different players, and the value of those spaces. The results were striking. The novelty was that they looked at *how* space was gained or lost by different players. Was it done *actively*, by making a run towards that space? Or was it done *passively*, with space appearing around a player but not as a result of his movements?

For the game they analysed in depth – a 1–1 draw between Barcelona and Villarreal – Fernández and Bornn found that Messi gained a lot of valuable space, but not an outlandish amount. The striking feature of Messi's generation of space was its passivity. Every other

Barcelona player generated the majority of their space actively, by running away from opponents or running into unoccupied spaces. But Messi generated two-thirds of his valuable space without running. He hung around or slowly wandered into valuable areas that defenders just so happened to vacate.

They also looked at losing valuable space – players being closed down by defenders, or moving to less valuable locations. Messi, along with the other attacking superstars Suárez and Neymar, lost the largest amounts of space. This chimed with a finding from our own tracking model: dribbling sometimes looks like a bad thing. This is a bit counter-intuitive – the best players on the planet are among the dribbliest. We spent some time trying to understand the paradox, and it all comes back to space. A dribble usually attracts the close attention of at least one defender. If I have the ball in midfield under no pressure and decide to go on a dribble, I will soon be under a lot of pressure. Often, the pressure that a player comes under while dribbling does not make up for the few yards closer to goal the dribble has taken him. The real value comes at the *end* of the dribble. When a pass is made after a successful dribble, it is into more space than usual. Defenders who might usually be covering that space have closed down the dribbler instead. Fernández and Bornn had found the same thing – the best dribblers lost the most space as they were closed down.

Their final piece of analysis looked at which players generate space for others. The runs of the forwards, Messi, Neymar and Suárez, added the most value by dragging defenders away from valuable space. This is not very surprising – those three players operated furthest up the pitch where the valuable space lies. The interesting thing to me was that Suárez and Neymar generated about 35% more space through dragging opponents away than Messi did. Suárez and Neymar are physically much more impressive players than Messi, and they used their physicality to generate the space for Messi to stroll into. Messi partly returned the favour, but the two other members of 'MSN' generated far more space for Messi than Messi produced for them.

To sum it up, not only was Messi a generational talent, he achieved it mostly at walking speed. Messi's strolls around the pitch and apparent uninterest in the game have attracted a lot of comment. The most entertaining came from The Athletic's Duncan Alexander. He noted that Messi, for all his achievements, had not scored in the first two minutes of a game (though in June 2023 he broke his duck, scoring after one minute and 20 seconds). Messi's scoring is significantly worse than Ronaldo's in the first 15 minutes of games. Ronaldo scores about 8% of his goals in the first 10 minutes of games, while Messi scores about 5%. Pep Guardiola has commented that Messi spends the first few minutes mapping out the defensive spaces and the defenders' tendencies before springing (or ambling) into action.

Messi and Ronaldo were the first superstars whose careers we had the privilege of analysing using data. As their careers end they have left statistical footprints of their brilliance, for the next generational talent to try to live up to. The challenge will be tough, but the top teams have increased their dominance since the start of Messi and Ronaldo's careers, giving new superstars a perfect environment and a head start as they try to surpass them.

And the Winner Is . . .

Messi. Obviously.

13

Zebra Farmers: Why Transfers Fail

Personally, I would have paid less for myself

Neymar

A Worthy Successor

In September 2016, I was completing our transfer window review. One of the first things you are taught as a scientist is to write down your hypotheses, your methods and your results. That way, if you find something interesting, there's a record of what you've done and you can repeat the work to see if the results can be replicated. There wasn't really an equivalent when it came to transfers. We'd discuss hundreds of players, go into lots of detail on about a dozen, but only sign a couple. All the players we didn't sign, the club collectively forgot about. I suggested we record our opinions about all transferred players immediately after each transfer window. Might the player have been suitable for Liverpool? Was the fee value for money? Did we think the transferred player would succeed at his new club? I hoped we'd be able to go back and see if our opinions turned out to be accurate, and if we had some blind spots.

One player I was very disappointed to have missed out on was Naby Keïta, who had moved from Red Bull Salzburg to Red Bull Leipzig. In the review, I'd written: 'Stats love Naby very much.' I didn't need to add any more detail – the rest of the Transfer Committee knew my feelings about Keïta because I'd been banging on about him for months. At age 19 he'd arrived in Salzburg from the French club Istres, following a similar path to Sadio Mané. Naby had performed brilliantly in his first season in Austria as a destructive central midfielder. Our Possession Value model rated him as above average Premier League level, which was very unusual for a player playing in Austria. Our league benchmarking model considered the Austrian league to be significantly lower quality than the Premier League, with the result that players there were rarely deemed to be playing at Premier League standard. The previous example had been Mané. Next season Keïta played a more attacking role and again looked way above the average Premier League level. I remember calling up Hans Leitert, later Liverpool's goalkeeping consultant, who was working for Red Bull at the time. 'What about this Naby Keïta, Hans?' 'Ah yes, young Naby, very talented. Very talented.'

I hounded Eddy, saying that if he really believed in a data-led approach he had to seriously consider signing Keïta. I was devastated when Keïta signed for Red Bull Leipzig, and the feeling was compounded when he went on to have an outstanding first season in Germany. Leipzig's best ever Bundesliga finish was in 2016/17, Keïta's first at the club, and he made the Bundesliga team of the season. I kept on harassing Eddy, and in summer 2017 we signed Keïta on the proviso that he could stay at Leipzig until summer 2018. He inherited Steven Gerrard's number 8 shirt, vacant since 2015, and I thought he would be a worthy successor.

Despite my sky-high expectations, Keïta did not succeed at Liverpool. Among Liverpool's big-ticket transfers in the Klopp era – Van Dijk, Alisson, Fabinho, Salah, Jota, Mané and Firmino – Keïta stands out as the least successful. This is not to say he played badly: when he played, he played nearly as well as I expected, and I expected him to be world-class. But he didn't play very much. He started only 16 Premier League games in his first season at Liverpool and started fewer than 16 in the four seasons that followed. From 2019/20 onwards, every time he had a run of games in the team, he suffered an injury. He'd had a couple of hamstring strains at Leipzig but at

Liverpool he suffered a whole range of problems, and from 2020 onwards missed a very large number of games. His bad luck even extended to getting caught up in an attempted military coup in Guinea while on international duty.

Keïta had some extenuating circumstances – if he could have stayed fit he might not have been considered a 'failure'. But lots of transfers fail for lots of reasons and, as our experience with Mohamed Salah had shown, it is a worthwhile endeavour to analyse these failures in detail.

The 50% Rule

Consider this benchmark for 'success': after transferring to a Premier League club, you are considered a 'success' if during the next two years you start in 50% of their Premier League games. That's a pretty low benchmark. If a team has decided to spend tens of millions on a new player, they must surely think he'll start half of all the games, and they'd probably be disappointed if he only just manages 50%.

Nevertheless, many transfers do not achieve even this modest definition of success. Considering all transfers of players to Premier League clubs of €10 million or more between its inception in 1992 and January 2021, you would find nearly half (46%) of them failed to start half the team's Premier League games in the next two years. As with Keïta, the term 'failure' is rarely a critique of a transferred player's talent or dedication, but rather the team that incorrectly thought they were making a purchase that would fit their needs.

These unsuccessful transfers were not cheap back-ups bought to sit on the bench as insurance against injury to a first-choice star. Clubs had paid at least €10 million to secure their services, yet nearly half of them failed to start in half the clubs' games. For every successful big-money transfer like Manchester City signing Kevin de Bruyne from Wolfsburg in 2015 (225 Premier League starts and

counting; six titles in nine seasons and counting) or Liverpool signing Roberto Firmino from Hoffenheim in 2015 (80 Premier League
goals excluding penalties and 50 assists in 211 starts), there was a failure, like Manchester United's signing of Angel di María in 2014
(three Premier League goals excluding penalties and 10 assists in 20
starts) or Liverpool's signing of Christian Benteke in 2015 (eight
Premier League goals excluding penalties in 14 starts is a perfectly
good goal rate, but 14 total Premier League starts after paying
£32.5 million is not good business).

To emphasise how modest our definition of success is, consider
Fernando Torres' transfer from Liverpool to Chelsea in January
2011. The transfer would be considered a failure by most, given that
Torres only scored seven goals in his first one and a half seasons at
Chelsea. But by our definition it was successful because Torres
started 50 of Chelsea's 77 Premier League games in the two years
following his move.

Spending more money does not guarantee success either: the fee
paid has very little to do with whether the move will be successful
or not. Just over two of every five Premier League transfers over
€20 million fail to start half their team's games during the following
two years. Di María at Manchester United, Alvaro Morata and
Christian Pulisic at Chelsea, and Naby Keïta at Liverpool were all
very expensive players who did not cross the 50% threshold.

I am not the first to point out the surprisingly large proportion of
failed transfers. Paul Tomkins' book *Pay As You Play* looked at transfer fee inflation in the Premier League.[1] A few years later, he revisited
the work in his blog, 'The Tomkins Times',[2] and compared transfer
fees to 'success'. His method for measuring success was more complicated than ours, with the benchmark depending on a weighted
mixture of transfer fee paid, inflation, transfer fee received and
number of games started. Tomkins' conclusion was that only 40%
of transfers succeed. This is a lower success rate than my simple
starts-based measure but is in the same ballpark.

Looking at transfers in financial terms rather than by number
of starts is also instructive. When a player is signed, the transfer

fee is spread over the length of his contract. In the accounts, a £50 million fee will be recorded at £10 million per year for a five-year contract, a process known as amortisation.[3] Every year, financial auditors will look at how much of the fee remains on the books and ask the club to decide if that represents a fair value for the player. If the remaining fee doesn't represent a fair value, an impairment (a loss in the accounts) is recorded. After three years, our £50 million transfer still has £20 million on the books. If the club believes the player would now attract a fee of only £5 million, the other £15 million remaining is recorded as an impairment. Kieron O'Connor recently noted that Premier League clubs recorded more than a quarter of a *billion* pounds of impairments between 2020 and 2022.[4] In 2021/22, Chelsea alone recorded £77 million of player impairments. What's more, these impairments don't even include the wages spent on 'impaired' players, who by definition don't play.

How come so many transfers fail? Football teams put an awful lot of time and effort into scouting but the huge variability of transfer success is often accepted as either an unfortunate fact of life or is forgotten by the time the next transfer window comes around.

There is no shortage of explanations after the fact for why a transferred player fails: maybe they were not as good as the team thought, or they couldn't fit into the manager's tactical system, or a player already in the team started playing well. It was a truth universally acknowledged within football clubs that some transfers would not be very successful. Teams just had to live with it.

At Liverpool we showed that teams did *not* have to live with it. A data-driven approach considers all players – including those currently employed by the team – on an equal footing. If the stats suggest a new prospect is not much better than the players currently available, a team owner should at least ask for further justification as to why such an (inevitably expensive) change is necessary.

The hottest players in the transfer market tend to be ones who have been on a scoring streak, or play for a team on a winning run, or who have had a successful World Cup. These streaks typically do not continue, and the performances that teams believe they are paying for are often unsustainable. Conversely, players who had a scoring streak or an impressive defensive record long before the transfer window opened, or who had been playing consistently but not as eye-catchingly, may have better underlying performances. Again, good data analysis helps: we have seen that one of its fundamental uses is to filter out short-term fluctuations – hot streaks – from longer term trends.

The malfunctioning transfer market was the prime candidate for exploitation using data analysis and it is where we concentrated our efforts at Liverpool. We've seen how the idea misfired badly when Brendan Rodgers was manager. Even so, we enjoyed some successes: signing Daniel Sturridge and Philippe Coutinho in January 2013 galvanised our title challenge in 2013/14. Roberto Firmino arrived in summer 2015, as did James Milner, on a free transfer.

But when Jürgen arrived we finally began to exploit our edge. Our transfer success rate, defined as the fraction of league starts in the next two years weighted by transfer fee, leapt from 41% to 58%. Our 41% was the worst success rate among the big six between 2012/13 and 2015/16, though it does ignore the contribution of free transfers Milner (64/76 starts) and Kolo Touré (22/76 starts).

Weighting number of starts by transfer fee in the Klopp era ignores the contribution of Joël Matip, who started 54 of Liverpool's 76 Premier League games in the two years following his arrival on a free transfer. It also downplays the importance of Andrew Robertson (58 starts out of 76) because his fee was so low. Manchester United (60%) and Arsenal (59%) achieved a higher fee-weighted success rate of signings than Liverpool in the Klopp era, but transferring in expensive players and having them play is not sufficient for success. Two of the biggest contributors to Manchester United's high success rate are Paul Pogba and Harry Maguire. Both players were expensive and started regularly in their first two seasons. Pogba and Maguire are fine players, but their performances did not help Manchester United to achieve much success on the pitch.

Taming the Beasts

To gain some more insight into why transfers fail, I turned to a very unlikely source. In his book *Guns, Germs and Steel*, Jared Diamond poses a question: why are there no zebra farmers? Only a few species of large mammal have ever been domesticated. The pig, cow, sheep, goat and horse have found use in cultures across the world. A few other species (including the camel, llama, yak and donkey) have some regional use. Given their potential as producers of food and clothing, and their use as transport, the absence of the zebra is strange. There are many other species that surely could have been put to the same use as the cow, horse or pig. Diamond suggests 148 species were potential candidates for domestication. But only 14 were ever domesticated – a success rate of less than 10%. It seems humans are even worse at domesticating animals than football clubs are at signing players.

It turns out that domesticating an animal is very difficult. Many modern attempts at domestication, of moose, deer, zebra and more, have failed. The reason is that successful domestication requires a species to be suitable in many different ways. To be domesticated and useful an animal must have a suitable diet, so they can be fed cheaply. They need a high growth rate and a high-density herd structure, so they are profitable to farm, and the inclination to breed in captivity. They must also be safe to farm – if they have a violent disposition or a tendency to panic they may kill themselves or the farmers. The absence of any *one* of these characteristics means the animal can't be domesticated. Zebras score brilliantly on five of the six characteristics, but have an unfortunate tendency to bite, kick and kill anyone trying to domesticate them. This is what makes domestication so difficult, and why you don't see any zebra farmers around.

Imagine a new animal is discovered, and its potential for domestication is studied. The researchers estimate that it's 70% likely the animal's diet is suitable, 70% likely their growth rate is high enough and 70% likely that they can be persuaded to breed in captivity. There's a 70% chance that they have a suitable temperament for domestication, a 70% chance that they will not panic easily, and a 70% chance they can be farmed at high density.

This animal looks like a great bet for domestication. On each characteristic, we have a good chance of success. But if the animal fails on any one of these characteristics, we are doomed to failure. Our chance of success on every characteristic is 70% x 70% x 70% x 70% x 70% x 70% = 12%. Even a promising species that looks favourable on every aspect of domestication is a 12% long shot. This is also why popular 'multiples' bets have such long odds. It might be 70% likely that Manchester City win next weekend, and 70% for each of Arsenal, Liverpool, Real Madrid, Barcelona, Bayern Munich, Borussia Dortmund, Internazionale and Paris Saint-Germain to win. But the chance that they all win is 4%. I wouldn't take that bet at odds of 20 to 1.

What does this have to do with signing players? Just like domesticated animals, footballers must succeed in every aspect in order to achieve a successful transfer. It is necessary to be a good footballer if you are to succeed. But it's not sufficient. You will not succeed if you are always injured. It's not enough to have a track record of success in France if you argue with your new manager and he drops you. And the more aspects a player needs to succeed on, the lower his chances of success. Thinking back on our experiences at Liverpool, I came up with the following list of possible explanations why a player's transfer may not succeed: the player may suffer injuries, he may have a 'difficult personality', he might be played out of position, or he might not be any better than others already at his new club. He might simply turn out to be not as good as his new club thought, or his style of play might not suit his new club, or perhaps his new manager will not rate him. Finally, he may be very young and need more than two seasons to become a regular starter.

Let's imagine that a team has done their scouting very well and there's a 92% chance that the player will not fail on each of these factors. Everything looks great but we can't be absolutely sure the player won't have medical problems, will get on with the manager, will be better than existing options etc. What is his chance of success? I have listed eight ways in which a player might fail. The overall chance of success, assuming each of the ways a player might fail is independent,[5] is 92% x 92% x 92% x 92% x 92% x 92% x 92% x 92% = 51%. Jared Diamond calls this the 'Anna Karenina principle' after a line in the Tolstoy book: 'All happy families are alike; each unhappy family is unhappy in its own way.' Similarly, all successful transfers are alike, and each unsuccessful one is unhappy in its own way.

Many Ways to Fail

We can browse through the list of historic expensive transfers to find out which factors may have been important in derailing their chances of success. At the top of the list is the most expensive of all time – Neymar. Paris Saint-Germain's transfer of Neymar in 2017 for a reported €222 million was supposed to transform the club into Champions League contenders. Neymar is a brilliant player, but injuries limited his impact in Paris and he started only 47% of their league games in his first two years there. His injuries also contributed to PSG's lack of success in the Champions League. PSG and their effectively unlimited transfer funds feature heavily in the list of high-profile transfers who failed to start for the team. The French club paid €25 million or more for Icardi, Paredes, Mendes, Kehrer, Diallo, Guedes, Krychowiak, Cabaye, Kurzawa and Jesé, who all started fewer than 50% of league games in their first two seasons.

Neymar's transfer also led to two other high-profile signings failing to make it to the 50% benchmark. Barcelona used Neymar's fee, and more, to sign Philippe Coutinho from Liverpool for £142 million and Ousmane Dembélé from Borussia Dortmund for €135 million. Dembélé suffered a series of hamstring injuries and only managed to start 33 out of 76 La Liga games. Coutinho was presumably the long-term replacement for Andrés Iniesta in midfield but in his first year at the club was mostly used on the left wing where Neymar had been playing. He'd also played that position for Liverpool, but he interpreted it in a very different way to Neymar. Coutinho was not a fast, direct wide forward like Neymar, but rather a number 10 who could also play wide. Barcelona already had Lionel Messi playing in a similar fashion and to a higher standard on the right. Despite Coutinho's raw numbers looking good, Barcelona gave up on their investment in 2019, and Coutinho joined Bayern Munich on loan.

Another expensive transfer who failed to hit 50% was João Félix (€127.5 million), signed by Atlético Madrid in 2019 as Antoine Griezmann's replacement. Griezmann had just been signed by Barcelona for €120 million. Félix is a very good player, but one whose style seemed more suited to tiki-taka Barcelona than to the defensive, counter-attacking Atlético. It's always hard to tell looking from the outside, but to me Félix seemed a player whose style just didn't suit Atlético's system.

Some classic Premier League transfers also feature highly in the list of expensive signings who didn't make the 50% grade. Robinho's fee of £32.5 million does not seem very high by today's standards but he was the most expensive transfer of summer 2008. He memorably thought he was signing for Chelsea rather than Manchester City, which may go some way to explaining his failure to become a regular starter. He did start regularly in 2008/09 but barely featured the following season and was loaned to Santos in Brazil after 18 months. Angel di María joined Manchester United in summer 2014 for approximately £60 million. He had been a regular starter for Real Madrid, helping them win a Primera División title and 'La Decima' – Real Madrid's 10th Champions League title. He only lasted one season at Manchester United, starting 20 games. He was often played out of position by Louis van Gaal, but his wife's comments about Manchester were possibly more revealing: 'I didn't like it at all . . . I can tell you. People are all weird. You walk around and you don't know if they're going to kill you. The food is disgusting . . . I just told him: "Darling, it's horrible, it's night-time at two o'clock." '

The other standout Premier League transfer is Romelu Lukaku's to Chelsea in 2021, reported to have cost £97.5 million. It was hailed as a masterstroke at the time, and seemed to be confirmed in his second debut at the club, when he scored against Arsenal. But he would only make 16 Premier League starts and went on loan to Internazionale after just one season. The player seemed unhappy at Chelsea and gave a strange interview describing his regret at leaving Inter. It was a case of déjà vu for both Lukaku and Chelsea. In 2011 they had signed him from Anderlecht for a reported £13 million plus add-ons. An 18-year-old prodigy, he had been starting and scoring in Belgium for two years. But he was too young to break into a Chelsea team featuring Torres, Sturridge, Anelka and Drogba, and only made one Premier League start. The transfer wasn't really a failure first time round, as Chelsea made a large profit by transferring Lukaku to Everton after a successful loan.

One of the stranger deals of recent times was the swap deal between Barcelona and Juventus involving Miralem Pjanić and Arthur Melo. Pjanić had been a regular starter for Juventus for four seasons, and Arthur had been a squad player for Barcelona for two. The swap deal valued Arthur at €72 million and Pjanić at €60 million. The deal happened during Covid – both clubs had financial issues and needed to balance their books. The large fees attached to the swap allowed each club to book a large transfer profit but spread the cost of the incoming player over five years by amortisation. As Sid Lowe, the English football journalist based in Spain, wrote: 'The accountancy is more creative than the midfielders are.'[6] Each player's career was disrupted by the move. Pjanić had started 108 Serie A games in four seasons for Juventus. He started only six La Liga games for Barcelona and has since joined Sharjah in the United Arab Emirates. Arthur fared a bit better at Juventus, starting 24 Serie A games in two seasons, but spent the following two seasons out on loan.

Physician, Heal Thyself

As entertaining as it is to speculate on the transfer failings at other clubs, we at Liverpool had our fair share of transfers that didn't work out.

Christian Benteke ticked most of the boxes to be a successful transfer. The only shortcoming was that his style did not suit Liverpool's, and this one factor led to him making only 14 starts. There was some hope that his style would change in a better team, despite my research showing that target men very rarely change their spots. Benteke might not have played as well as Brendan Rodgers hoped but his rate of goals and assists at Liverpool was as high as any other Premier League season he played, except for 2012/13. Similarly, Joe Allen also ticked nearly every box. His only problem was that, as good a player as he was, he was not quite as good as Steven Gerrard, Lucas Leiva or Jordan Henderson. He also suffered a few injuries at Liverpool, which limited his availability. Mario Balotelli could easily be pigeonholed into the 'personal issues' category but didn't really behave badly at Liverpool. His signing was a result of the Transfer Committee being unable to agree on other options, and he was no one's first choice (through no fault of his own). His past personal issues also gave an easy excuse for any shortcomings.

Lazar Marković did not tick nearly every box but was the hottest young prospect in scouting departments across Europe. The manager didn't really rate him, and played him out of position at wing-back, but they were secondary issues. The main problem was that he wasn't as good as we'd thought. Eddy knew that he was not an outlier in our statistical ratings. His video analysis had also showed a player much more variable than the scouting reports implied. Eddy cites signing Marković as his biggest regret, but at least we learned from the experience. This was the failure that led to an extra layer of detailed video analysis being added for every serious transfer target Liverpool considered from that point on.

In the Klopp era, most of the 'failures' have been due to injury.

Luis Díaz and Diogo Jota didn't quite hit 50% of starts in their first two seasons – both suffered unlucky on-pitch injuries. Naby Keïta arrived at Liverpool without much history of injuries but simply could not stay fit. We also signed two players who had long histories of suffering injuries: Alex Oxlade-Chamberlain and Thiago Alcântara. Their injury issues did not improve at Liverpool, which is not a surprise, given Jürgen's physical, high-energy pressing style in both training and games.

The other 'failures' in the Klopp era are not really failures: Kostas Tsimikas, Xherdan Shaqiri and Takumi Minamino were bought as squad depth options. Transfer fee inflation meant that the price for Champions League level squad players had crept up to over €10 million by the late 2010s. Ibrahima Konaté suffered some injuries, but his lack of starts was also due to having to share game-time with Joël Matip and Joe Gomez.

Getting to 70%

In Chapter 10 we saw that there is a high correlation between wage bill and success, but a much smaller correlation between net transfer spend and success. That only half of transfers start 50% of their new clubs' league games goes some way to explaining the low correlation. The 50% of players who are successful will get offered new contracts on better terms or be sold for a profit. But 50% are not successful. Any club that can raise their success rate to 70% will have an enormous advantage over their competitors.

Looking through the range of risk factors, data analysis can mitigate against most of them. I had found that target men do not change their style of play at a new club and we used this analysis as an argument against signing Christian Benteke. Our objective analysis of players already at the club also helped avoid unwise transfers. The old saying that familiarity breeds contempt is true for players: if a player plays for your club then you see them at their worst as well as their best. All of their flaws that were unknown to you when they signed sooner or later become apparent. They might complain about the training regime or the quality of the food in the canteen. A shiny new transfer prospect has none of these issues. Their upsides are highlighted and their downsides are downplayed or just unknown. The natural human biases against a current player who is a bit of a pain or towards a transfer prospect who has a nice high-lights reel are reduced by using data analysis.

As our team got better and better, fewer and fewer players were rated as good enough to make a difference to our first team. As a result, we stayed out of the transfer market except on the rare occa-sions when a promising player was available. In a game where the average success rate is 50%, refusing to play unless you have a good reason to can be a good strategy for success.

Some of the risk factors are more difficult to address using data. Player injury risk is hard to predict, and for big-ticket transfers it is probably the most important cause of failure. No one doubts that Neymar is a great player, but he couldn't stay fit at Paris Saint-Germain. The other two 'softer' risk factors – personal issues and the manager's opinion – depend on the skills of the sporting dir-ector. They have to decide how much attention to pay to negative personal opinions about a player, which is not an easy task. They also have to discuss signings with the manager and be confident the manager will play new players and play them in the right position.

Eddy often said that if scouting, data and manager are aligned in their opinion of a player, then that player rarely fails. It turns out that the committee-based approach can be a recipe for success, with the blind spots of each member covered by the others. Liverpool moved from a situation where there was rarely alignment between the members of the committee to one where alignment was the norm (even if alignment required hours of arguments). We reaped the rewards, as did Brighton and Brentford. Given the appallingly low benchmark of success for transfers, other clubs have the oppor-tunity to reap the rewards too.

The concept of 'marginal gains' has become popular in sport. The idea is that if we can make improvements of 1% in 10 areas, then we will get an improvement of at least 10%, and maybe more if there are synergies between these improvements. I disagree with the concept of marginal gains because it ignores opportunity cost: time and effort you spend doing one thing is time and effort you could have spent doing something else. I think a better approach is to make a list of all the possible gains you might make, rank them in order of most impactful to least impactful, and concentrate on the important ones. In football, 65% of revenue is spent on wages, and 25% on transfer fees. We've seen that a huge fraction of that money is wasted. Player recruitment and development is the place to expend time and effort in a football club: the gains can be huge rather than marginal.

14.

Home Is Where 30% More Goals Are

I never, ever felt I was influenced by the crowd

Jeff Winter, former Premier League referee

Kicking Off Early

In November 2020, Liverpool played out a 1–1 draw at Brighton. Brighton missed a penalty in the first half and we were lucky to go ahead in the second half. We'd created next to nothing. Brighton equalised with a last-minute penalty but probably deserved to win. Our models rated Brighton as the better performing team. It was a bad performance and a bad result, compounded by a hamstring injury to James Milner. Jürgen was livid after the game and placed the blame squarely on the 12.30 kick-off time.

In his mind, playing early on a Saturday after playing on a Wednesday, as we had, was a recipe for disaster. He rather unfairly had a pop at the BT Sport interviewer for always choosing Liverpool to play at 12.30. It certainly wasn't the interviewer's fault that his TV station had chosen Liverpool for the early kick-off slot. Really, the early kick-offs were part of the price we paid for success. At the time, BT Sport had the second choice of which fixture to televise. Sky Sports would choose the highest profile clash for Sunday afternoon, often a game between two of the big six. If Liverpool were not chosen for Sunday, we were often the most attractive remaining fixture for BT Sport. If we were rubbish or played boring football, we would not have had to play so often at 12.30 and Jürgen would not have felt compelled to have running arguments about it with TV interviewers.

Jürgen's obsession with early kick-offs started long before his spat with BT Sport. Late in the 2017/18 season I was asked by Harrison Kingston, then Liverpool's head of post-match analysis, to investigate our performances in early kick-offs. Jürgen felt we performed badly in these early games. The raw data indeed looked bad – we'd won only 29 points in 21 early kick-offs. That pace was equivalent to a 52-point season, way below our typical 76-point return at that time. Fifty-two points is what an average Premier League team wins in a season, while 76 more or less guaranteed a top-four finish. On first inspection, those 12.30 kick-offs were causing Liverpool to decline from a Champions League quality team to an average Premier League team.

As we've seen many times in this book, context is everything in football. Aggregating points in early kick-offs tells us something, but I needed to dig deeper to understand the reasons *why* our points return was poor. Early kick-offs are special: they are nearly all televised in the UK which, until recently, wasn't true of the majority of games.[1] If a match is televised, that might mean the opposition is strong – TV stations often like to show games between good teams. So I used our match forecasting model to see how bad that 29 points return really was. I'd fully expected a 30% drop in points return to be extremely unusual, even if our opponents were better than average, but the forecasting model indicated that the result was far from unexpected. A points return of 29 points was below par, but not very far below the 32.4 points that the model indicated to be the average points return from those games. All in all, the chance of winning 29 points or fewer from those 21 early kick-offs was estimated at 31% – not at all an unusual occurrence.

I thought that Liverpool's low expected points return would be explained by a particularly difficult set of opponents, but it wasn't. Yes, we'd played Manchester United, Manchester City, Tottenham and Chelsea in the early kick-offs. But we'd played each of Bournemouth, Crystal Palace and Southampton twice, and Swansea three times. There was nothing special about the identity of the opponents, but there was something special about their *location*: we'd played 17 out of the 21 games away from home, probably because a big team playing away against a small team makes for better TV than the other way round. And it turns out that teams typically earn 60% of their points at home and 40% away from home. A 76-point team can expect about 46 points from their home games and 30 from their away games. Our 17 away games had generated 24 points, only a couple of points below expectations for a Champions League level team playing away against a random selection of opponents. This 'home advantage' was included in our forecasting model – playing at home constitutes a 30% increase in goal-scoring rate for the home team compared to the away team. Our early kick-off results were not expected to be great simply because we played away so often.

Fast forward to 2023/24 and Jürgen was still arguing with TV interviewers about early kick-offs. In December 2023, a TNT Sports interviewer joked that 12.30 was Jürgen's 'favourite kick-off time'. Jürgen responded by calling the interviewer 'completely ignorant'. Liverpool had scored a last-minute winner in that particular game, but the important point was that the game was played at Selhurst Park, not Anfield. In the Klopp era Spurs, Arsenal, West Ham and Manchester United have played more early kick-offs than Liverpool. But Liverpool still have the greatest fraction of early kick-offs played away from home – 63%.

Messi in Your Team

The effect of home advantage is very strong. It's like having Messi at his peak in your team. The downside, of course, is that when you play away, it's like having Messi play against you. Today, the average Premier League team scores about 1.2 goals when they play away, and about 1.6 when they play at home. This extra 0.4 goals is more than nearly any individual player on the planet brings to a team. Home advantage for defence is the same. The swing between home and away in terms of goal difference is an enormous 0.8 goals.

Home advantage leads to about a 47% chance of winning on average, compared to about a 29% chance of winning away from home (assuming two average Premier League teams playing against each other). If there was no such thing as home advantage, each team would have about a 37.5% chance of victory. Home advantage has existed since football began and, even though its impact has diminished, it is still a crucial factor in deciding the outcome of games. In the early days of football, more goals were scored. At the start of the 20th century, in the English First Division, home teams scored about 1.9 goals compared to 1.1 for away teams. There was a drop in home scoring after the Second World War to about 1.75 goals, but home advantage bounced back a little in the 1950s and 1960s. Since the 1970s it has been decreasing, with home teams in the 2000s scoring 1.5 goals compared to 1.1 for the away team. The proportion of *points* won by the home team has declined from nearly 70% in the 1900s to 60% in the 2000s.[2]

Historically, differences in home advantage between the divisions in England have been small. Until the 1980s, a consistent pattern was that the lower divisions had slightly higher home advantages, but that pattern has disappeared. Today the Premier League has the highest home advantage of the English leagues, and there is not much difference between the others, from the Championship down to the National League.

Every league I've ever looked at has had a positive home advantage, although it varies considerably by continent and by competition. African leagues in Nigeria, Ghana and Algeria have very large home advantages, but others, such as Egypt and South Africa, have less home advantage than the English Premier League. Across the world, there is some correlation between size of country and variety of playing conditions and home advantage. Outside of Africa, the leagues with the largest home advantages are Brazil, Colombia and the United States. These are very large countries with a wide variety of climates, so travelling is more punishing and playing conditions are more variable. In Europe there is much less variation in home advantage. For most of the top leagues it hovers around 30%, though it does vary from 22% in small, mild-mannered Denmark, to 44% in passionate Greece, maybe not a surprise in a country where, in 2018, the owner of PAOK Salonika confronted a referee while having a holstered gun on his belt.[3]

Throughout Europe the general trend today is that lower divisions have smaller home advantages and youth competitions have even smaller home advantages. This suggests that the size and the passion of the crowd at a game may have something to do with home advantage.

Home Comforts

Home advantage was the reason behind my very first football forecast. As an eight-year-old I had been given the Ladybird book of the 1986 World Cup before the tournament began. The book contained results and tables of all the qualifying competitions and I was mesmerised by the offhand way in which oddities like 'Costa Rica v Barbados: Walkover' and Iran's disqualification (apparently for refusing to play home matches on neutral ground) were listed. The book included space to write the results of each game, and it also invited readers to write their prediction for the tournament winner. I knew that England had won the World Cup at home in 1966 (an event so far in the past that English people rarely mention it these days), and the book also listed all the past winners. Argentina had won at home in '78, Germany in '74 and England in '66. In my mind there could only be one winner of Mexico '86: Mexico!

There has been a wealth of academic research on home advantage. Kerry Courneya and Albert Carron conducted a wide-ranging review of home advantage in 1992.[4] They identified various 'location factors' that cause the game to look different to the away team compared to the home team. A partisan crowd may affect the away team differently to the home team. The home team's familiarity with their surroundings is another difference, as is the travelling that the away team have to do. They also identified that psychological and behavioural factors affect the players, coaches and referees. Their work revived academic interest in studying home advantage in football, and it was a topic I looked at several times while researching articles for Danny Finkelstein's 'Fink Tank' column in *The Times*.

There was usually a 'newsy' reason for looking at home advantage, and one of these came in the qualifiers for Euro 2008. England ended up failing to qualify, but their penultimate game was a crucial away fixture against Russia. The game was to be played on a plastic pitch that had been installed at the Luzhniki Stadium in Moscow. The English FA were not very happy about it, but Fifa decided the game could go ahead. In England there was a collective memory of the terrible plastic pitches that Queens Park Rangers, Luton Town, Oldham Athletic and Preston North End had played on in the 1980s. The academic researchers Stephen Clarke and John Norman had shown in a 1995 paper that these four clubs enjoyed an enormous home advantage.[5] At the time in England, teams scored 1.5 goals at home and 1.0 goals away. A team with a plastic pitch playing at home against an equally strong opponent could expect to score 1.7 goals and concede 0.9, increasing their chance of winning from about 47% to 56%. The FA were certainly worried enough to move the England team's training to Blessed Thomas Holford Catholic College in Altrincham, which had installed the same brand of artificial pitch as England would play on in Moscow.

There were three teams in Russia who played on a plastic pitch: Spartak Moscow, Torpedo Moscow and Amkar Perm. It was an ideal opportunity to test if these three Russian teams enjoyed the same huge advantages as the four 'plastic' English teams had in the 1980s. It turned out that they did not. The 'plastic' Russian teams' home advantage was not significantly different to the other teams in the league. There were plausible explanations for this very different result in Russia. Plastic pitch technology has progressed a long way since the 1980s, and by 2007 plastic pitches played a lot more like grass. And even though only three Russian teams played games on plastic, others, like CSKA Moscow and Lokomotiv Moscow, trained on plastic, perhaps negating the familiarity with the playing surface that QPR enjoyed in the 1980s. Despite the lack of evidence for an extra home advantage, the Russian FA were at pains to point out that only two of the national team players regularly played on artificial turf. They neglected to mention that many of the squad were CSKA and Lokomotiv players who regularly trained on it. England ended up losing 2–1 in Moscow, but our 'Fink Tank' article had made it clear that the plastic pitch was not to blame.

Another game that fired the imagination was the 2012 Champions League final between Bayern Munich and Chelsea. The game would be played in Bayern's home stadium, leading to many newspaper articles discussing the home advantage they would enjoy. It occurred to me that data analysis could help to answer this question. They might be at home, but instead of a stadium with a huge majority of Bayern fans, there would be approximately equal numbers of Bayern and Chelsea fans, plus a very large number of Uefa's VIP guests.

As it turned out, there had been a few European finals played at the home stadium of one of the teams. The last of these had been Sporting Clube de Portugal's 3–1 Uefa Cup final loss 'at home' against CSKA Moscow in 2005. All in all, there had been six European finals played at home stadiums, and four had been won by the 'home' team. It wasn't enough data to draw any conclusions. There had to be some more data available somewhere. I discovered that the domestic cup finals in Sweden, Denmark, Norway and France were played at a club stadium, and that the stadium's 'home' clubs had played in multiple cup finals. AIK had played eight Swedish Cup finals at the Råsunda Stadium. FC Copenhagen had played seven finals at Parken. Lyn played eight and Vålerenga played two finals at the Ullevaal Stadion they shared. And Paris Saint-Germain had played five finals at Parc des Princes.

With a decent number of 'home' cup finals available, I could run our forecasting model on old Scandinavian and French seasons to find out if these teams really did enjoy a home advantage. Tracking down data for old league games played decades ago in Norway and Sweden was a challenge, but I was able to find enough to predict 19 of the 30 finals. In France, it looked like Paris Saint-Germain had a large home advantage in finals – they'd won four, drawn one (in 90 minutes) and lost only one, against a much stronger Monaco side in 1985.

But the Scandinavian clubs had fared much worse in their home finals. They'd won 12 but drawn five (in 90 minutes) and lost nine of the finals. Overall, the results were more consistent with there being no home advantage in effect than a normal home advantage. But the home teams' cup final results were not quite bad enough to discount the possibility that full home advantage was in effect. It was possible that the 'home' teams had just been unlucky to win so few of the finals.

Another avenue of research focused on distance travelled. In their 1995 work, Clarke and Norman had also shown that home advantage increased as the distance the away team had to travel increased. We realised there was a famous game played on neutral territory where one team often travelled a much shorter distance than the other: the FA Cup final. Between 1947 and 2000 London clubs won 11, drew eight and lost five Wembley cup finals. And for England we had a full record of league and cup results that allowed us to retrospectively forecast each team's chances in each cup final. London clubs averaged 0.33 more goals than their opponents in the cup finals, much higher than the equal goal difference we predicted if there was no home advantage at play. If the London club experienced full home advantage, we'd have expected them to score 0.53 more goals than their opponents. The results were not quite statistically significant, but they were consistent with some form of home advantage being in effect. Since the FA Cup final returned to the new Wembley in 2007, 10 out of 17 finals have featured one London club.[6] The London clubs' goal difference since 2007 has averaged +0.8 per game.

The evidence, though not conclusive, suggested that Bayern

might enjoy some form of home advantage against Chelsea in the 2012 final. They were the stronger team and would have been favourites at a neutral stadium, with about a 57% chance of winning the Champions League. Full home advantage would increase their winning chance to 67%. Chelsea ended up winning the game on penalties, but Bayern certainly played like the home team – they generated 4.4 Expected Goals to Chelsea's 0.7. In a classic case of paying more attention to the result than the performance, Chelsea awarded victorious caretaker manager Roberto Di Matteo a two-year contract. He was sacked just 21 games after signing his new contract.

Keep It Tight, Lads

The academic literature on home advantage and our attempts at the Fink Tank to understand it showed that things like distance travelled and familiarity with the stadium may affect home advantage. But the size of the effects was small. A large distance travelled could increase home advantage a bit but there was still a huge chunk of unexplained home advantage between next-door neighbours. Most of the academic literature was concerned with results or goals. But I had access to detailed event data to help me explore aspects of play beyond goals.

In the Premier League playing at home gave about a 33% boost to goal-scoring. Looking at Expected Goals, there was also a 30% boost. But the mechanism by which the extra goals came about was instructive. The *number* of shots was 24% higher at home than away, as was the number of shots on target. But the shot accuracy – how many tested the goalkeeper – was no different for the away team. However, the shot *conversion* – how many shots hit the back of the net – was 11.3% compared to 10.5% for away teams: 8% higher for home teams in relative terms. It seemed that the biggest contributor to home advantage was the volume of attacking that the home team was doing. When a shot happened, it was no more likely to be accurate at home compared to away, but a lot more shots occurred at home than away.

I tried to measure the teams' 'attacking intent' by calculating the number of shots per pass. If teams are happy to defend, they will pass the ball around without trying to attack or make a couple of passes before kicking the ball up field. Shots per pass also showed a strong and significant home advantage of 17%. This 'attacking intent' home advantage was much stronger than a simple measure of number of passes made, where the home total exceeded the away teams' by only 5%.

I have a pet theory that home advantage is partly a self-fulfilling prophecy. In the old days, a long journey to the opposition stadium, a very different pitch, and a passionate and possibly violent crowd probably had a big effect on the away team. Manager instructions to 'keep them quiet for the first 10 minutes' or 'keep it tight, a draw is a good result' were likely very sensible. But travel has become easier, pitches more standardised and crowds less violent. The value of a draw has also decreased since the introduction of three points for a win, but today's teams often persist in playing much more defensively away from home, with much less justification.

However, the 'self-fulfilling prophecy' didn't explain the whole story. A 7% higher conversion of shots into goals for home teams suggested there was something more to home advantage than just the *amount* of attacking home teams were doing. So I also looked at *expected* conversion rates through the lens of Expected Goals. It turned out that home teams were converting more of their shots because they were taking shots from higher quality locations. The players were not executing their shooting skills any better at home, they were simply able to take shots from more advantageous locations and situations. The discovery that a big chunk of home advantage is due to volume of attacking rather than execution of skill chimed with results from another sport. Baseball has a small home advantage compared to other major sports, and it is the sport that most depends on individual skill execution. Every action in a baseball game pits the pitcher's skill against the batter's. In their book *Scorecasting*, Toby Moskowitz and Jon Wertheim showed that pitchers and batters pitch and bat about as well away from home as at home.[7] I'd found the same for shot-takers in football: they convert their shots about as well away from home as at home, they just get fewer opportunities from inferior situations.

Crowding the Ref, Reffing the Crowd

The other statistics that leapt out were referee-influenced events. Home teams were awarded 70% more penalties than away teams. This compared to 10% more free-kicks leading to a direct attempt on goal. Free-kicks further away from the opposition goal did not display much of a home advantage. Some of the increased shot quality that home teams enjoyed was due to the larger number of penalties and direct free-kicks they were awarded.

The behaviour of referees is very difficult to measure, but a brilliant paper published in 2002 by Alan Nevill, Nigel Balmer and Mark Williams had shed some light on the matter.[8] They recruited 40 qualified referees from the North Staffordshire Referees Club and played them a video of Liverpool versus Leicester City from the 1998/99 Premier League season. Twenty-two of the referees were shown the game with the volume turned up, and the rest with the sound muted. The game was paused after each one of 47 'contentious incidents' and the refs were asked whether a foul should be given against Liverpool or against Leicester, or whether there was no foul. They could also say that they weren't certain if a foul should be given.

The results were striking. The refs who watched the game on mute were significantly more likely to give a foul against the home team (an extra 2.3 fouls, a 15% increase), and were more likely to say there was no foul. They were also significantly less likely to say they were uncertain whether a foul should be given. It must have been very satisfying for the researchers to find that the numbers of home and away fouls actually given in the game were almost identical to the decisions given by the refs watching the game with the volume turned up. The simple act of playing crowd noise while watching a game on video influenced referees. Surely the effect of the crowd in a live game would be even stronger.

The former Premier League referee Jeff Winter said in a 2008 *Observer* interview: 'I can only speak for myself, but I never, ever felt I was influenced by the crowd.'[9] Referees act in good faith and try not to be influenced by the crowd, but Nevill's research suggested that they are, and the strong and significant home advantage for penalties and cards also suggested that referees are the medium through which the crowd can exert its influence. Of course, correlation doesn't imply causation, but as Randall Munroe put it: 'It does waggle its eyebrows suggestively and gesture furtively while mouthing "look over there".'

My friend Natxo Palacios-Huerta found more eyebrow-raising referee behaviour in 2005 by studying injury-time.[10] He found that referees add less injury-time when a home team is leading in a close game than when they are behind. When the home team is behind by one goal, there is 35% more injury-time. When they are ahead by one there is 29% less injury-time. If the game is not close, with a goal difference of at least 2 heading into the final minute, there is no significant difference in injury-time. The favouritism shown to the home team in injury-time persisted even after the researchers controlled for the number of substitutions and cards, and the strengths and budgets of each team.

Behind Closed Doors

It seemed an impossible task to properly disentangle the true causes of home advantage but in 2020 the world changed with the onset of Covid-19. A trivial and unexpected side effect of the pandemic was that football games were played with no fans in attendance. Elite football returned first in the German Bundesliga and shortly after in the Premier League. The Bundesliga games were watched with great interest because they were just about the only football games in the world being played. Almost all other live entertainment had been curtailed in the efforts to curb the spread of the virus.

Very soon after its restart, lots of people realised that German home teams were winning much less often than they had before the pandemic. I took a look at the data in mid-June when 47 Bundesliga games had been played behind closed doors. The Premier League would soon resume and I wanted to know if there were any differences to playing behind closed doors that we needed to be aware of. The results were weird. Bookmakers had been taken by surprise by the Bundesliga results – their odds implied they had not expected home advantage to change with no fans present. In the second division the home teams were winning as often as usual, but third division teams had seen a drop in home wins similar to the Bundesliga. The reason behind fewer wins in the Bundesliga and the third tier was that both teams were producing fewer shots on target, but the home team's decline was much steeper.

The results were different enough to normal German football that I decided we had to revise our forecasting model to allow for a different home advantage when games were played behind closed doors. Instead of one home advantage effect per competition we would have two, and we would also allow for an 'away advantage' because the Bundesliga had shown away teams might also score at a different rate in an empty stadium.

Across Europe, home scoring behind closed doors dropped by 10%. In addition, there was an away advantage compared to a normal game. Away teams scored about 10% more behind closed doors. The effect was particularly strong in the Premier League, where home advantage was wiped out almost entirely. Home teams' chance of a win reduced from 47% to 38% and away teams' chance leapt from 29% to 37%. Not every league saw a decrease in home advantage. In Denmark home teams were more likely to win behind closed doors than in front of a crowd. But the vast majority of leagues saw fewer home goals and more away goals.[11] The same pattern was seen in the Americas, with a large decline in home advantage in Brazil, Argentina, Colombia, Ecuador, Mexico and the US.

Splitting home advantage into quantity and quality – the amount of shots and the conversion of shots into goals – showed that home teams in Europe shot about 22% more than away teams, and converted at about a 6% higher rate. Behind closed doors, home teams shot at a rate only 13% higher than away teams. The conversion advantage also disappeared, because away teams had increased their conversion to the same level as the home teams.

The Devil in the Detail

The picture of home advantage behind closed doors had been complicated by another novelty: the video assistant referee. VAR had been introduced in Germany in the 2017/18 season and in 2019/20, before lockdown, home advantage had gradually slumped to only 7%. By contrast, 2019/20 was the first season of VAR in the Premier League and home advantage had not decreased. Since the world reopened, home advantage in both leagues has returned to pre-VAR levels. The difference in crowds and the difference in VAR lets us look more closely at the changes in home advantage for different aspects of play.

In the Bundesliga, the large home advantage seen in penalties had declined before lockdown. Before the pandemic started in 2019/20, away teams received more penalties than home teams. The relative lack of home team penalties continued when audiences were limited, and then bounced back when stadiums reopened. The Premier League underwent a similar journey. The league's first season of VAR, 2019/20, was extremely unusual in that more penalties were awarded to away teams. In lockdown, penalty home advantage more or less disappeared, and then made a partial comeback since reopening. In both leagues we see the strange effect that penalty home advantage is stronger today than it was in 2019/20, the early days of VAR. Yellow cards show the same pattern, with home and away teams having much more parity in empty stadiums than in front of crowds, and yellow card home advantage bouncing back to pre-Covid levels since reopening.

The pandemic did not only affect referees. Teams felt the effects too, though in subtle ways. The 'attacking intent' metric of shots per pass was the place where the signal was clearest. In Germany home teams had historically shown 15% more attacking intent than away teams. This dropped to about 5% in empty and limited audience situations. And since reopening, it shot back up to 17%. Exactly the same thing happened in the Premier League. Historic extra attacking intent of 17% for the home team dropped to 5% and immediately rebounded to 17% upon reopening.

The results hinted that referees certainly seemed to behave differently in empty stadiums, but then so did teams. It is perfectly understandable that both referees and players are influenced by the conditions in which they play. Referees are not *intentionally* biased, but they are biased towards the home team. And even without the intervention of the referee, the teams themselves help to cause home advantage through their defensive away tactics. Brentford's Matthew Benham wants his teams to attack, even when 1–0 up in the 90th minute. An even more important situation in which to attack is away from home: reducing the home team's advantage could be worth half a Lionel Messi. We have seen that, referees aside, home advantage mostly plays out in the *amount* of attacking a team does away from home, rather than their ability to convert the chances they concede. And we've seen that away teams appear to have less attacking intent than home teams. Away teams who unshackle themselves from the traditional mantra of 'keep it tight' stand to win a few more points, and a few points can mean the difference between winning the Premier League and coming second.

15.

Stats and Snake Oil[1]

*The amount of energy necessary to refute bullshit is an order
of magnitude bigger than to produce it*

Paul Kedrosky

We Should Have Sold Suárez?

After Brendan Rodgers was sacked in October 2015, the football
world lined up to give the Transfer Committee a good kicking, and
my Research department received its fair share of the criticism. I
didn't really mind criticism in the press, or even from ex-managers
and players. We were trying to do something new and we didn't
expect it to be welcomed with open arms, especially when the
results looked so bad. The slings and arrows we received from the
analytics community did sting, though. The media policy in place
at Liverpool meant (quite rightly) that we couldn't explain how or
why things had gone wrong, but external consultancies were quick
to point out how awful our data analysis must have been.

Just after Brendan's departure, an article was published by a consultancy business raising the possibility that the analytics team at
Liverpool was simply not very good and that our analysis may
amount to no more than just counting tackles. I can take criticism,
and if I was looking at Liverpool from the outside I may well have
written a similar blog post. But I'd had previous experience of this
company that caused this particular piece to stick in my throat.

In July 2013, they had sent Liverpool an analysis asking how much

Luis Suárez was worth to the club. Arsenal had offered us a transfer fee of just over £40 million for Suárez a few days before. Our internal analysis considered Suárez to be Liverpool's best player and one who would cost more than £40 million to replace. This was not at all controversial. It was completely in line with conventional wisdom and with the opinion of the rest of the Transfer Committee. But their analysis had a different take.

They pointed out that Liverpool's goal difference was better when Suárez didn't play than when he did, and that the club should seriously consider selling. I couldn't believe what I was reading. I was amazed to see that in 2013 a professional analytics company was using 'plus-minus' analysis to recommend selling a player. This was the same sketchy analysis the English football press had used years before to suggest that Gareth Bale was a poor player. By 2013, detailed performance data had been available for a long time, but the consultancy's analyst ignored it in favour of the observation that Liverpool's goal difference had been +0.5 per game when Suárez played and +1 when he didn't.

Suárez had only missed 10 Premier League games through injury and suspension, and Liverpool's brilliant +1 goal difference per game when he didn't play had been entirely due to a 6–0 thumping of Newcastle in April 2012, just after he began his ban for biting Branislav Ivanović. The analysis didn't stand up to scrutiny. To be fair, they did point out that the results were not statistically significant. But if results are not statistically significant, the conclusion must be 'the results aren't significant' rather than 'you should consider selling Suárez'. Suárez signed for Barcelona in 2014 for £65 million. If we'd followed their bad statistical advice it would have cost us nearly £25 million.

During the explosion of interest in football data analysis in the 2010s, we were faced with many more incorrect arguments about football from a new breed of football consultant, keen to jump on the data bandwagon. Most of the incorrect arguments were wrong in ways more subtle than the 'sell Suárez' analysis. If you are not trained in data analysis it can be difficult to see where the missteps in a bad analysis are. Using data to analyse football is a bit like using dynamite. It has the potential to be very powerful, but unless handled carefully it can blow up in your face.

Are Corners Worthless?

The Numbers Game, written in 2013 by Chris Anderson and David Sally, was the first book to cover the burgeoning interest in football data analysis. I was excited to read it. It was full of provocative statements that were catnip to the budding online football data community. But reading the book I found myself agreeing with conventional wisdom more often than with the analysis being presented. This was unnerving to me: if I was coming to different conclusions to other data analysts then one of us was wrong. And worse, to the traditional football world it might look like data analysis is just another opinion. If analysts can't even agree among themselves then why should owners or managers trust what they say?

One of the strongest conclusions in *The Numbers Game* was that the number of goals a team scores does not increase with the number of corners they win. My work on Possession Value had shown that set-pieces were valuable and that for the average team a corner kick was often a higher value situation than having the ball in open play. But *The Numbers Game* was adamant: 'The total number of goals a team scores does not increase with the number of corners it wins. The correlation is essentially zero. You can have one corner or you can have seventeen corners: it will have no significant impact on the number of goals you score.'

My colleagues at Liverpool were reading this book and wondering why it was saying something very different to what I'd told them. I'd have to reconsider my analysis of set-piece situations and issue a mea culpa if I'd made a mistake. The conclusion that corners were not correlated with goals hinged on looking at the average number of goals scored for a given number of corners won. In the

Premier League between 2001/02 and 2011/02, teams who won zero corners scored 1.24 goals per game. But teams who won exactly one corner scored only 1.03 goals. After that, the number of goals creeps up with the number of corners, but not by much. Teams winning exactly eight corners scored 1.41 goals on average. And beyond eight corners won there is no further increase in goals. These results do look pretty unimpressive and the correlation between the number of corners and average points gained does seem to be about zero.

There is, however, a big problem with analysing average data. Teams win exactly one corner in a game far more often than they win zero corners. A team wins between one and eight corners 78% of the time, and between one and eight corners was exactly where the average number of goals *did* increase. We should pay much more attention to the places where there is more data available, by weighting each number of corners by the frequency with which that number of corners happened. Performing this weighting changes the results dramatically. Instead of zero correlation, one extra corner won was associated with 0.024 extra goals scored, beyond any statistical doubt. The extra 0.024 goals was broadly in line with the 2% goal probability that I'd found for corners in my Possession Value model.

Still, 0.024 goals doesn't sound like much. But the question is always 'Compared to what?' For example, a 2.4% chance of a goal is higher than most teams have when they have midfield possession against a set defence. I convinced my colleagues that corners were worthwhile, and years later it became apparent to the world that Brentford, the other analytics pioneers, felt the same way.

Are Clean Sheets More Important than Goals?

One of the conclusions of *The Numbers Game* was 'o>1'. That is to say 'a clean sheet is worth more than a goal scored'. This conclusion was a big surprise to me, as all my work had found that defence and attack were about equally as important as one another when it came to winning. I certainly believed that defenders and goalkeepers were undervalued compared to attackers, but I didn't believe they were fundamentally *more* important than attackers. The authors of *Scorecasting* had analysed various sports and found that the influence of attack was about the same as the influence of defence in each and every one. And 'o>1' must have also come as a surprise to Matthew Benham and others in the analytics vanguard who believed in 'attack, attack, attack'. The promise of soccer analytics was to discover and exploit knowledge that conventional wisdom ignored. And this discovery of the large value of defence compared to attack was a prime candidate for an early analytics 'aha' moment. After all, a Chelsea executive told the *Financial Times* in 2009: 'If you look at 10 years in the Premier League, there is a stronger correlation between clean sheets and where you finish than goals scored and where you finish.'[2]

The Numbers Game expanded on this clean sheets theme. The argument went like this. The relationship between goals scored and points won over a Premier League season is strong. And the impact of one extra goal scored is worth about one extra point. The correlation between clean sheets and points is not as strong as between goals and points, contrary to what the Chelsea executive claimed. But one extra clean sheet has a bigger impact than one extra goal. Clean sheets are worth 2.5 points, goals scored are worth 1, defence is more important than attack, end of story. The analysis kind of makes sense. If you have a clean sheet, the worst you can do is draw 0–0. Any other scoreline guarantees three points.

Unfortunately, the analysis was wrong. The first problem was in the measurement of how many points a goal scored is worth. If you plot goals scored against points won for a few Premier League seasons, you will find that teams who score more tend to win more points (obviously). And teams who score one extra goal win one extra point on average. The same goes for defence – an extra goal conceded costs about a point. But something strange happens when you look at the relationship between goal *difference* and points. The correlation between goal difference and points is extremely strong, much stronger than the correlation between goals scored and points. But the impact of increasing your goal difference by 1 is worth only about 0.7 points. How can this possibly be the case if a goal scored is worth one point and a goal conceded is worth one point? It is because the teams who are good at scoring are usually also good at not conceding. And, related to that, some goals mean more than others.

We can double check this result that an extra goal is worth about 0.7 points by using the Dixon-Coles forecasting model. In a Premier League game between average teams, the home team is forecast to win 1.6 points and the away team 1.1. What would the points return be if one of the teams scored immediately from kick-off? Dixon-Coles predicts that the home team should expect 2.3 points if they effectively start the game one goal up, and the away team should expect 1.8 points if they were to score from kick-off. Each team's expected points return from a goal scored at the start of the match has increased by 0.7 points, in line with the season-long term relationship between goal difference and points.

But not all goals are scored at the start of the game. Some are completely meaningless, such as when Daniel James scored in injury-time for Manchester United in their 9–0 win against Southampton in 2021, or when Ashley Cole made it 8–0 for Chelsea against Wigan Athletic in 2010. Those goals were effectively worth zero points, as the game was already won. Other goals are crucial, like Alex Iwobi's last-gasp winner for Everton against Newcastle United in 2022. The only goal of the game, it was effectively worth two points. Penalties can even be scored after the final whistle as Brighton found out to their cost in 2020. The referee had blown the final whistle, but a VAR check awarded a penalty to Manchester United. Bruno Fernandes converted to make it 3–2, a goal worth exactly two points.[3]

A goal might be worth 0.7 points if it's scored right at the start of the game, but we should check the times and the scorelines when goals are actually scored just in case there is a glut of meaningless ones or a surplus of highly important ones. I looked at every goal scored in the Premier League between 2008/09 and 2022/23 and calculated the expected points return before and after each goal,[4] based on the current scoreline and the time remaining in the game. On average, a goal for the home team was 0.67 expected points and a goal for the away team was worth 0.72. The average impact of a goal in the Premier League is about the same as the impact of a goal scored straight from the kick-off: the extra impact of those crucial goals is cancelled out by the meaningless late goals in 3–0 and 4–0 wins.

The second problem with *The Numbers Game*'s analysis of clean sheets is that they are a poor way of measuring defence. We know that a game ending with a clean sheet is better for our team than a game that ends without one. But measuring defence by 'clean sheet or not' leaves a lot of information on the table. After all, it must be important to know how many goals a team concedes on the occasions they do not keep a clean sheet. To find out if clean sheets tell us anything that goals conceded doesn't, I performed a simple statistical analysis.[5] The number of goals scored and conceded over a Premier League season explained 92% of the variation in points won. An equivalent model that used goals scored and clean sheets to estimate points won explained 90% of the variation in points won over a season. Both models were very good at explaining the number of points won, but the goals conceded model did a slightly better job than clean sheets.

Finally, what about the observation that a clean sheet is worth more than a goal scored? Again, using goals scored and clean sheets to predict points won, I found that one extra goal is worth 0.72 points, and one clean sheet is worth 1.67. Superficially, one clean sheet *is* worth more than one goal. But we are not comparing apples with apples. There are usually more goals in a game than there are clean sheets. The correct question to ask is 'What is the impact when a team improves from average to good in a particular aspect of play?' And going from average to good is very different for goals and clean sheets. On average, Premier League teams score 51 goals and keep 11 clean sheets per season. An 80th percentile team, i.e., the fourth best in the league, scores 64 goals and keeps 14 clean sheets.

The increase in the number of clean sheets between the average team and a Champions League contender is small because a clean sheet is a limited resource that is difficult to improve. One extra goal scored may be worth less than one extra clean sheet kept, but goals are not as rare as clean sheets or as difficult to generate. In terms of goals scored, going from average to good means 13 extra goals, and 13 x 0.72 = 9.4 extra points. In terms of clean sheets, going from average to good means three extra clean sheets, and 3 x 1.67 = 5 extra points scored.

The supreme importance of clean sheets turned out to be a statistical illusion. If we consider clean sheets to be the most important measure of a team's success, then Middlesbrough's 2016/17 season was successful – their 11 clean sheets was mid-table. But they only managed to win 28 points while getting relegated. Clean sheets did not translate to points because their goal-scoring was poor. At the other end of the spectrum, Manchester United's 1999/2000 team only managed 12 clean sheets, but won 91 points and the league.

Darren Bent Versus Wayne Rooney

Teams that want to win more should look for the players whose goals matter the most. This was the argument that led to *The Numbers Game* claiming that Darren Bent was the standout player in the Premier League. The idea was to weight the number of goals scored by their impact on the game outcome – after all, the first or second goal a team scores is usually much more valuable than the third or fourth. This can be quantified by looking at the average number of points a team wins when they score zero, one, two, etc. goals. Teams who score one goal in a game on average win 0.85 points more than teams who score zero. Teams who score three goals in a game win 0.55 more points than teams who score two. Therefore the third goal is usually worth less than the first, and this was the weighting that *The Numbers Game* used to value strikers' contributions.

At the time I thought Bent rated among the Premier League's

best forwards, but I didn't think he was the league's best striker. Using the method of rewarding the first and second goals more than others showed that Bent's goals were extremely valuable for Sunderland. A few other players scored more goals than him, but adding up the points contributions of those goals placed him second in 2009/10 and in 2010/11, and top when looking at both seasons together. The idea of looking for players who can produce in the critical moments – so-called 'clutch' players – is seductive. Every team would like a player who can be relied upon to score when it matters. So I decided to investigate the differences between the number of goals strikers scored and their impact further.

The first thing I found was that the impact-adjusted goals followed the actual number of goals very closely. The correlation between the two exceeded 98%. That's not a surprise – if you don't score a lot, then you can't affect your team's chance of winning much, and vice versa. The way to find the 'clutch' players is to calculate if players are generating more points for their teams than expected given the number of goals they scored. Darren Bent was the best player in the league by this measure, scoring goals that were about 15% more valuable than those of the average striker. But there was a peculiar pattern in the rankings spat out by this method. The top of the list was dominated by players from smaller teams – Darren Bent at Sunderland, Clint Dempsey at Fulham, D. J. Campbell at Blackpool and Hugo Rodallega at Wigan. And near the bottom of the list, scoring less meaningful goals, were Andrey Arshavin, Nicolas Anelka and Florent Malouda, all playing for Champions League teams.

It would be a wonderful thing if the strikers at smaller teams really were better than those at Champions League giants – a team could simply hoover up the talent at Sunderland and Blackpool and win the league in true *Moneyball* fashion. But I didn't believe the results, because the method of weighting goals by their impact had not adjusted for *opportunity*. If you play for a terrible team, then every goal you score is likely to be the first or second and likely to be quite important. In other words, the quality of your team goes a long way to deciding how important the goals you score are.

Let's take Darren Bent and Wayne Rooney in 2009/10 as an example. Both players scored goals that were more important than average, but Bent's contribution was 14% more important than average while Rooney's was only 8% more important. Sunderland scored 48 goals that season, and 79% of Sunderland's goals were the first or second they scored. Manchester United scored 86, and only 65% of their goals were the first or second. Bent had much more opportunity to be the first or second goal-scorer than Rooney. Thanks to their greater firepower, the impact of a goal is expected to be lower for Manchester United than for Sunderland, and Rooney was being punished for it.

After adjusting for differences in opportunity, both Bent's and Rooney's contributions remained more important than average. But Rooney now looked the more impactful player. And the rest of the league table changed. Anelka, who had looked a less impactful player than average, was revealed to be much more impactful than expected given Chelsea's 103 goals that season.

The answer to who is the most impactful striker varied a lot depending on how it was measured and, even worse, the strikers could not seem to repeat their level of impact in one season the following season. This is not very surprising – the circumstances in which strikers score their goals are often outside their control. They cannot easily choose to score more of their goals when it's 0–0 and fewer when the team is 3–0 up. Goal rate, Expected Goal rate and Possession Value added per 90 minutes are all far more repeatable season to season than any measure of 'impact'.

The Tyranny of Metrics

One of the problems with statistics, according to the writer Marilyn vos Savant, is that they can be used to support or undercut any argument. This is especially true of football statistics. In the good old days when data was limited, the analyst's task was to wring every drop of signal from meagre data sources to try to say something meaningful about performance. Today a torrent of data arrives for every game and the analyst's task is to make sense of it. In the era of 'big data' there is a pervading belief that the 'bigness' of the data will somehow magically give the answer to any question you might ask of it. I do not share this belief. I prefer Nate Silver's approach to analysis: 'Statistical inferences are much stronger when backed up by theory or at least some deeper thinking about their root causes.'

Log on to any data provider's platform today and search for your favourite player. You will be bombarded by a plethora of basic and advanced statistics: goals, assists, Expected Goals, headed shots, touches in box, key passes, progressive carries, blocks, pressures, clearances, interceptions and so on. All the data you could ever want is at your fingertips. Most clubs would like to find a player who scores as highly as possible on as many metrics as possible but it turns out that they are guaranteed to run into problems, thanks to a mathematical concept called the Pareto Frontier.

As an example, imagine a team is looking for a midfielder and that they would like a player with a high rate of Expected Assists and a high rate of Pressure Regains. The players who are on the Pareto Frontier are those who have the highest rate of Pressure Regains for a given rate of Expected Assists. In the 2020/21 season in the big five European leagues, Kevin de Bruyne had the highest rate of Expected Assists but an unspectacular rate of Pressure Regains. At the other end of the spectrum, no midfielder matched Everton's hard-tackling Allan for Pressure Regains, but he had a low rate of Expected Assists. And somewhere in between were players like Thiago Alcântara and Giovani Lo Celso. They had lower Expected Assists rates than De Bruyne and lower Pressure Regains than Allan, but if you wanted more regains than Lo Celso offered, you'd have to compromise on Expected Assists. If you wanted more assists than Thiago, you would have to compromise on regains.

In all, 13 of the 492 midfielders were on the Pareto Frontier. They are the outlying data points right on the edge of a cloud of midfielders. Each of the 13 represented a combination of Expected Assists and Pressure Regains that could not be beaten. Once you find the set of players on the Pareto Frontier you will find that there is a negative correlation between the metrics, no matter which metrics you have decided to look at. Players that are better on one metric will look worse on the other. Among midfielders there is not much correlation between Expected Assists and Pressure Regains. But if we are only interested in players who look better than average on one of these two aspects, the correlation magically becomes negative. This is because we've removed the 25% of players who look bad on both aspects. Now we are left with the 25% who look good on both aspects, and the 50% who look good on one aspect and bad on the other.[6] This majority of players who look good in one way but bad in another is what drives the negative correlation. And by selecting only the most extreme players on the Pareto Frontier we make the correlation more negative still: you can have a player that looks brilliant on one aspect of play or the other, but not both.

Now let's say we also want our midfielder to have a high pass completion rate (we know by now this is not a very important metric, but some teams still pay attention to it). The number of players on the Pareto Frontier increases to 28. Our original 13 remain as, no matter how bad their pass completion rate, they cannot be beaten on the first two metrics. But 15 new midfielders appear on the frontier. Marco Verratti and Sergio Busquets had lower Pressure Regains and lower Expected Assists than Thiago, but they had a higher pass completion rate than him so they get added to the list. Maxime López and Arthur Melo looked completely unremarkable on the first two metrics but they had a higher pass completion than any of the 13 originally on the Pareto Frontier: the higher the pass completion we want, the more we have to compromise on our first two metrics.

By asking for three metrics to be optimised instead of two we've more than doubled the size of our shortlist. And this increase in shortlist size gets worse and worse as you add more metrics. Thirteen out of 492 players could not be beaten on a combination of two metrics. Twenty-eight could not be beaten on three. That increases to 70 when you look at five metrics, 133 when you look at seven and 240 when you look at 10, and at this point the shortlist is useless. Data analysis can't be advertised as a tool to filter players if 240 players are on the 'short' list.

This is the tyranny of metrics. If you look at enough of them, most players will look extremely good in one way or another, to the point that half of all midfielders are 'optimal' when you compare them across 10 metrics. By 'optimal' I mean that if you want to find a player who looks better than, say, Allan on one of the 10 metrics, then he will look worse than Allan on some of the other metrics. And this is one of the reasons why statistics can be used to support or undercut any argument about players. There will be some combination of metrics that the player under discussion will look particularly good or particularly bad on. I think this is how 'data' is used at lots of clubs. The manager or sporting director takes a look at the data of the player they want to sign, and cherry picks the metrics they look good on to support their decision. Or they are presented with a player they don't wish to sign and sift through the data to find a convenient metric he looks bad on.

A team looking for success must narrow their search to a few important metrics if they want to be efficient at finding suitable players. Goal probability added and saved from a Possession Value model, split into a few categories like passing, dribbling, shooting, ball-winning and defending space, is enough. This is what we did at Liverpool: avoiding the mistake of weighing up many different metrics allowed us to focus on what was important, and it was a successful approach. Once we had a shortlist we could study players' ratings in fine detail, but only once we had our shortlist.

Written in the Stars

The analyses discussed above were performed in good faith, and the missteps were only obvious to a trained statistician. The same goes for some other misuses of statistics, such as commentators on

Bundesliga games highlighting a team's 'efficiency' by compliment-
ing them for outscoring their Expected Goals rather than praising
the team that generated more Expected Goals. But there is a range
of products and services available to football clubs that do not perform their analyses in such good faith.

Igor Stimac played as a centre-back for West Ham United and
Croatia. In 2022, he was managing the Indian national team and was
reportedly convinced to take the advice of an astrologer to help
with his team selection.[7] The astrologer allegedly 'delved into the
astrological realm and provided a verdict for each player listed, from
"good" to "not recommended for the day"',[8] though Stimac later
denied the reports. Whatever the truth, we had been through a
similar experience at Liverpool. One of the coaching staff had been
approached by someone calling himself 'the football astrologer'
and my department was asked for its view. I was in another meeting, and in my absence the coach asked my colleague Tim what he
thought of the astrologer's website. The site included an astrological explanation of the inevitability of Germany winning the 2014
World Cup given the combination of star signs in their squad. Tim,
an astrophysics Ph.D., naturally assumed that the question was a
joke so replied: 'Yes, this looks totally legitimate.' The coach immediately invited the astrologer to come and present his methods at
the training ground. Astrology is obviously nonsense[9] and we were
thankfully able to stop horoscopes having any effect on our team.

Ironically, there is a significant correlation between star sign and
success in football, but it is mundane rather than celestial in its
nature. The 'relative age effect' is seen in most sports:[10] the oldest
children in a cohort tend to be the most physically developed, and
so have an advantage compared to their team-mates. The result of
this is that there is an excess of Librans in the Premier League,
because the age cut-off for youth football is 1 September, and an
excess of Aquariuses on the Continent, because the age cut-off is 1
January.[11] In the top divisions in France, Germany, Italy and Spain,
more than one-third of starts are made by players born in the first
three months of the year, and less than one-fifth are made by players

born in the last three months of the year. The relative age effect is a bias that stops players born late in their school year from flourishing, but most clubs are yet to do anything about it.[12] The Basque team Athletic Club de Bilbao were an exception when my friend Natxo Palacios-Huerta was head of talent ID there. Natxo insisted that youth scouts be split into four groups. The first group could only scout players born in the first three months of the year, and the last could only scout players born in the last three months of the year. The relative age effect declined when equal resources were put to work on the youngest players in each age group.

Relative age effect aside, astrology has no predictive power when it comes to improving team selection or results, yet football clubs are strangely prone to seeking out easy answers like astrology promises to provide. Football is fundamentally a noisy, capricious business and it is difficult to control results. Services that promise to increase that control, even if it is only an illusion of control, are seductive.

Data analysis by contrast does not offer easy answers, or at least honest data analysis doesn't. Teams must invest time and money in raw data and in expertise to turn that data into predictive insights. The insights are probabilistic in nature, not absolute promises. A club may use good data analysis to recruit players who increase their promotion chance from 25% to 50%. Even then, there is a 50% chance promotion will not happen. At Liverpool we believed the processes we put in place increased our chances of success, but in 2016/17 and 2017/18 our Champions League qualification came down to the wire, and was decided on the final day. But crucially, we would have stuck with the process even if we hadn't qualified, and appreciated that our work had not guaranteed success, it had just shifted the odds in our favour.

16.

Stats and Crude Oil: The Future of Football

If people do not believe that mathematics is simple, it is only because they do not realise how complicated life is

John von Neumann

The Football Loop

I've written a lot about using data to help identify players and esti-mate the strength of teams. But this is not at all how coaches view the game. During the season the squad cannot be changed very much. The coach is concerned with maximising the talents of his current squad through teamwork and instilling a tactical plan. The quality and quantity of data now available for teams across the world mean that it can finally be used to impact tactics and teamwork.

To my mind, tactical evolution in football is not about three at the back or the inverted forward, but the philosophical approach to the game. Do teams want to play a possession game, a pressing game, a gegenpressing game, or defend deep? After Jürgen Klopp arrived at Liverpool in October 2015 our tactical approach shifted from Brendan Rodgers' brand of controlled possession. We played a mix of gegenpressing and all-out attack. It was thrilling to watch the gegenpress against big teams – a high-risk, high-reward strategy where a team tries to regain possession immediately after losing it. When it fails it fails badly, often allowing the opposition to create a dangerous chance as our players are stranded upfield. But when it works it can be sensational – 'No playmaker in the world can be as good as a good gegenpressing situation,' according to Jürgen.

It was also thrilling to watch an attacking approach working against defensive teams. I was on the edge of my seat in 2016/17 and 2017/18 as central defenders Dejan Lovren and Joël Matip pushed well into the opposition half whenever we had possession. Intellectually, I knew it was the right way to play against opponents with limited ambition, but it could be nerve-racking to experience live. I remained on the edge of my seat for the next three years as I watched our full-backs, Trent Alexander-Arnold and Andy Robertson, play like wingers, and Naby Keïta risk possession again and again by attempting a killer pass. Despite the high level of anxiety it caused, it maximised our chances of success. A team that wants to win the title must aim for three points in every game, not one.

Football philosophy can be defined by the cycle of attack and defence, and managers can be characterised by where they like to concentrate their efforts. In open play, there are four phases for a team to cycle through. Possession of the ball, transition into defence when the ball is lost, out-of-possession defence, and transition into possession when the ball is won. As a team cycles through the phases, so does their opponent. But the opposition experiences the opposite phase of play. Our opponent loses possession as we win it, and they defend as we attack.

The four-phase principle has its roots in Johan Cruyff's Barcelona and was systematised by Louis van Gaal. Its popularity has spread throughout football, via José Mourinho, Brendan Rodgers and others, demonstrating that the idea is useful no matter your preferred style of play. The cycle is an insightful way to characterise teams. Defensive teams concentrate on out-of-possession organisation and positioning. Attacking teams, meanwhile, concentrate on possession: upon winning possession, Barcelona's players are apparently told to find a safe pass that will secure the possession and allow the team time to organise an attack. Traditional pressing teams concentrate on the transition between out of possession and in possession, focusing on winning the ball back.

Tactical innovations are the result of disrupting the four-phase cycle. The gegenpressing game popularised by Ralf Rangnick and Jürgen attempts to disrupt the opponent's transition from defence to attack. Barcelona's strategy of finding a safe pass upon winning possession becomes hard to execute when the team that's just lost the ball swarms forward. Transitions are ripe for exploiting because teams tend to be positionally disorganised when possession is won or lost – precisely the reason why 'Look for a safe pass' was very good advice.

With the advent of tracking data, we data analysts can finally weigh in. Gegenpressing requires a high degree of teamwork. If the ball-winning player has at least one easy pass, gegenpressing will not work efficiently. The pressing players must press together, forcing a loss of possession, or forcing a rushed pass backwards and keeping up the pressure on the ball. This collective behaviour of players can be measured and analysed. If one of the players did not press, and an easy pass was made, we can replay the game inside our computer, and see what might have happened if the player did press. Using ideas like Pitch Control and Possession Value, we can measure the impact of a press that should have happened but didn't.

Analysing the collective behaviour of players can also suggest further innovations. Pitch Control shows that when players rush forwards they leave space behind them. The counter-strategy to gegenpressing might be to play a 'percentage ball' forwards into the space that the pressers have just vacated. During Covid, Liverpool lost a bizarre game against Aston Villa 7–2. Villa seemed uninterested in possession and, under pressure, often just kicked the ball forward. Whether through luck or good judgement the ball often found itself in a huge amount of space for a Villa player to run on to. Villa's contentment to kick the ball away turned into an advantage against a gegenpressing team.

Strategies and counter-strategies can be found for any phase of the possession cycle. Diego Simeone's Atlético Madrid concentrate on the defensive side of the game – we saw that, in 2012, they had low overall possession but a high level of 'dangerous possession'. But the approach does not work so well against a similarly defensive manager. Atlético faced José Mourinho's Chelsea in 2014 in the Champions League quarter-finals. It was suggested to Atlético captain Gabi that Chelsea's tactics may be to let Atlético have the ball. His response: 'We'll give it back.'[1] Atlético's success made teams nervous about attacking them, with the result that Atlético started to see more of the ball. Conversely, Pep Guardiola is the master of the possession phase of play, using it to control the game, pull the defence out of position, and wait for a high-value scoring opportunity to appear. In 2022/23, Manchester City's possessions lasted nearly 50% longer than the average Premier League team, and nearly 20% longer than second-placed Arsenal's. This controlled, probing nature of possession is a good compromise between playing high up the pitch and limiting the risk of a counter-attack, but requires very skilful players to be able to execute it.

The beauty of analysing the tactical movements and teamwork of the players is that it may finally allow us to measure the impact of managers properly. The dominant factor in success in football is the difference in skill and athleticism between the opposing players. The original edge in data analysis was to find more impactful players for less money, as we did at Liverpool. Having better players than your opponents can take you a long way. Real Madrid under Zinedine Zidane did not appear to have a sophisticated tactical plan, but they did have better players than nearly every other team on the planet. Teams like Manchester City and Liverpool have great players *and* good tactical plans, which leads to tactics and teamwork becoming the next edge. Gegenpressing is a good example of a tactic that requires teamwork, and this teamwork can compensate to some extent for inferior skills and athleticism. But the possibilities for advancements in teamwork, collective behaviour and counter-strategies have barely begun to be explored in football. Strategies to counter the 'percentage ball' solution to gegenpressing can be found, but will require more training and teamwork, and more analysis. Data will be the fuel for a tactical weapons race in football. The way to succeed in sport (and in business) is by being able to modify your tactics in the face of uncertainty.

The four-phase cycle has some similarities to the 'OODA loop'[2] theory of combat developed by US Air Force Colonel John Boyd. One of Boyd's conclusions was that if you can decide what to do and act quicker than your opponent you will have an advantage. Techniques like Barcelona's 'find an easy pass' and Liverpool's gegenpress are trained as an automatic way to get to the next phase of the game quicker than the opponent and therefore generate an advantage while they are disorganised. Another one of Boyd's conclusions was that you should invent new tactics designed to confuse the enemy. In football the question to ask is: 'How can we mess with our opponent's possession cycle?' This question is not asked enough: counters to gegenpressing and tiki-taka could have been found long before they were. In the future data analysis will accelerate the speed of tactical evolution and lead to more effective teamwork and collective movement among players.

Levelling the Playing Field

Given the increasing financial firepower of the biggest teams, what hope is there for smaller teams? One source of hope is the transfer market, but another might be set-pieces. The highest wages and transfer fees tend to pay for individual skill: the star players who can create chances and score goals earn the most money and transfer for the highest fees. But plenty of goals come from set-pieces, where individual skill makes less of a difference. Of the 52 goals that the average Premier League team scores, 41 come from open play, direct free-kicks and penalties. But 11 come from corners, crossed free-kicks, passed free-kicks and long throw-ins. Thinking in terms of Pitch Control, these set-piece situations are highly contested. When the box is packed with attackers and defenders neither team has much certainty that they will be the first to make contact with the ball. And if they do make contact, often it is not with a skilful controlled touch of the ball. In set-piece situations players have little time to react and insufficient space to bring the ball under control.

Set-pieces therefore appear to represent a way to level the playing field between richer teams and poorer teams. We can examine the data to see if this is really the case. In the Premier League there is a very, very strong correlation between goal difference and points – obviously if you score more goals than you concede you'll win more points. Separating out goal difference between open play and set-pieces shows there is no difference between them when it comes to winning points. It would be extremely surprising to find there was a difference. The number of goals you score and concede is what's important – it doesn't matter how you scored them!

This is the point at which set-piece goals begin to look different to open-play goals. There is not much correlation between teams' open-play goal difference and their set-piece goal difference. And the modest correlation is entirely driven by the big six. These teams win a lot more corners and free-kicks than the other 14 teams, so have more opportunities to score set-piece goals. For the 14 smaller teams there is *no* correlation between open-play goal difference and set-piece goal difference.

This means that the *proportion* of goals scored through set-pieces is higher the worse you are in attack, and concentrating on set-pieces can be a rewarding strategy.[3] For example, West Bromwich Albion, with Roy Hodgson in 2011/12 and with Tony Pulis in 2015/16, finished 10th thanks to set-piece goals. If the league was decided on only open-play goals they would have been relegated on both occasions.

We can also examine the relationship between wages and set-pieces, by flipping the wage question on its head. Instead of predicting team performance using wages, we can predict wages using team performance. The first result is that goal-scoring has a larger effect on wages than goal-conceding. Teams who score a lot tend to spend more on wages than teams who concede few. This is in line with our player salary and transfer fee predictions – goalkeepers and defenders are paid less and transfer for less than forwards.

The second result is that for the 14 smaller Premier League teams there is *no* correlation between wages and set-pieces. Teams who spend more money do not appear to have a better record when it comes to set-piece goal difference. The implication is that it is a cheap way to score more and concede fewer goals. Most teams spend a very small fraction of their time training for set-pieces. One exception might be Brentford. When I watched Liverpool lose 3–1 away to Brentford in early 2023 I was impressed by their corner routines. On one occasion they loaded all of their outfield players (except the corner taker) into our six-yard box. Some of them retreated before the corner was taken but we were clearly unsettled by Brentford's approach. In the game, Brentford generated more than one Expected Goal from corners, and scored one actual goal. Another Brentford goal from a corner was ruled out for offside and did not count towards their Expected Goals total.

Brentford have packed their team with giants. Defenders Ajer (196cm), Collins, Zanka and Goode are all over 190cm, and nine more of their 2023/24 squad are over 183cm in height. Until 2023 they also had Pontus Jansson (194cm) in their squad. Height is a feature that is relatively more important in set-piece situations than in open play. Their 2021/22 squad was the third tallest in the Premier League. After replacing the giant Jansson with Ben Mee (a rare centre-back under 183cm), they were a short team in 2022/23, but in 2023/24 were back to being one of the tallest squads.

Set-pieces give a free opportunity for the tallest players, often centre-backs, to join the attack. Anecdotally, qualities like height and strength that make players effective at attacking and defending set-pieces may make them less suitable to play the fast, possession-heavy football that the best teams play. Big defenders are often more comfortable defending deep than holding a high line, and tall attackers are often target men. The tallest squads over the past 10 Premier League seasons have been Tony Pulis-era Stoke City, and Tony Pulis-era West Bromwich Albion. These teams were very effective at set-pieces, but played a style of football that fans of other teams may not appreciate.

Set-piece goals are not a panacea for small teams. Scoring a lot of them this season is no guarantee of scoring a lot next season. Partly this is due to there being not very many of them. Even so, they are fundamentally less stable year to year than open-play goals. This may reflect the approach of the head coach. Some, like Pulis and Sam Allardyce, are known for the value they attach to set-piece situations. Others do not care so much for set-pieces and so when the coach changes, the team's attitude to set-pieces may change. But the high variation in set-piece goals year on year also reflects the greater element of chance at play in such situations. Own goals and lucky deflections occur more often in set-piece situations than in open play, making them less predictable.

I believe that data analysis has improved the watchability of football. But there is a risk it may become less watchable, or at least a slightly different sport, when more teams cotton on to the value of set-pieces. A set-piece dominated game might well be less aesthetically pleasing than today's open-play dominated game.

Petrochemical Football and the European Elite

Liverpool's achievements in the Klopp era have been remarkable. But the second, fourth and eighth highest points totals in Premier League history only led to one Premier League title.

At the same time, Manchester City, with the backing of its Abu Dhabi owners, have assembled the best football team ever seen. To get a sense of their long-term brilliance we can look at five-year average Premier League tables – and Manchester City have the best three in history. They achieved an incredible 91.7 points per season on *average* between 2017/18 and 2021/22. The best non-Manchester City performance is Chelsea in the early Abramovich years; between 2004/05 and 2008/09 they averaged 87.4 points per season. But even the first hydrocarbon-powered club was not too far ahead of its rivals: Alex Ferguson's Ronaldo-powered Manchester United averaged 86.8 points per season between 2005/2006 and 2009/10. Our super Liverpool team peaked at 86.4 points per season between 2017/18 and 2021/22. Manchester City's historical competitors all peaked between 86.4 and 87.4 points, within a single point of each other. But between 2020/21 and 2022/23 Manchester City have recorded five-year averages of 88.6, 91.6 and 89.4 points.

Despite their unprecedented Premier League success, Manchester City have, for the large part, been massively underrated by the football media and the public for years. In 2019/20, Liverpool won the Premier League title by 18 points and were at their historical apex in terms of team strength. But our models still rated Manchester City as 20% stronger than Liverpool and clear favourites to win a game against us at a neutral stadium.[4] The bookmakers agreed. After the title win, they predicted Manchester City to finish three points ahead of Liverpool in 2020/21. This was in line with our internal view that City's poor 2019/20 season was unusually bad by their own incredible standards. In fact our view was even more pessimistic. We thought we would end up six points behind City. After an injury-plagued season, Liverpool actually ended 2020/21 18 points behind them. An obvious answer to 'How to win the Premier League' is: 'First, make sure you're not competing against Pep Guardiola's Manchester City, or hope they become sated with success.'

Since 2009 Manchester City have used owner funding of £1.3 billion to build and maintain a world-class team able to spend very heavily in the transfer market and pay their players high wages. To put that funding into context, Roman Abramovich – the original oil-backed owner of a Premier League team – funded Chelsea to the tune of £800 million between 2009 and 2021. Abramovich's total funding of Chelsea since 2004 totalled £1.5 billion, with £700 million arriving between 2004 and 2009.[5] The difference between Abramovich and Abu Dhabi United Group is that Abramovich continued funding Chelsea directly throughout his reign. Abu Dhabi injected the vast majority of its funding between 2009 and 2014. Since 2015, Abu Dhabi has pumped only £81 million directly into Manchester City. [6,7]

To stand a chance of competing with Manchester City's financial power, we had to find some kind of edge, and that meant employing untried, sometimes risky techniques, such as data analysis and a Transfer Committee. We had to spend our money extremely wisely, despite having a revenue of €306 million back in 2015, the ninth highest in world football at the time.[8] In 2015, Manchester City were sixth, with a revenue of €414.4 million. We were very lucky to find Jürgen Klopp when he was undervalued and out of work. Competing against a team with, for all intents and purposes, unlimited resources is difficult when your owners sensibly demand that you live within your means. If a European giant like Liverpool finds it difficult, then most teams will find it impossible.

The arrival of Saudi billions into football in summer 2023 has dwarfed even Manchester City's rate of investment. In summer 2023 Liverpool players Fabinho and Jordan Henderson signed for Saudi clubs, where they earned much, much more than they did at Liverpool. Abu Dhabi with Manchester City, Qatar with Paris Saint-Germain and Saudi Arabia with Newcastle United have been accused of 'sportswashing'. Saudi Arabia's Crown Prince and Prime Minister, Mohammed bin Salman, is unequivocal about it. He told Fox News: 'If sportswashing is going to increase my GDP by 1%, then we'll continue doing sportswashing. I don't care [about the term]. I have 1% growth in GDP from sport and I am aiming for another 1.5%.'[9]

Sportswashing might actively seek to help a club dominate its league, but TV revenue has also helped increase inequality in football. The TV broadcast and prize money on offer in the Champions League has put the bigger clubs in every European country on a different financial plane to the rest. Owner funding has led to Manchester City dominating England and Paris Saint-Germain dominating France. But Champions League revenue has helped the big teams in every country dominate their domestic leagues too. Champions League qualification is a virtuous circle for the clubs who qualify. The huge revenue boost it brings allows good players to be retained with higher salaries and transfer fees to be spent to bring new talent to the club. Clubs who haven't qualified cannot compete financially. This was why we valued fourth place above anything else at

Liverpool: it was our route to financial firepower. But the result has been that, for the most part, the same teams qualify every year, which makes them even more likely to qualify next year. Champions League revenue also varies widely across countries, which cements the inequality between nations as well as within them. The result has been a gradual decrease in competitiveness, with the same teams winning domestic leagues year after year, and the same teams progressing to the Champions League knockout stages.

There is no easy solution to this problem. A more even spread of money across teams and leagues may be seen as 'rewarding failure', though the Premier League's success has been built on a much more equitable distribution of TV broadcast revenue than other European leagues. In 2022, the Premier League paid over £100 million to Norwich City in TV revenues, the lowest earners that season. Manchester City, the highest earners, received only 53% more. The disparity between the highest and lowest TV revenues is much greater in other leagues. It is also important to note that the Premier League's revenues dwarf those of every other domestic league. Just as smaller clubs find it difficult to compete financially with their domestic Champions League rivals, other European leagues cannot compete with the Premier League.

Football often experiences seismic financial disruptions, from Colombia's 'El Dorado' of the 1950s, which attracted world stars by paying huge wages, to China's government-funded programme to popularise football in the 2010s, which did much the same. The level of Saudi spending dwarfs that of Colombia and China, but football has always found ways to adapt and survive. Every team always has a hope of winning, even if crude oil money makes that hope a little smaller; they just need to find new edges to exploit. Over the last decade, smart teams like Brentford, Brighton and Liverpool have proven that when competing against the ever-greater spending power of petrochemical football, innovation and intelligence can be used to fight back.

Conclusion

How Not to Win the Premier League

Laziness is built deep into our nature

Daniel Kahneman

The football world has dramatically changed its attitude to data in the past few years. As recently as 2016, the England manager, Roy Hodgson, was happy to insist that statistical analysis had no place in the game. At a conference in Leicester in February 2016, his view on data analysis was unashamedly old-school. Hodgson told the audience: 'When shots on goal determine the outcome of a game, England will be shooting from kick-off', suggesting ignorance or at best a misunderstanding of the whole concept of Expected Goals. Today, few managers or executives publicly criticise the adoption of data analysis at football clubs.

Richard Pollard and Charles Reep wrote in their 1997 paper: 'Soccer is now a big business, and it is difficult to think of any other business activity in which vital decision-making would be tolerated in the almost total absence of the collection and analysis of numerical data.' It took many years for the footballing world to catch up to this way of thinking, but despite Liverpool's success, and Brentford and Brighton's, many teams and executives continue to do what they always did. Remarkably few football teams have truly embraced the data revolution. Sports club executives, like everyone else, are subject to a host of cognitive biases that make it difficult for them to accept statistical analysis. The vividness and emotional impact when one player played brilliantly against you, the optimism and excitement that take control when you think about signing him, and the fear of missing out on the next potential superstar, are all powerful forces that are difficult to combat.

Barcelona assembled a very impressive collection of scientists and analysts to help better understand their game. The quality of their work – including Javier Fernández's analysis of Lionel Messi's ability to occupy space – was very good. Simon Kuper, writing in the *Financial Times* in March 2019, was also impressed with the detailed analysis that was done at the club.[1] But when he asked the analysts about their impact, they were unconvinced. When asked about the size of the edge their work gave to the team, one analyst replied: '0.01 per cent.' Looking from the outside, their recruitment process certainly did not seem to be data-driven. Many of the big signings of the past few years – Coutinho, Dembélé, Paulinho, Semedo, Malcom, Arthur, Pjanić, Griezmann – are no longer at Barcelona and were not very successful when they were there. It appeared as if players were signed for their prestige rather than for the needs of the team. At Liverpool, our rule of thumb when it came to recruitment was that replacing a poorly performing starter with a good one is worth about two points per season. That is a 4% difference to the average team *per player* – an edge worth having. The quality of Barcelona's analysis was almost certainly good enough to generate such an edge, but it didn't have an impact on player recruitment at the club. The edge really was small, but only because the decision-makers did not listen to the data analysts.

Every team in the Premier League will tell you that they've embraced the data revolution, that they've hired a data department, and that they are using its insights. But saying you use something and actually using it are two different things. Using insights generated by data analysts means that decision-makers must change their approach and humans, as a rule, dislike change. There is a huge temptation for every executive with a new data department to look at the insights it generates, say 'That's interesting', and continue doing things the same way they were always done. In this case the adoption of data analysis is nothing more than a box-ticking exercise designed to placate a new owner who has just watched *Moneyball*. Or even worse, executives pretend to use data by cherry-picking metrics that support a decision they were going to make anyway. The metrics that might challenge their decision are conveniently ignored.

I believe the job of data analysis is to challenge subjective opinions using objective evidence. But that challenge can be difficult to live with. The psychologist Gary Klein recently told the *Freakonomics* radio podcast that, in business, management teams 'want to be harmonious, so they make decisions where everybody agrees. A harmonious decision is a terrible idea . . . your chance of coming up with an innovation has been severely compromised.'[2] At Liverpool we were anything but harmonious. We had many arguments about many players but the disagreements eventually led to better decisions being made.

The other job of data analysis is to separate long-term underlying performance from short-term unrepeatable fluctuations. Most teams cannot tell the difference between signal and noise, and it's lethal for their long-term health. I speak to many teams who have objectives like 'We want to be promoted' but have no idea of how they are currently performing compared to these objectives or what changes are needed in order to meet them. A team I recently spoke to believed they were favourites for promotion after a good start to the season. Their underlying performances, however, were poor. In time-honoured tradition the manager was soon sacked, but his replacement was unable to improve results, mostly because those good early-season results were a statistical blip.

I hope that reading this book has encouraged you to think about football a little more probabilistically and with a little more appreciation for the short-term variation in results that all clubs suffer. Looking through the lens of data analysis, football is still the Beautiful Game, but its beauty can be appreciated more quantitatively. We've broken down the game into its constituent parts, understood the importance of each one, and seen how each contributes to a team's success. To quote the Greek poet Agathon: 'Art loves chance, and chance loves art.' Football is often described as art. By understanding the probability and chance involved, I think we can appreciate that art even more deeply.

Acknowledgements

The Liverpool story told in this book would not have happened without Michael Edwards. Eddy was instrumental in kickstarting Liverpool's use of data. I am grateful to him for that and for being open to my writing in some detail about our experiences at Liverpool. Likewise, I am indebted to John Henry, Tom Werner and Mike Gordon at FSG for believing in and funding the data project at Liverpool. They continued to believe in our work even when results were bad. Many football club owners would have given up on us but they did not. The work of the Transfer Committee and the Football Operations department at Liverpool – Ian Ayre, Dave Fallows, Barry Hunter, Matt McCann, Julian Ward and David Woodfine – was instrumental in our success.

Henry Stott hired me at Decision Technology in 2005. It was through Henry that I met Danny Finkelstein at *The Times*. The publicity that Danny's 'Fink Tank' column gave us was invaluable, and he was one of the first champions of data analysis in football. His enthusiasm and encouragement convinced me to write *How to Win the Premier League*.

Much of the work described in the book was done by my colleagues in the Research department at Liverpool: Tim Waskett, Daf Steele, Mark Stevenson, Will Spearman, Ian Jenkins and Ben Hervey all made me look good. And we only made an impact because of the hard work and dedication of all my colleagues at Liverpool including Besim Ali, Tony Barrett, Jenny Beacham, Gareth Chappell, Kenny Dalglish, James French, Billy Hogan, Tim Jenkins, Laura Jones, Preston Jones, Harrison Kingston, Mark Leyland, Greg Mathieson, Patrick Montgomery, Conall Murtagh, Lee Richardson, Paddy Riley, Nikki Sanders, Julia Scott, Danny Stanway, Kyle Wallbanks and Andrea Wilkinson.

Acknowledgements

Damien Comolli and Ryan Groom were excellent team-mates at Tottenham Hotspur, as were Jin Chen, Benny Cheung, Paul Jackson, Mark Latham and Gabriella Lebrecht at Decision Technology.

It was a privilege to be able to work with DeepMind, and in particular with Demis Hassabis, Karl Tuyls and Zhe Wang.

My agent Toby Mundy helped me turn a hazy collection of ideas into a coherent book proposal. My editor at Century, Callum Crute, showed great enthusiasm for the book. Thanks also to Joanna Taylor and Aoifke McGuire-France at Century. David Edwards' diligent copy-editing caught many errors and improved my writing. John Muller spotted an error with the text that I'd missed.

Over the years, John Coulson, Richard Ewing, Ted Knutson and Jens Hegeler have helped me out with requests for data. Paul Gornall and Steve Palmer were the champions of tracking data at the Premier League. David Eccles was the go-to person for tracking data, and even provided me with Jürgen's running statistics.

I have been inspired by the work of Richard Pollard, Charles Reep, Bill James and Dean Oliver. Some concepts in this book were motivated by the ideas of Erik Bernhardsson, John Cook, Garry Gelade, Ben Torvaney and Dinesh Vatvani.

Thanks to Hans Leitert, Damian Murphy, Seamus Brady, Natxo Palacios-Huerta, Giles Pearson and Nagulan Saravanamuttu for their moral support over the years.

I am grateful to my family, especially my mother Auriol Graham and my brother Neil Graham.

Last but not least, thanks to Sara.

Notes

1. The Best Team in the Land

1 Barcelona, Opposition Team, LFChistory.net, https://lfchistory.net/Opposition/Team/Profile/91

2 Richard Pollard and Charles Reep, 'Measuring the effectiveness of playing strategies at soccer', *Journal of the Royal Statistical Society: Series D (The Statistician)*, 1997, vol. 46, no. 4, pp. 541–550.

3 Buster Olney, 'Could Theo Epstein help MLB fix its pace-of-play problem?', ESPN, 22 November 2020, https://www.espn.com/mlb/insider/story/_/id/30359574/could-theo-epstein-help-mlb-fix-pace-play-problem

2. Tottenham Hotspur

1 Polymers are long, chain-shaped molecules. A famous example of a polymer is DNA.

2 Nick Wright, 'Tottenham's lasagne-gate against West Ham remembered', Sky Sports, 6 May 2017, https://www.skysports.com/football/news/11675/10860462/tottenhams-lasagne-gate-against-west-ham-remembered

3 Transfer fees are difficult to find accurate information for. The numbers reported in the press are not always accurate – they often report what clubs want the public to think about the fee rather than the real fee. Throughout the book I have used transfer fees reported in the press. We can eventually discover the transfer spending of clubs through their company accounts, but it is usually difficult to assign a completely accurate fee to each player.

4 Daniel Kahneman, *Thinking, Fast and Slow*, Farrar, Straus and Giroux, 2011.

5 'Harry: Bent sulked over "my wife could have scored" remark . . . but it was the truth!', *Daily Mail*, 13 March 2012, https://www.dailymail.

co.uk/sport/football/article-2114003/Harry-Redknapp-Darren-Bent-wanted-Spurs-exit-Sandra-comment.html

6 'Van der Vaart: "Data people must get out or I'll quit watching football in 3 years"', Tribuna, 17 May 2023, https://tribuna.com/en/news/football-2023-05-17-van-der-vaart-data-people-must-get-out-or-ill-quit-watching-football-in-3-years

3. False Red Dawn

1 Rory Smith, *Expected Goals: The Story of How Data Conquered Football and Changed the Game Forever*, Mudlark, 2022, p. 86.

2 Andy Hunter, 'Brendan Rodgers: My Liverpool terms were full control or nothing', *Guardian*, 1 June 2012, https://www.theguardian.com/football/2012/jun/01/brendan-rodgers-liverpool-control

3 Sam Carroll, '15 of Brendan Rodgers' most infamous quotes as Liverpool manager', *Liverpool Echo*, 4 October 2019, https://www.liverpoolecho.co.uk/sport/football/football-news/brendan-rodgers-quotes-liverpool-envelopes-17012384

4 Example inspired by Rob Eastaway and John Haigh, *How to Take a Penalty: The Hidden Mathematics of Sport*, Robson Books, 2005.

4. Heavy Metal Football

1 Duncan Castles, 'Inside Line: Liverpool's Transfer Committee Has Been a Spectacular Failure', Bleacher Report, 15 December 2014, https://bleacherreport.com/articles/2296954-inside-line-liverpools-transfer-committee-has-been-a-spectacular-failure

2 This assumption is not realistic as teams play differently when leading compared to when level and when behind. But it is an easy way to convert Expected Goals into Expected Points.

5. Winning the Lot

1 Including Neil Critchley (Blackpool and QPR), Michael Beale (QPR, Rangers and Sunderland), Steven Gerrard (Rangers and Aston Villa), Gary O'Neil and Tim Jenkins (Bournemouth and Wolves).

2 We can also ask how much a player's estimated goal rate has changed from our prior assumption. Le Fondre's estimate increased from our prior assumption of 0.25 goals per game to 0.40 quickly, because his actual scoring rate was much higher than 0.25. Under Bayes' theorem, estimates change a lot when there is little evidence available, but only a little when there is lots of evidence available.

3 'TGG Podcast #55: Sarah Rudd – Arsenal's analytics pioneer', Training Ground Guru, 14 September 2023, https://trainingground.guru/articles/sarah-rudd-arsenals-analytics-pioneer

4 Kahneman, *Thinking, Fast and Slow*.

5 Nate Silver, *The Signal and the Noise: Why So Many Predictions Fail – But Some Don't*, Penguin, 2012.

6. Gambling on Data

1 Since 1995/96 there have been 20 teams in the Premier League. From 1992/93 to 1994/95 there were 22.

2 Kevin McCarra, 'Is searing attack or slack defence behind Premier League goal glut?', *Guardian*, 31 October 2011, https://www.theguardian.com/football/blog/2011/oct/31/premier-league-goal-glut

3 Mark J. Dixon and Stuart G. Coles, 'Modelling association football scores and inefficiencies in the football betting market', *Journal of the Royal Statistical Society: Series C (Applied Statistics)*, 1997, vol. 46, no. 2, pp. 265–280.

4 Some adjustments were necessary to control for the number of low-scoring results, which did not follow the predictions of the Poisson distribution.

5 The 2023/24 season has just ended, with 1,246 goals being scored, 15% higher than the previous record of 1,084 set in 2022/23. This was a real goal glut, beyond any statistical doubt.

6 I estimated about a 1% chance of observing 295 or more goals in the first 99 games of 2006/07.

7 Kahneman, *Thinking, Fast and Slow*.

8 Ian Graham, 'Premier League Goal Glut – What Goal Glut?!', Decision Technology's Football Blog, 3 November 2011, https://web.archive.org/web/20120318072558/http://dectech.org/blog/football/2011/11/premier-league-goal-glut-what-goal-glut/#more-574

9 Bookmakers love to offer bets that increase their cut: multiples, accumulators and cash-outs all offer bookmakers the opportunity to increase their margins, and so are heavily advertised.

10 There was a chance that the positive profit they found in their analysis could have been a fluke.

11 Andy Naylor and Jay Harris, '"A Cold War": The rivalry between Brighton's Tony Bloom and Matthew Benham at Brentford', The Athletic, 30 March 2023, https://theathletic.com/3029279/2023/03/30/cold-war-brighton-tony-bloom-matthew-benham-brentford

12 Mark J. Dixon and Michael E. Robinson, 'A birth process model for association football matches', *Journal of the Royal Statistical Society: Series D (The Statistician)*, 1998, vol. 47, no. 3, pp. 523–538.

13 Naylor and Harris, 'A Cold War'.

14 Silver, *The Signal and the Noise*.

15 Naylor and Harris, 'A Cold War'.

16 In 2020 Brentford moved from Griffin Park to Brentford Community Stadium, capacity 17,250.

17 Correct as of 21 May 2024.

18 Christoph Biermann, *Football Hackers: The Science and Art of a Data Revolution*, Blink Publishing, 2019.

19 This seems to be a dose of bad luck – they were mid-table according to Expected Goals.

20 Brighton & Hove Albion Holdings Limited Report and Financial Statements Year Ended 30 June 2023, https://resources.brightonandhovealbion.com/bhafc/document/2024/03/28/d328df45-1e6a-4947-9ffc-52a3b00b25f1/Brighton-and-Hove-Albion-Holdings-Limited-30.06.2023-EV.pdf

21 Annual Report and Financial Statements for the year ended 30 June 2023 for Brentford FC Ltd, https://res.cloudinary.com/brentford-fc/image/upload/v1707846734/Brentford_FC_Ltd_-_web_version_wqsaey.pdf

22 'Premier League clubs to ban gambling sponsorship on front of match-day shirts', BBC Sport, 13 April 2023, https://www.bbc.co.uk/sport/football/65260002

7. *What to Expect if You're Expecting Goals*

1 John Cohen and E. J. Dearnaley, 'Skill and Judgment of Footballers in Attempting to Score Goals: A Study of Psychological Probability', *British Journal of Psychology*, 1962, 53, pp. 71–86.

2 Pollard and Reep, 'Measuring the effectiveness of playing strategies at soccer'.

3 Charles Reep and Bernard Benjamin, 'Skill and Chance in Association Football', *Journal of the Royal Statistical Society: Series A (General)*, 1968, vol. 131, no. 4, pp. 581–585.

4 Ben Torvaney, 'Dixon Coles and xG: together at last', Stats and Snakeoil, 22 June 2018, https://www.statsandsnakeoil.com/2018/06/22/dixon-coles-and-xg-together-at-last/. I stole my title for chapter 15 from Torvaney's blog.

5 My old Decision Technology colleague Mark Latham wrote about this on the company's blog, but the article is no longer available.

8. *The Value of Possession*

1 Matt Ladson, '"Death by football" – Rodgers explains his Liverpool vision', This Is Anfield, 7 September 2012, https://web.archive.org/web/20120909210420/https://www.thisisanfield.com/2012/09/death-by-football-rodgers-outlines-his-liverpool-vision/

2 Pollard and Reep, 'Measuring the effectiveness of playing strategies at soccer'.

3 David Hytner, 'Arsenal's "secret" signing: club buys £2m revolutionary data company', *Guardian*, 17 October 2014, https://www.theguardian.com/football/2014/oct/17/arsenal-place-trust-arsene-wenger-army-statdna-data-analysts

4 'Markov chain', Wikipedia, https://en.wikipedia.org/wiki/Markov_chain

5 The worst was Derby County, who suffered the worst Premier League season ever, winning only 11 points.

6 Dean Oliver, *Basketball on Paper: Rules and Tools for Performance Analysis*, Potomac Books, 2003.

7 The previous three actions in a possession are taken into account in the 'Valuing Actions by Estimating Probabilities' model developed by Tom Decroos, Lotte Bransen, Jan van Haaren and Jesse Davis at KU Leuven. See 'Valuing actions in soccer', DTAI Stories, 16 May 2020, https://dtai.cs.kuleuven.be/stories/post/sports/exploring-how-vaep-values-actions/

9. Track Your Man

1 A game contains about 3,000 on-ball events. The same game contains over 3 *million* player and ball coordinates.

2 Going from event to tracking data increased the number of data points from 3,000 to 3 million. Pose data increases that to 90 million data points.

3 Shayegan Omidshafei, Daniel Hennes, Marta Garnelo et al, 'Multi-agent off-screen behavior prediction in football', *Scientific Reports*, 2022, vol. 12, pp. 1–13, https://doi.org/10.1038/s41598-022-12547-0

4 Similar work had been attempted before, but only one team's positions were allowed to vary, which limited its usefulness. See Hoang M. Le, Peter Carr, Yisong Yue and Patrick Lucey, 'Data-Driven Ghosting using Deep Imitation Learning', Disney Research Studios, 3 March 2017, https://studios.disneyresearch.com/2017/03/03/data-driven-ghosting-using-deep-imitation-learning/

5 Zhe Wang, Petar Veličković, Daniel Hennes et al, 'TacticAI: an AI assistant for football tactics', Nat Commun 15, 1906 (2024), https://doi.org/10.1038/s41467-024-45965-x

10. Paying for Performance

1 If that seems like a large number, it's not. Tesco recorded £61.5 billion of sales in 2023/24, making a profit of £2.8 billion (https://www.tescoplc.com/preliminary-results-202324/).

2 I collected this information from Kieron O'Connor's excellent Substack site, The Swiss Ramble (https://swissramble.substack.com/).

3 In football clubs' financial accounts only total wages are shown. This includes all employees, not just the players (though players account for the vast majority of the wage bill).

4 The best players play in attack. Many Premier League midfielders and defenders started their youth careers as a number 9 or a number 10. As young players move to bigger and better academies, they come up against more competition for the coveted attacking roles and often have to find a new position in which to play.

5 Loans are clouded by the fact that the loaning club often covers a fraction of the player's wages.

6 Raffaele Poli, Roger Besson and Loïc Ravenel, 'Econometric Approach to Assessing the Transfer Fees and Values of Professional Football Players', *Economies*, 2022, vol. 10, no. 1, pp. 1–14.

7 The correlation is a lot lower over one season, and it's also a lot lower when the Premier League and Championship are considered separately.

8 Gregg Evans, 'City's team deal, United's 25 per cent pay-cuts: Football bonuses and how they work', The Athletic, 4 May 2022, https://theathletic.com/3279361/2022/05/04/citys-team-deal-uniteds-25-per-cent-pay-cuts-football-bonuses-and-how-they-work/

11. *Schrödinger's Manager*

1 Their *actual* goal difference was only +5 so maybe this isn't too surprising.

2 Ronaldinho, Ronaldo and Beckham also had cameo roles at Ancelotti's Milan.

3 Daniel Yankelovich, 'Corporate Priorities: A continuing study of the new demands on business', 1972.

4 His tenure as England manager was also fairly disastrous, but somehow lasted four years.

12. Goat War

1 'Castrol performance index', Wikipedia, https://en.wikipedia.org/wiki/Castrol_performance_index

2 Maybe one reason why Real Madrid were open to selling him to Tottenham Hotspur at the end of the season.

3 Simon Kuper and John Burn-Murdoch, 'Cristiano Ronaldo vs Lionel Messi: who was the greatest footballer?', *Financial Times*, 3 June 2023.

4 I included a slightly different set of competitions so my numbers are slightly different to those that appear in the *Financial Times* article.

5 Assists are not straightforward. Different data providers have different definitions for exactly what does or does not count as an assist. I used the website Transfermarkt, which has a generous definition of assists, and also considers the winning of a penalty to be an assist. Most official competition statistics do not count winning a penalty as an assist, despite its high value.

6 It is difficult to find detailed data on Ronaldo's early career. By the time Opta started selling event data in 2007, he had already played for Manchester United for four full seasons. Unfortunately, early-era Ronaldo is something of an unknown, though we can see that he did start quite slowly. The first time he scored more than 10 goals in a Premier League season was 2006/07, his fourth at United.

7 Ian Graham, 'Is Spanish Football Broken?', Decision Technology's Football Blog, 4 October 2011, https://web.archive.org/web/20120106164515/http://dectech.org/blog/football/2011/10/is-spanish-football-broken/

8 The Uefa Nations League has recently increased the level of competition for the big European nations.

9 RedBird bought a stake in FSG in 2021.

10 Javier Fernández and Luke Bornn, 'Wide Open Spaces: A statistical technique for measuring space creation in professional soccer', MIT Sloan Sports Analytics Conference 2018, http://www.lukebornn.com/papers/fernandez_ssac_2018.pdf

13. *Zebra Farmers: Why Transfers Fail*

1 With Graeme Riley and Gary Fulcher.
2 'The Tomkins Times', https://tomkinstimes.com/2014/06/tomkins-law-only-40-of-transfers-succeed/
3 I recommend reading Kieran Maguire's *The Price of Football* for all the gory details.
4 'Premier League 10 Years (2013-22)', The Swiss Ramble, 20 July 2023, https://swissramble.substack.com/p/premier-league-10-years-2013-22
5 It's an oversimplification to assume that all the ways a player might fail are independent of one another. Calculating the overall chance of success by multiplying together each individual chance is only valid if every facet is independent from all the others, as in multiple flips of a coin. Football is not like flipping a coin: if a player is played out of position, it may lead the club to thinking he's not very good. If he's very young, the manager may be reluctant to allow him to start many games. The calculation of transfer success is meant to illustrate why we shouldn't be surprised that many transfers fail – the details of the calculation should not be taken too seriously.
6 Sid Lowe, 'Barcelona swapping Arthur for Pjanic was a business move but for all the wrong reasons', ESPN, 29 June 2020, https://www.espn.co.uk/football/story/_/id/37584543/barcelona-swapping-arthur-pjanic-was-business-move-all-wrong-reasons

14. *Home Is Where 30% More Goals Are*

1 In 2017/18, 168 of the 380 Premier League games per season were televised in the UK. In 2024/25, 267 live games will be televised.
2 Assuming three points for a win.
3 Helena Smith, 'PAOK owner who stormed pitch with gun ordered to testify', *Guardian*, 16 March 2018, https://www.theguardian.com/football/2018/mar/16/paok-owner-ivan-savvidis-stormed-pitch-gun-ordered-to-testify

4 Kerry S. Courneya and Albert V. Carron, 'The Home Advantage In Sport Competitions: A Literature Review', *Journal of Sport & Exercise Psychology*, 1992, vol. 14, pp. 13–27.

5 Stephen R. Clarke and John M. Norman, 'Home Ground Advantage of Individual Clubs in English Soccer', *Journal of the Royal Statistical Society: Series D (The Statistician)*, 1995, vol. 44, no. 4, pp. 509–521.

6 I included Crystal Palace's 2016 final loss to Manchester United as a London club loss, but excluded Watford's 2019 6–0 shellacking by Manchester City.

7 Stephen J. Dubner, ' "Football Freakonomics": How Advantageous Is Home-Field Advantage? And Why?', Freakonomics, 18 December 2011, https://freakonomics.com/2011/12/football-freakonomics-how-advantageous-is-home-field-advantage-and-why/

8 A. M. Nevill, N. J. Balmer and A. M. Williams, 'The influence of crowd noise and experience upon refereeing decisions in football', *Psychology of Sport and Exercise*, 2002, vol. 3, no. 4, pp. 261–272.

9 David Runciman, 'Home Sweet Home?', *Observer*, 3 February 2008, https://www.theguardian.com/sport/2008/feb/03/features.sportmonthly16

10 Garciano, Palacios-Huerta and Prendergast, 'Favouritism under social pressure', *Review of Economics and Statistics*, 2005, vol. 87, pp. 208–216.

11 Luke Benz and Michael Lopez published a paper in 2021 with different results: https://link.springer.com/article/10.1007/s10182-021-00413-9. In contrast to Benz and Lopez, our model allowed for time-varying team strength, and for the away teams to change their goal-scoring rates away from home.

15. Stats and Snake Oil

1 I stole this chapter title from Ben Torvaney's football analytics blog https://www.statsandsnakeoil.com

2 Simon Kuper, 'Baseball's love of statistics is taking over football', *Financial Times*, 21 November 2009, https://www.ft.com/content/2b1ee75c-d855-11de-b63a-00144feabdc0

3 Brighton would get their revenge in 2023, when Alexis Mac Allister scored a last-minute penalty against Manchester United to win the game 1–0.

4 Assuming average scoring rates.

5 A multiple linear regression.

6 In statistics this is known as Berkson's Paradox.

7 'India football head coach Igor Stimac took astrologer's advice in picking team for crucial matches in 2022', ESPN, 11 September 2023, https://www.espn.co.uk/football/story/_/id/38383816/igor-stimac-indian-football-head-coach-astrologer-advice-afc-asian-cup

8 Samaan Lateef, India's national football team 'hired astrologer to pick star players', *Telegraph*, 12 September 2023, https://www.telegraph.co.uk/world-news/2023/09/12/india-national-football-team-hired-astrologer-asian-cup/

9 As a Capricorn, I would say that, wouldn't I?

10 For example, see Jochen Musch and Simon Grondin, 'Unequal Competition as an Impediment to Personal Development: A Review of the Relative Age Effect in Sport', *Developmental Review*, 2001, vol. 21, no. 2, pp. 147–167.

11 Raffaele Poli, Loïc Ravenel and Roger Besson, 'Relative age effect: a serious problem in football', CIES Football Observatory, Monthly Report 10, December 2015, https://football-observatory.com/IMG/pdf/mr10_eng.pdf

12 Musch and Grondin, 'Unequal Competition as an Impediment to Personal Development'; Werner F. Helsen, Jan van Winckel and A. Mark Williams, 'The Relative Age Effect in Youth Soccer Across Europe', *Journal of Sports Sciences*, 2005, vol. 23, no. 6, pp. 629–636.

16. Stats and Crude Oil: The Future of Football

1 Sid Lowe, 'Chelsea and Mourinho draws Diego Simeone's Atlético into war of attrition', *Guardian*, 22 April 2014, https://www.theguardian.com/football/2014/apr/22/chelsea-jose-mourinho-diego-simeone-atletico-madrid

2 Observe, Orient, Decide, Act.

3 Conversely, the better defensive teams concede a *higher* proportion of their goals via set-pieces.

4 See Chapter 14 on home advantage.

5 'How Much Money Did Chelsea Really Spend?', The Swiss Ramble, 6 February 2023, https://swissramble.substack.com/p/how-much-money-did-chelsea-really

6 'Manchester City charged by the Premier League', The Swiss Ramble, 13 February 2023, https://swissramble.substack.com/p/manchester-city-charged-by-the-premier

7 Manchester City were accused in February 2023 of 115 breaches of Premier League rules, including effectively falsifying their accounts and artificially inflating commercial sponsorship deals. The club denies the charges.

8 'Deloitte Football Money League 2015', Deloitte, January 2015, https://www2.deloitte.com/tr/en/pages/consumer-business/articles/deloitte-football-money-league-2015.html

9 'Mohammed bin Salman: "I don't care" about "sportswashing" accusations', BBC Sport, 21 September 2023, https://www.bbc.co.uk/sport/66874723

Conclusion: How Not to Win the Premier League

1 Simon Kuper, 'How FC Barcelona are preparing for the future of football', *Financial Times*, 1 March 2019, https://www.ft.com/content/908752aa-3a1b-11e9-b72b-2c7f526ca5d0

2 'How to Succeed at Failing, Part 4: Extreme Resiliency', *Freakonomics* radio podcast, Episode 564, 1 November 2023, https://freakonomics.com/podcast/how-to-succeed-at-failing-part-4-extreme-resiliency/

Index

'A Birth Process Model for Association Football Matches' (Dixon/Robinson) 108–9

Abramovich, Roman 274, 275

Abu Dhabi United Group 275

AC Milan 182, 197

academies, football 10, 31, 32, 80, 91, 92, 154, 179, 184–5, 186

Adebayor, Emmanuel 35, 104

Adrián 90, 91, 183

age
  ageing curve 201
  Brentford squad and 114–15
  Dortmund squad and 194
  relative age effect 264–5
  skills changing with 44–5
  transfer fees and 181
  wages and 178–9, 181

agents 76, 77, 177, 179, 184

Agüero, Sergio 104, 121, 193

AIK Fotboll 241

Alba, Jordi 5, 8

Alberto, Luis 51, 53, 54, 95

Alcântara, Thiago 231, 261

Alcorcón S.A.D. 205–6

Alexander-Arnold, Trent 5, 15, 80, 89, 91, 92, 154, 268

Alexander, Duncan 217

algorithms 4, 6, 155, 158, 161, 172

Allan 261, 263

Allardyce, Sam 104, 274

Allegri, Massimo 193–4

Allen, Joe 46–7, 50, 149, 230

Amisco 22

Amkar Perm 240

Ancelotti, Carlo 197–8, 199, 200

Anelka, Nicolas 229, 259, 260

Anna Karenina principle 227

Antonio, Michail 152

Aquilani, Alberto 42, 180

Arsenal 19, 22, 23, 30, 43, 52–3, 54, 56, 62, 77–8, 79, 82, 103, 104, 106, 229
  performance analysts 159
  points per season 93, 186
  possession 142, 270
  revenue 176
  shots 139
  StatDNA and 145
  total expenditure 94, 186
  transfers 116, 126, 183, 185, 186, 203, 224, 226, 252
  wages 176

Arshavin, Andrey 259

artificial intelligence (AI) 170–73

Ashton, Neil 65

Asian Handicap 107–8

Aspas, Iago 51, 53–4, 95

Aston Villa 31, 36, 52, 56, 90, 113, 139, 159, 186, 269

astrology 264, 265

Athletic Club de Bilbao 265

Athletic, The 217

Atlético Madrid 51, 57, 88, 143, 212, 228, 269

attacking intent 244, 249

Aubameyang, Pierre-Emerick 68, 183, 196

availability bias 28
Ayre, Ian 46, 61

Bale, Gareth 25, 29–30, 47, 95, 114, 197, 209, 252
ball control 164–7
Balmer, Nigel 245
Balotelli, Mario 56–8, 95, 182, 230
Barcelona, FC
    Champions League semi-final vs Liverpool (2019) 3–5, 7, 8, 9, 89, 96
    four-phase principle 268, 269, 271
    GOAT and 206, 207, 211, 212, 213, 215–16
    managers 193, 194
    possession and 143, 155
    transfers 11, 14, 28, 54, 55, 86–7, 136, 181, 227, 228, 229, 252, 280
Barnet 30
Barton, Joey 126
baseball 16, 22, 39–40, 43–5, 96, 159, 244–5
Basel, FC 80–81
basketball 16, 29, 33, 152
Bayer Leverkusen 82
Bayern Munich 44, 68, 69, 73, 78, 155, 193, 196, 226, 228, 241
Bayes' theorem 84, 105
Beane, Billy 22, 39, 40
Beck, Kent 101
Becker, Alisson 8, 11, 88, 137
behind closed doors, playing 10, 246–9
Bellamy, Craig 42–3, 48
Benfica 57
Benham, Matthew 107, 108, 109, 110, 111, 112, 117, 118, 119, 249, 255
Benítez, Rafa 145
Benjamin, Bernard 137
Benrahma, Saïd 113, 114

Bent, Darren 30, 31, 258–60
Benteke, Christian 52, 56, 58, 59, 61–3, 65, 76, 95, 181, 222, 230, 231
Berbatov, Dimitar 25–6, 30, 61, 186
Berg, Sepp van den 183
betting/gambling 101–20, 145–6
Bielsa, Marcelo 199–200
Birmingham City 150–51
Blackpool 50, 96, 259
Bleacher Report: 'Liverpool's Transfer Committee Has Been a Spectacular Failure' 58
Bloom, Tony 107, 108, 109, 110, 111, 115, 119
bookmakers 106, 107, 108, 109, 110, 111, 119, 120, 189, 190, 191, 192, 193, 197, 247, 275
Borini, Fabio 48, 50
Bornn, Luke 215, 216
Borussia Dortmund 64, 66–9, 70–73, 75, 76, 86, 183, 189–91, 192, 193, 194–5, 196, 197, 201, 208, 226, 227
Boston Red Sox 40, 43, 44
Bournemouth 113, 236
Box, George 39
Boyd, Colonel John 271
Brandt, Julian 82
Bray, Ken: *How to Score* 122
Breitner, Paul 119
Brentford FC 14, 111, 112–16, 117, 118–19, 176, 232, 249, 254, 273, 277, 279
Bridcutt, Liam 116
Brighton & Hove Albion 14, 111, 113, 115–19, 139, 232, 235, 256, 277, 279
Britton, Leon 47, 149
broadcast tracking 170–73
Bruyne, Kevin de 81, 221–2, 261
BT Sport 235–6
Buckley, Will 116

Bundesliga 11–12, 13, 24, 35, 63, 64, 65, 66, 76, 89, 118, 181, 189, 195, 196, 209, 263–4
  Covid-19 and 246–7, 248
  (2010/11) 70, 194
  (2011/12) 70, 195
  (2014/15) 66–9, 70, 72–3, 189, 190, 192, 193
  (2016/17) 220
Burnley FC 113, 176
Burn-Murdoch, John 207
Busquets, Sergio 262

Caicedo, Moisés 116
Cameron, William Bruce 199
Campbell, D. J. 259
Campbell, Fraizer 26
Can, Emre 57
Carragher, Jamie 65–6
Carroll, Andy 42, 48–9, 56, 61, 180
Carron, Albert 239
Castilla 205–6
Castrol Index 126–7
Castrol Rankings 205–6
Centre International d'Etude du Sport 180, 182
Champions League 22, 24, 27, 65, 77, 79, 80, 91, 92, 114, 171, 182, 185, 193, 202, 205, 210, 211, 215, 227, 228, 231, 236, 237, 243, 258, 259, 265
  (2010–11) 36, 50–51
  (2011–12) 241
  (2012–13) 36, 70, 72
  (2013–14) 270
  (2014–15) 52
  (2017–18) 3, 86, 87–8, 115
  (2018–19) 3–11, 89–90, 154, 168–9, 183
  (2021–22) 10

  qualification as a virtuous circle 276–7
  TV broadcast deals 176, 276, 277
Championship 50, 85, 112–13, 114–16, 118, 176, 177, 184, 185, 238
character references 77, 83, 95–6
Charlton Athletic 30
Chelsea FC 43, 53–4, 84, 90, 106, 270
  Abramovich and 274, 275
  Champions League final (2012) 241
  clean sheets and 255
  early kick-offs 236
  Expected Goals 93
  goals 256, 260
  home advantage and 243
  managers 197, 200
  performance analysts 159
  points per season 93, 274
  possession 142
  scoring rates 104
  transfers 11, 12, 13, 14, 48, 50, 81–2, 88, 94, 96, 116, 118, 180, 181, 183, 185, 222, 223, 228, 229
  wages 94, 186
Chiellini, Giorgio 54
China 180–81, 277
ChyronHego 159
Clarke, Stephen 240, 242
clean sheets 52, 135, 254–8
Club World Cup (2019), Fifa 10, 91
cognitive bias 14, 47–8, 279
Cohen, John 122–4, 127
Cole, Ashley 198, 203, 256
Coles, Stuart 103, 106, 107, 109
Colombia 214, 238, 248, 277
Comolli, Damien 22, 40, 41, 150, 154
computer vision 6, 158, 161
Copa América 214
Copa del Rey 206

Copenhagen, FC 118, 241

corners 5, 8, 24, 27, 52, 53, 60, 127, 161,
173, 178, 253–4, 271, 272, 273

Costa, Diego 51–2, 66, 84–5, 181–2

counter-attacking 52, 127–8, 142, 228

Courneya, Kerry 239

Coutinho, Philippe 8, 11, 14, 50–51, 52,
55, 63, 66, 78, 86–7, 88, 96, 121–2,
128, 132, 134, 135, 139, 181, 186, 224,
227, 228, 280

Covid-19 10, 15, 195, 229, 246–9, 269

Crouch, Peter 30–31

Cruyff, Johan 75, 152, 166, 175, 193, 268

Crystal Palace 53, 200, 236

CSKA Moscow 240

Cucurella, Marc 116, 118

Curran, James 3

Dagenham & Redbridge 30

Daily Mail 65

Dalglish, Sir Kenny 43, 46, 90, 158

Damião, Leandro 30

Dangerous Possession 141–3, 270

Dangerous Possession Dominance 142

data analysis *see individual area of data
analysis*

deadline day 35, 183

Dearnaley, E. J. 122–4, 127

'death by football' 52, 141

Decision Technology 21, 28–9, 31,
35–6, 39, 40, 41, 43, 94, 103, 105–6,
131, 212–13, 283, 284

DeepMind 172

Defoe, Jermain 30

Dembélé, Ousmane 86, 181, 227

Deming, W. Edwards 177

Dempsey, Clint 259

Deutsche Fußball Liga (DFL) 67–8

Diamond, Jared: *Guns, Germs and
Steel* 225, 227

Díaz, Luis 231

di María, Angel 181, 209, 222, 228

Di Matteo, Roberto 243

director of football 22, 29, 40, 46, 76

Dixon-Coles 103–5, 107–9, 112, 114, 134,
155, 189, 190, 214, 256

Dixon, Mark 103, 106, 107, 108–9

domestication 225–7

Downing, Stewart 29

dribbling 12, 15, 34, 60, 85, 89, 150, 153,
211, 213–14, 216

Džeko, Edin 61, 104

early kick offs 235–7

Edwards, Michael 'Eddy' 10, 13
Alexander-Arnold and 89
Alisson and 88
Benteke and 56, 62, 95
Coutinho and 50–51, 87
Firmino and 63, 64, 65
Keïta and 220
Klopp and 66, 70, 75
Konaté and 170
Liverpool, joins 41, 42, 43,
45–6, 48
Luis Alberto and 54
Mané and 76–7, 78
Marković and 57, 95, 230
Matip and 78
Mendy and 83
others' opinions and 96
Portsmouth and 31–2
Research department and 79–80,
91, 92, 151
Salah and 80, 82
salary model and 179
sporting director, promoted to
Liverpool 75
Tottenham Hotspur and 31–2, 33,
34, 35, 36–7, 126

Elo, Arpad 141

emotional tone setting 199–200, 202–3

England (international football team)
29, 85, 113, 239, 240, 241, 279
Epstein, Theo 16
Espanyol 51
Estupiñán, Pervis 118
Europa League
(2013–14) 76
(2015–16) 3, 75, 77
European Championship 80, 114, 127
(2008) 26, 205, 240
European Super Cup (2019/20) 10, 90, 91
event data 22–4, 59, 127, 144–5, 151, 161,
169, 170, 243
Everton 19, 34, 61, 92–3, 104, 113, 135,
157, 159, 185, 229, 256, 261
evidence, player's performance and
83–5
Exeter City 113, 114
Expected Assists 261–2
Expected Goals (xG) 14, 23, 121–39,
150, 279
author's model, origins of 122–8, 144
Brentford and 112, 119
Bundesliga and 68–9, 71, 72
context and 132–4
Coutinho and 121–2
databases, first 110
defined 7–10
Dortmund and 190, 192
Expected Goal Difference 68, 93, 192
Expected Goals Shadow 133–4
GOAT and 210, 211–12
home advantage and 243, 244
league position, xG 119
outcome bias and 134–6
possession and 152–4
Post-Strike Expected Goals 8, 9,
26–7, 129–30, 134, 135, 136, 139, 148,
192, 210
Pre-Strike Expected Goals 128–9,
132, 133, 135–6, 139, 192, 211–12

relative value of versus actual goals
136–7
Salah and 82
shot distance and 138–9
Smartodds and 114, 119
World Cup (2010) and 195–6
Expected Points 68–9, 236–7, 256–7
Expected Possession Value 15
Expected Threat 23, 141, 145
expenditure, total 63, 93–4, 186
extreme characteristics, game-changers
and 85–6, 202

FA Cup
(2014–15) 58
(2021–22) 10, 91
home advantage and 242
Fabinho 12, 88–9, 91, 92, 161, 220, 276
failure, concept of 81–2, 95, 221, 230–31,
277
fair score 7, 72, 134–6
fair value 180–81, 222–3
Fallows, Dave 13, 46, 82, 92
Falmer Stadium 116
false 9 59, 95, 213
fans
conservation of fan joy 45
'fanalysts' 45
games without 246–9
home advantage and 15, 237–49
Félix, João 228
Fenway Sports Group (FSG) 10, 11, 40,
42, 43, 45, 46, 91–2, 94, 125, 186, 189
Ferguson, Alex 202, 203, 210, 274
Fernandes, Bruno 139, 256
Fernández, Javier 215–16, 280
Fifa 240
50% Rule 221–4
finance, football 175–86
revenue, increases in 175–6
salary model 177–80

finance, football – *cont.*
   success and 184–6
   transfer fees *see* transfer fees
   TV broadcast deals 176, 180, 276, 277
   wages *see* wages
Financial Times 207, 255, 280
Finkelstein, Danny 21, 22, 124, 240, 283
Firmino, Roberto 9, 12, 13–14, 59, 63–5, 75, 79, 86, 91, 92, 95, 153, 183, 201, 220, 222, 224
First Division 20, 238
first touch 127
Football Association (FA) 157, 240
Football Hackers (Christoph Biermann) 112
Formula One 16
Forshaw, Adam 113
Foster, Ben 121
fouls 60, 124–6, 161, 213, 245–6
four-phase principle 268–9, 271
Frank, Thomas 112
Freakonomics radio podcast 281
free-kicks 24, 124, 125, 128, 178, 211, 213, 245, 271–2

Gaal, Louis van 228–9, 268
Gabi 270
game changers 85–6
game state 142, 143–4, 146–8, 154, 162
gegenpressing 16–17, 67, 70, 267–71
Gerrard, Steven 9, 47, 48, 50, 52, 58, 80, 89, 121, 122, 124, 149, 220, 230
Gervinho 126
Gillett, George 42
goalkeeper 11, 52, 83–4, 87–8
   Expected Goals and 8, 9, 26–8, 69, 71, 121, 122, 123, 128, 129, 130–37, 148, 210, 211
   wages and 178, 272

goals
   betting and 101–10
   clean sheets and 254–8
   corners and 253–4
   Expected Goals *see* Expected Goals
   fair score and *see* fair score
   'goal glut' 101–6
   Goal Probability Added 23, 141, 263
   goal-scoring probability 23, 141, 166–9, 263
   Goal Yield 144–5
   GOAT and 207–12, 214–16, 217
   home advantage and 237–8, 240, 242, 243, 244, 245, 246, 247–8
   impact-adjusted 258–60
   importance of 108–9
   Poisson distribution and 101–4
   possession and 141–56
   rare events 101
   scoring rate 84–5, 102, 109, 207, 237
   set-piece 271–4
   tracking data and 162, 164, 166–7, 168–9
Gomes, Heurelho 27–8, 35
Gomez, Joe 91, 231
Gordon, Mike 10, 45, 91–2, 94, 96
Gornall, Paul 159
Götze, Mario 67, 76, 83–4, 194, 196
Gray, Andre 113, 114
Greatest of All Time (GOAT) 205–17
   basic numbers 207–10
   chances, taking and creating 210–11
   Messi's deceleration 215–17
   physicality of game and 212–14
   set-pieces and 211–12
   winner 217
Greek Super League 155–6
Griezmann, Antoine 57, 228, 280
Griffin Park 112
Großkreutz, Kevin 194

Index

Groom, Ryan 30
Gross, Pascal 118
Guardian 65
Guardiola, Pep 89, 138–9, 189, 193, 194, 201, 217, 270, 275
Gündoğan, Ilkay 195

Haaland, Erling 59, 193, 208, 209
hallucination of player trajectories 172–3
Hanover FC 72
Hazard, Eden 81
heavy metal football 70, 75
height 273
Henderson, Jordan 5, 52, 55, 91, 154, 168–9, 230, 276
Henry, John W. 10, 33, 40–41, 42, 43, 44, 45, 54, 67, 70, 94
Henry, Thierry 206
Heung-min, Son 137, 169
Hicks, Tom 42
Hill, Jimmy 52
Hodgson, Roy 42, 46, 121, 200, 272, 279
Hoffenheim, TSG 1899 13, 63, 64, 65, 73, 222
Hogan, Scott 113
Holmes, Sherlock 19, 160
home advantage 15, 237–49
    behind closed doors 246–9
    Champions League final (2012) and 241–3
    Euro (2008) qualifiers and 240–41
    location factors 239–40
    Messi in your team, like having 237–9
    referee and 245–6
    shots/goals and 243–5
    VAR and 248–9
Houghton, Ray 103
Houllier, Gérard 125
Hull City 12, 85, 113
Hume, David 16

Hummels, Mats 67, 194
Hunter, Barry 13, 46, 51, 82, 92, 162
hybrid strikers 61

'iBob' ('in-box-outside-box') model 125, 127, 136–7
Ibrahimović, Zlatan 61, 197, 208
Immobile, Ciro 72
impact-adjusted goals 258–60
in-running or in-play markets 108–10
Ince, Tom 50, 51
Independent 65
information leak 155
Inglethorpe, Alex 80
injury-time 121, 122, 157, 246, 256
intercepting passes 167–8
Internazionale 11, 50, 182, 200, 226, 229

Jabulani ball 196
James, Bill 43–4, 159
Jansson, Pontus 118, 273
Jenkins, Ian 171
Jordan, Joe 30
Jota, Diogo 220, 231
Journal of the Royal Statistical Society: Series C (Applied Statistics) 103
Juventus 213, 229

Kagawa, Shinji 67, 194, 195, 196, 201
Kahneman, Daniel 28, 50, 105, 279; *Thinking, Fast and Slow* 123
Kane, Harry 9, 121
Karius, Loris 72
Keane, Robbie 26, 30, 186, 202, 203
Keïta, Naby 89, 91, 92, 168, 169, 219–21, 222, 231, 268
Kent, Ryan 186
King, Ledley 29
Kingston, Harrison 236
Klein, Gary 62, 281

Klopp, Jürgen 13, 14
  early kick-offs and 235–7
  Expected Goals and 139
  GOAT and 205, 208
  Liverpool, arrival at 10, 14, 15, 66–7,
    68, 69, 70–73, 75, 189–91, 192, 194,
    195, 196, 197, 198, 199, 200, 201,
    202, 203, 224, 276
  Liverpool's achievements in era of
    274
  physical statistics of 157
  tactics and 16–17, 59, 67, 70, 75, 95,
    267–71
  transfers and 11, 12, 75–9, 82, 85, 86,
    87, 88, 89, 92, 95, 220, 224, 230–31
Kompany, Vincent 139
Konaté, Ibrahima 170, 231
Konsa, Ezri 113
Kranjčar, Niko 31
Kuper, Simon 184, 207, 280
Kuyt, Dirk 43, 48

La Gazzetta dello Sport 179
Lacazette, Alexandre 82, 183
La Liga 24, 54, 143, 207, 209, 212,
  228, 229
Lallana, Adam 55–6, 78, 87
Lambert, Rickie 56–8, 61, 87
Latham, Mark 34
Le Fondre, Adam 84–5
League Cup 150
  (2007–8) 25
  (2011–12) 46
  (2015–16) 75
  (2021–22) 10, 91
League One 111, 112, 113, 119
Leeds United 118, 199
Leicester City 116, 139, 192, 245, 279
Leitert, Hans 88, 131, 220
Leiva, Lucas 47, 149, 230
Levy, Daniel 36

Lewandowski, Robert 67, 69, 153, 193,
  194, 195, 200, 201, 208, 209
Lewis, Michael: *Moneyball* 16, 22, 39–40,
  43, 63, 65, 175, 259, 281
Leyton Orient 30, 53, 114
Ligue 1 24, 118
Ligue 2 114, 118
Lille, LOSC 126
Liverpool FC
  Academy 10, 31, 32, 80, 91, 92, 154,
    179, 184–5, 186
  competitions *see individual*
    competition name
  Decision Technology discussions
    with 40–45
  director of football 40, 46
  early kick offs and 235–7
  Edwards and *see* Edwards, Michael
  Expected Goals and *see* Expected
    Goals
  Fenway Sports Group (FSG) and
    10, 11, 40, 42, 43, 45, 46, 91–2, 94,
    125, 186, 189
  home advantage and 15, 237–49
  managers *see individual manager*
    name
  players *see individual player name*
  possession and *see* possession
  Premier League seasons *see*
    Premier League seasons
  recruitment process, manager
    66–73, 189–203
  recruitment process, player *see*
    transfers
  Research department 71, 80, 125,
    135, 171, 251
  revenue 175–6
  Scouting department 9, 10, 12, 13,
    14, 27–8, 46, 51–2, 56, 57, 71, 76, 78,
    87, 89, 91–2, 94, 95, 96–7, 151, 154,
    162, 171, 230, 232

sporting director 10, 13, 46, 70, 75, 96

tracking data and *see* tracking data

Transfer Committee 46, 55, 56, 58, 62, 63, 65–6, 219–20, 230, 251–2, 276

transfers under Klopp 75–97, 219–33

transfers under Rodgers 46–66, 251–65

Video Analysis department 5–9, 10, 13, 30, 31, 36, 56, 71, 78, 97, 125, 131, 135, 151, 154, 230

wages 176, 177, 185, 186

Lloris, Hugo 26

Lo Celso, Giovani 261

Lokomotiv Moscow 241

Lonergan, Andy 183

long-range shooting 110, 121, 124–5, 128, 137, 139, 211

Lovren, Dejan 57, 87, 268

luck 7, 13–14, 50, 63, 69, 72, 73, 83–4, 92, 96, 102, 104, 111, 135, 185, 190, 191, 221, 269

Lukaku, Romelu 61–2, 82, 183, 229

Luton Town 107, 114, 240

Lyn 241

Maguire, Harry 11, 85, 224

Maguire, Kieran: *The Price of Football* 119, 176

Mainz (FSV Mainz 05) 72, 189, 190–91

Malouda, Florent 259

manager 189–203

ageing curve of player and 201

Ancelotti 197–8, 199, 200

Bielsa 199–200

coaching qualities, difficulties measuring 200–201

emotional tone setting and 200, 202–3

forecasting future manager performance, difficulty of 198–9

Klopp *see* Klopp, Jürgen

long-term performance of 189–91

manager buy-in 95

manager reports 124

personal relationship with players 201

picking the best players 200

players as most important factor in football and 193–5

points per season added by 201–2

Premier League Manager of the Season award 191–3

Schrödinger's cat and 203

tactics and 199–200, 202–3, 223, 267, 269, 270–71

wages of 201

Manchester City 10, 53, 89, 90

Abu Dhabi owners 274–6

'big six' 36, 43

early kick-offs and 236

Expected Goals 138–9

goal-scoring 90–91, 104, 106

performance analysts 159

points per game 93

possession 142, 155, 270

revenue 175–6

total expenditure 94

transfers 12, 46, 51, 58, 83, 86, 93, 104, 185, 221–2, 228

Manchester City – *cont.*

TV revenues 277

wages 186

Manchester United 19, 22, 43, 90, 94

clean sheets 258

early kick-offs 236

expenditure 63

goals 106, 107, 256, 260

GOAT and 209, 212, 213–14, 215

Manchester United – *cont.*
    managers 200, 203
    points per season 274
    possession 142
    revenue 175
    shots 122, 139
    transfers 25, 26, 77, 81, 82, 85, 93, 181,
       183, 185, 186, 196, 222, 224, 228
Mané, Sadio 5, 9, 12, 13–14, 55, 57, 75–9,
    83, 86, 87, 91, 92, 95, 153, 183, 202,
    220
Maradona, Diego 166, 196, 207
marginal gains 232–3
market values 180–81
Markov assumption 145–6, 154–5
Marković, Lazar 57–8, 95, 230
Martial, Anthony 181
Martínez, Roberto 43, 46, 142, 143
Mata, Juan 81
Match of the Day 28, 144
Matip, Joël 11–12, 78, 79, 91, 92, 152,
    224, 231, 268
Maupay, Neal 113, 114
Mbappé, Kylian 208, 210
McCann, Matt 51–2
McCarthy, Mick 32
McNamara, Robert/McNamara
    fallacy 198–9
Melo, Arthur 229, 262
Melwood 41, 57, 62, 70–71, 78, 125, 135,
    145, 195
Mendy, Benjamin 12, 83, 86
Mepham, Chris 113
Messi, Lionel 4, 8, 9, 15, 54, 61, 155, 164,
    166, 193, 194, 228, 249, 280
    GOAT 205–17
    home advantage and 237–8
Midtjylland, FC 118
Mignolet, Simon 51, 52, 53
Milner, James 63, 64, 65, 82–3, 91, 92,
    115, 149, 161, 224, 235

Minamino, Takumi 231
MIT Sloan Sports Analytics
    Conference 43
Mitoma, Kaoru 118
Mkhitaryan, Henrikh 196
'Modelling Association Football
    Scores and Inefficiencies in the
    Football Betting Market'
    (Dixon and Coles) 106
Modrić, Luka 25, 34, 35, 186, 209
Monaco, AS 12, 88, 242
'Moneyball Derby' 118–19
Morata, Alvaro 82, 183, 222
Moreno, Alberto 57, 82, 83, 85, 86, 152
Mosteller, Frederick 55
Mourinho, José 81, 104, 200, 268, 270
Munroe, Randall 246
Mwepu, Enock 118

negative expected return 106–7, 120
Neuer, Manuel 69
Neumann, John von 267
Nevill, Alan 245, 246
Newcastle United 12, 78, 104, 126, 143,
    192, 252, 256, 276
Neymar 11, 14, 86, 208, 209, 210, 216,
    219, 227–8, 232
NFL 20
Nice, Olympique Gymnaste Club 26,
    114
Nightingale, Florence 16
Norman, John 240, 242
North Staffordshire Referees Club 245
Norwich City 52, 53, 176, 185, 277
Numbers Game (Anderson/Sally) 253–8

Oakland A's 22, 39–40
Oblak, Jan 88
O'Connor, Kieron 223
Odubajo, Moses 113
off-ball movement 161–2, 169

Oldham Athletic 114, 240
Oliver, Dean: *Basketball on Paper* 33, 152
Olympiacos 156
on-ball event data 161
Onyeka, Frank 118
OODA loop 271
opportunity, controlling for 83
Opta 22–4, 124, 127, 131, 132, 144, 150
    Opta Forum 162–3
Optical Tracking Data 158
optimism, bias towards 123
Origi, Divock 5, 9, 57, 91, 157
outcome bias 134–5
overperformance 69, 190, 193
Over-Under 107–8
Oxlade-Chamberlain, Alex 91, 231
Ozil, Mesut 35

Palacios-Huerta, Natxo 246, 265
Palmieri, Emerson 83
PAOK Salonika 239
Parc des Princes 241
Pardew, Alan 191–2
Pareto Frontier 261–2
Paris Saint-Germain (PSG) 11, 14, 86,
    197, 208–10, 226, 227, 232, 241, 242,
    276
Parken 241
passing
    pass completion 32, 47, 148, 149, 262
    Possession Value and *see* Possession
    Value
Pavlyuchenko, Roman 26, 35
Pelé 166, 207
penalties 27, 28, 31, 52, 68–9, 72, 84
    Expected Goals and 7, 8, 121, 124–6,
    128, 130, 133, 137
    GOAT and 207, 211, 212
    home advantage and 245, 246, 248
percentage ball 269, 270
perfect hindsight model 137

Peterborough United 32
Peters, Steve 56–7
physical abilities 157, 163, 215–17
Pitch Control 163–7, 168, 172, 201, 215,
    269, 271
Pjanić, Miralem 229, 280
plastic pitches 240–41
Player Classification 58–61, 64, 178
Player Rating 24, 80, 147–9, 155, 178
plus-minus analysis 29, 252
Pochettino, Mauricio 51
Pogba, Paul 65, 183, 224
points
    per game 42, 50, 68–70, 93
    per season 36, 93, 186, 191, 201,
    274–5, 280
    three points for a win 52, 244
Poisson distribution ('Law of Small
    Numbers') 101–5
Pollard, Richard 7, 8, 23, 123–4, 126–7,
    137, 144, 279
Porto 168–9
Portsmouth FC 30, 31, 32, 33, 37
Portugal (international football team)
    214
pose data 171, 173
possession 141–56
    controlled possession 24, 33,
    52, 267
    Dangerous Possession 141–3, 270
    Dangerous Possession Dominance
    142
    defensive actions and 150–52, 156
    Expected Possession Value 15
    Expected Threat and 23, 141, 145
    game state and 142, 143–4, 146–8,
    154, 162
    Goal Probability Added and 23, 141
    Goal Yield and 144–5
    information leak and 155
    Markov assumption and 145–6, 154–5

pass completion percentage 32, 47, 148, 149, 262

Player Rating and 147–8

Possession Value 15, 23–4, 32, 33, 34, 47, 48, 56, 61, 67, 76, 78, 79, 85, 89, 141–2, 144–7, 150, 152, 153–6, 161–3, 166, 168, 178, 195, 200, 205, 211, 220, 253, 254, 260, 263, 269

Safe Possession Dominance 142

success, relationship between possession and 155

usage 152–3

Post-Strike Expected Goals 8, 9, 26–7, 129–30, 134, 135, 136, 139, 148, 192, 210

Potter, Graham 116

Poyet, Gus 116

praise model 177–8, 180

Premier League seasons

(1998–99) 245

(1999–2000) 258

(2001–02) 254

(2004–05) 274

(2005–06) 25, 274

(2006–07) 25, 26, 104, 274

(2007–08) 25, 57, 150, 274

(2008–09) 30, 228, 257, 274

(2009–10) 36, 191, 259, 274

(2010–11) 42, 106, 139

(2011–12) 36, 42, 46, 103, 104, 106, 126, 149, 191, 192, 254, 272

(2012–13) 46–50, 52, 84, 93, 135, 142–3, 192, 224

(2013–14) 3, 50–54, 55, 57, 63, 81, 93, 121–2, 135, 136, 191, 224

(2014–15) 57–8, 85, 91, 93, 135–6, 159, 196, 224, 276

(2015–16) 65–6, 75, 79, 92, 93, 181, 191, 192, 202, 224, 267, 272

(2016–17) 79–80, 83, 85, 92, 93, 192, 258, 268

(2017–18) 82, 83, 85, 86, 87–8, 92, 115, 268, 274, 275

(2018–19) 89, 92, 139, 274, 275

(2019–20) 10, 89, 90, 91, 92, 93, 248, 274, 275

(2020–21) 10, 91, 235, 261, 274, 275

(2021–22) 10, 91, 175, 176, 223, 273, 274, 275

(2022–23) 101, 138, 139, 270, 273, 275

Pressure Regains 261–2

Pre-Strike Expected Goals 128–9, 132, 133, 135–6, 139, 192, 211–12

Principal Component Analysis 60

Prozone 32, 158–9

PSV Eindhoven 27

psychology 56–7, 62, 102, 105, 122, 123, 200, 240, 281

Pulis, Tony 59, 165, 191, 272, 273, 274

Pulisic, Christian 222

Qatar 276

Ramos, Juande 28

Ramsey, Aaron 47, 65

Rangnick, Ralf 76, 269

Ranieri, Claudio 191, 192

RasenBallsport Leipzig *see* Red Bull Leipzig

Råsunda Stadium 241

Real Madrid 3, 30, 34–5, 54, 87–8, 89, 117, 143, 194, 197, 200, 205–6, 207, 209–10, 212, 213, 226, 228, 270

RedBird Capital Partners 215

Red Bull 88, 131

Red Bull Leipzig 89, 170, 219–20

Red Bull Salzburg 55, 76, 89

Redknapp, Harry 28–9, 30–31, 34, 36, 43, 191

Reep, Charles 7, 8, 23, 48, 123–4, 126–7, 137, 144–5, 279

referee
home advantage and 245–6, 248–9
video assistant referee (VAR) 248–9,
256
relative age effect 264–5
relegation 12, 19, 20, 44, 68, 78, 79, 85,
96, 114, 150, 185, 258, 272
Research department 71, 80, 125, 135,
171, 251
Reus, Marco 196
Ridgewell, Liam/Ridgewell Problem
150–52, 154
'risky' players 117
Robertson, Andy 12, 13, 15, 83, 85–6,
90, 91, 92, 96, 156, 202, 224,
268
Robinho 228
Robinson, Michael 108–9
Robinson, Paul 26
Rochdale AFC 113, 114
Rodallega, Hugo 259
Rodgers, Brendan 14, 43, 46, 141, 224,
230, 251, 267, 268
Rodríguez, Maxi 42, 48
Roma 13, 81–2, 88, 96, 182, 200
Ronaldo (Luís Nazário de Lima)
208
Ronaldo, Cristiano 15, 54, 197, 205–6,
207–17, 274
Ronay, Barney 65
Rooney, Wayne 209, 210, 260
Rosenfeld, Jaeson 94
Rudd, Sarah 94, 145
Ruhl, Holger 67
Russia (international team) 240–41

Sacchi, Arrigo 90
Safe Possession Dominance 142
Sahin, Nuri 67, 194–5
Saint-Etienne, AS 22, 114
Sakho, Mamadou 51, 53, 152

Salah, Mohamed 6, 9, 12–13, 14–15, 53,
80–81, 82, 86, 87–8, 89, 91, 92, 95,
96, 153, 168, 169, 182, 183, 202, 220,
221
salary model 177–80
Salman, Mohammed bin 276
Santos 207, 228
Santos, Giovani dos 28, 51, 57
Sánchez, Alexis 55, 56, 65, 66, 77–8
Sánchez, Robert 116
Saudi Arabia 276, 277
Savant, Marilyn vos 260–61
Schrödinger's cat 203
Scorecasting (Moskowitz/Wertheim)
245, 255
scoring streak 104, 223–4
Scouting department, Liverpool 9, 10,
12, 13, 14, 27–8, 46, 51–2, 56, 57, 71,
76, 78, 87, 89, 91–2, 94, 95, 96–7,
151, 154, 162, 171, 230, 232
Sensible World of Soccer 20
Serie A 24, 179–80, 182, 229
set-pieces 15, 24, 48, 60, 127–8, 133, 146,
147, 166, 178, 211–12, 253, 271–4
Sevilla FC 77
Shaqiri, Xherdan 231
Sharjah 229
shots
conversion 127, 133, 137, 138, 243–4
data 132
distance 138–9
Expected Goals and *see* Expected
Goals
long-range 110, 121, 124–5, 128, 137,
138, 139, 211
number of 138–9, 243, 244
shot situation 133
Weighted Shots 8, 126–8, 137
Sigurdsson, Gylfi 47–8
Silver, Nate: *The Signal and the Noise* 96,
111, 154, 261

Singh, Karun 23, 145
Sissoko, Moussa 169
'Skill and Chance in Association
    Football' (Reep/Benjamin) 137
Skrtel, Martin 52
Sky Sports 66, 235
Sky Sports News 183
Smartodds 108, 110, 111, 114, 120
Soccernomics (Kuper/Szymanski) 184
Southampton FC 13, 29, 55, 56, 57, 76,
    77, 87, 170, 175, 236, 256
Spartak Moscow 26, 240
Spearman, Will 215; 'Physics-Based
    Modelling of Pass Probabilities
    in Soccer' 162–3
Sporting Clube de Portugal 241
sporting director 10, 13, 22, 46, 66, 70,
    75, 80, 96, 172, 232, 263
sportswashing 276
Spurs Lodge 24–5, 30, 31, 33, 150
Starlizard 108, 110, 111, 120
StatDNA 94, 145
state-owned clubs 15, 276
statistical models 4, 6, 7, 75, 82
'Stats and Snakeoil' blog 137
StatsBomb 132, 155
Steele, Dafydd 59, 64, 88–9, 118, 130–
    31, 132
Sterling, Raheem 52, 55, 58, 80, 114,
    135, 186
Stevenson, Mark 80
Stimac, Igor 264
Stoke City 31, 36, 52, 58, 186, 194, 212, 273
Stott, Henry 21, 103
strike-back effect 109
Sturridge, Daniel 48, 50, 51, 52, 57, 63,
    66, 135, 136, 224, 229
Suárez, Luis 4–5, 9, 50, 52, 54, 55, 56, 61,
    80, 114, 135, 136, 186, 208, 216, 252
Subbuteo 20
Subotić, Neven 67, 194

success
    measuring 92–4
    'skill plus luck' equation 50
    transfers and *see* transfers
    wages and *see* wages
Sunderland AFC. 30, 31, 32, 36, 116, 259,
    260
surprising events, frequency of 109
Swansea City 19, 46, 47, 48, 112, 141,
    142, 149, 236–7
Swedish Cup 241
Szymanski, Stefan 184

tactics, managers and 199–200, 202–3,
    223, 267, 269, 270–71
target man 56, 58–9, 61, 62, 178
Tarkowski, James 113
Taylor, Graham 48, 157, 163
team player 211
teamwork 96–7, 153, 267, 269, 270–71
'10' 55, 60, 64–5, 121, 149, 228
Thaler, Richard 121
The Times 21, 22, 124, 240; 'Fink Tank'
    column 21, 124, 240, 241, 243
tiki-taka 211, 228, 271
Tioté, Cheick 126
Tippett, Tom 44
TNT Sports 237
Tomkins, Paul: *Pay As You Play* 222;
    'The Tomkins Times' 222
Torfabrik ball 196
Torpedo Moscow 240
Torres, Fernando 42, 48, 180, 222,
    229
Torvaney, Ben 137
Tottenham Hotspur 52, 104, 114, 142,
    149, 169, 185, 200, 236
    Champions League (2010–11) and
        50–51
    Champions League (2018–19) and 9,
        10, 154

Decision Technology and 14, 19–37, 39, 40, 41, 43, 46, 67, 90, 93, 94, 95, 126, 139, 150, 186, 191
'touch' 165–6
Touré, Kolo 122, 224
Touré, Yaya 121
tracking data 32, 132, 152, 157–73, 215, 269
  artificial intelligence and 171, 172–3
  broadcast tracking 170–71, 172
  computer vision 158, 161
  goal-scoring probability and 166–7
  hallucinates player trajectories 172–3
  Klopp and 157
  lobbying campaign to make available to clubs 158–9
  off-ball movement of players 161–2
  on-ball event data and 161
  Opta Forum 162–3
  Optical Tracking Data 158
  origins of 158–9
  pass interception and 167–8
  physical statistics and 157
  Pitch Control 163–6, 167, 168, 172
  pose data 171, 173
  Prozone and 158–9
  superiority of, example of 169–70
  video cameras and 158
transfer market
  Anna Karenina principle and 227
  deadline day 35, 183
  failure of 15, 219–33
  fair value/impairment 222–3
  50% Rule 221–4
  Liverpool under Klopp 75–97, 219–33
  Liverpool under Rodgers 46–66, 251–65
  marginal gains and 232–3

  scoring streak/winning run and 223–4
  70% success rate 231–3
  spending and success 222, 231–2
  Tottenham Hotspur and 25–6, 30–31, 34–7, 39
  Transfer Committee, Liverpool 46, 55, 56, 58, 62, 63, 65–6, 219–20, 230, 251–2, 276
  Transfermarkt 180
  transfer tax 184
  zebra farmers/domestication and 225–7
  See also individual player name
triple threat 153
Tsimikas, Kostas 156, 231
Tuchel, Thomas 69
TV broadcast deals 176, 180, 276, 277
  early kick-offs and 235–7
tyranny of metrics 260–63

Uefa 161, 182, 207, 241
Uefa Champions League *see* Champions League, Uefa
Uefa Cup 24, 27, 241
Uefa Super Cup 10, 91
Ullevaal Stadion 241
Ulloa, Leonardo 116
University of Cambridge Local Examinations Syndicate 21
University of Lancaster 103
usage 152–3

Vålerenga 241
valuable space 169, 215–16
value for money 116, 175, 177–9, 219
van der Vaart, Rafael 34–5, 37, 95, 206
van Dijk, Virgil 8, 11, 14, 87, 91, 92, 96, 152, 169, 170, 202, 220

Vatvani, Dinesh 155
Verratti, Marco 197, 262
Victor Chandler 108
video analysis 5–9, 10, 13, 30, 31, 36,
      56, 71, 78, 97, 125, 131, 135, 151, 154,
      230
video assistant referee (VAR) 248–9,
      256
video cameras 32, 158
Villarreal 215–16

wages 81, 93–4, 201
      Brentford 111, 112, 115
      Brighton 111, 116, 117, 119
      Championship 116
      individual skill and 271, 272–3
      inflation 184
      Liverpool 58, 86, 93–4, 176, 177–9,
            184–6
      managers 201
      Manchester City 58, 77, 275
      player wage model 177–80, 181
      Premier League spending 175
      revenue and 176, 233
      Serie A 179–80
      set-pieces and 272–3
      success and 93–4, 177–9, 184–6,
            231
      Tottenham Hotspur 36
      value for money 177–9
Walker, Kyle 35
Ward, Julian 80, 186, 283
Waskett, Tim 125, 160
Watkins, Ollie 113, 114
Weighted Shots 8, 126–8, 137
Wells, H. G. 3
Wenger, Arsène 22, 56, 78, 94, 203
Werner, Tom 10, 41, 48
West Bromwich Albion 49, 121, 122,
      150, 200, 272, 273

West Ham United 49, 113, 139, 152, 158,
      185, 264
White, Ben 116
'Wide Open Spaces: A Statistical
      Technique for Measuring Space
      Creation in Professional Soccer'
      (Fernández/Bornn) 215
Wigan Athletic 34, 46, 113, 142, 149,
      256, 259
Wijnaldum, Gini 5, 12, 78, 79, 91,
      92
Wilks, Samuel S. 3
Williams, Mark 245
Williams, Neco 186
Wilson, Harry 186
Winter, Jeff 235, 246
Winterburn, Nigel 103
Wissa, Yoane 118
Wolfsburg, VfL 68, 72, 81, 221–2
Women's Super League (WSL) 15
Woodfine, David 'Woody' 90, 158–60,
      186
Woodgate, Jonathan 29
World Cup 21, 54, 199, 214, 224
      (1966) 239
      (1974) 239
      (1978) 239
      (1986) 19, 127, 239
      (2010) 195–6
      (2014) 56, 264

xG *see* Expected Goals

young players 46, 56, 57, 65, 67, 76, 115,
      117, 178, 186, 196, 197, 200

Zanka 118
zebra farmers 225
Zidane, Zinedine 270
Zweite Bundesliga 67, 189